The Collect
of
Bernard Pomerance

By the same author

The Elephant Man
We Need to Dream All this Again

BERNARD POMERANCE

The Collected Plays
of
Bernard Pomerance

Superhighway

Quantrill in Lawrence

Melons

Hands of Light

Grove Press
New York

Published simultaneously in Canada
Printed in the United States of America

FIRST EDITION

Library of Congress Cataloging-in-Publication Data

Pomerance, Bernard.
    [Plays. Selections]
    The collected plays of Bernard Pomerance / Bernard Pomerance.—1st ed.
        p. cm.
    Contents: Superhighway—Quantrill in Lawrence—Melons—Hands of light.
    ISBN 0-8021-3845-4
    I. Title
PR6066.O48 A6 2001
822'.914—dc21   2001033239

Grove Press
841 Broadway
New York, NY 10003

01 02 03 04   10 9 8 7 6 5 4 3 2 1

CONTENTS

To my children, Eve and Moby,
and to Susan Bergholz,
who believes gathering enough no's
adds up to a bigger yes.

Quantrill in Lawrence played at the ICA Theatre in London in the spring of 1980. It was directed by Roland Rees.

Melons opened at The Royal Shakespeare Company, The Pit, in London, December of 1985. It was directed by Alison Sutcliffe. Subsequently it opened at the Yale Repertory Theater in New Haven in October 1987, directed by Gitta Honnegger.

Superhighway and *Hands of Light* have not been staged.

INTRODUCTION

William Quantrill's destruction of Lawrence, Kansas, in 1863 made him the leading candidate for worst man of the Civil War until John Wilkes Booth, a theater man, beat him at the wire by the length of a derringer.

Quantrill was a Northerner. He was an Ohio boy with gifts for violence, who found in the slavery issue the trigger that would complete him as a lethal weapon. On his arrival in Kansas to fight for a free state, he wrote earnestly to his mother that abolitionist Jim Lane, the governor, was the greatest man in Bleeding Kansas—called so for the bloody border warfare with pro-slavery Missouri. The border raiding was the sort of conflict that becomes self-sustaining on mutual atrocities. It had over time less and less to do with causes, or the Union, or secession, and more and more to do with the merciless behavior of the border raiders. The idealism of the letters to his mother may have died at the sight of Lane's brutalities in Missouri. It may be the Lawrence abolitionists understood Quantrill was more a trouble-prone opportunist than a committed free stater. Little evidence the welfare of black people, or the Union, was much on his mind. Lawrence imprisoned Quantrill and pondered how he'd hang. He escaped in a foul mood.

Quantrill's bruised ego made James Lane and Lawrence his prime furies in life, and he turned coat; he declared himself for the Confederacy. The Confederacy repeatedly rejected his pleas for a commission as a regular officer. Something . . . hm . . . is not quite right about this boy. However, the raid on Lawrence and the inclusion among Quantrill's Raiders of Jesse and Frank James and Cole and Jim Younger made him legendary in Missouri.

★ ★ ★

Harry Truman reports that as a young Missouri politician he was taken to veterans' homes and shown near-religious shrines to Quantrill, with the anarchist flag, black candles aflame, and crossed 1860 Navy Colts. Truman recalls that his mother, as a baby, was incarcerated in a prison camp as a reprisal for the raid on Lawrence. Truman himself, of course, proved another great bringer of fire to cities at dawn. In the end, James Lane escaped Quantrill's vengeance and the destruction of Lawrence by hightailing through cornfields disguised as a woman. After the war, Lane's hopes to create an empire for himself having been thwarted, he killed himself in a rage. The destruction of Lawrence is taken to be one more atrocity of Bleeding Kansas, one more appalling event of the Civil War. I thought I saw something else basic in it, well worth fiddling with and fictionalizing; therefore the play.

Upon opening, Roland Rees, who directed, began immediately to rehearse a reprise of his 1977 original Foco Novo production of *The Elephant Man* for the National Theatre. At night William Quantrill was played by the brilliant David Schofield. By day, David was rehearsing a reprise of his original portrayal of Mr. Merrick in *Elephant Man*. That portrayal, devised together with Roland off a few basic hints from me, became the standard way of playing Merrick. My own reluctance to do publicity is the primary reason neither of them has received the proper credit for their contribution to the play. It was groundbreaking.

Every night I was in to see and work on *Quantrill,* an American friend of David Schofield's was present. He was reputed to occasionally carry a .38, although I found that doubtful in London. I was curious. I finally approached him and asked what brought him back night after night. With great midwestern shyness, he told me that he in fact was from Lawrence, Kansas, and he liked nothing better than to see it wiped out nightly. Local pride. I asked David once how he felt to be rehearsing Merrick by day and playing Quantrill by night. He said he'd recently told his parents that he was being Jesus by day and the Devil by night. I liked that, problems of accuracy notwithstanding.

Superhighway was finished in 1978. Despite appearances or resemblances, it is not autobiographical. It is fiction.

Melons was sparked off by reading Geronimo's memoirs and accounts of turmoil instigated on New Mexico pueblos by U.S. authorities, both civil and religious. This subject matter was and is problematic for a non-Indian to enter. I had to learn a measure of appropriateness on the job. When you go to the Indian world, it has to do with the nature of the American earth and elements, the knowledge of it, the respect due it, and who knew it best, and what became of it. To draw on legal occupancy terms which are somehow appropriate, you may not enter as a proprietor merely because it is "American" history, but you may find a place in time as a tenant-in-common. It is good to be fortunate in your friends, as I was. Simon Ortiz, the poet from Acoma, asks, Once we know these truths, what are our relations to be now? How are we to treat each other? Yeats put it: After such knowledge, what forgiveness?

I called Ben Kingsley in London asking him to read *Melons* and to play the lead, Caracol. In the early eighties, there were no Native American actors with the stage experience to carry the role, and the great Canadians from the Red Earth Theatre were as yet unknown outside Canada. I knew Ben from London theater. He had just returned home from shooting *Gandhi*. He had met a Cherokee man in London and had expressed his desire next to play an American Indian. The man considered this, then told him that if he wanted to, it was certain he would, and soon. Ben's embrace of the part and the play was surely the main reason it opened at the Royal Shakespeare Company. His then-wife Alison Sutcliffe directed, and it opened in December 1985. It was a staggering performance. For the Yale Repertory Theater production in 1987, the director Gitta Honnegger brilliantly brought out the choreography needed to realize the play.

The actress who played Edna at Yale, Victoria Racimo, was one highlight of a production that had some highs, some lows. We stayed in touch over the years. This March, Victoria telephoned me in New Mexico just as I was about to leave on a trip. I passed through New York and left her a copy of *Hands of Light* for fun. *Hands* is a takeoff on the King Midas myth, which, although I had sketched it out in 1970, I had not been able to grasp what to do until my immersion in the native world. To turn stuff into gold is a metaphor. It is to remove matter from the natural cycles of the natural world, for the creation of an artificial value, which in turn overwhelms all previous values—an emblem perhaps for many peoples' passage on this earth.

On my return, there was a message from Victoria asking me to meet her at a mysterious address. As Victoria herself is kind of a mysterious address, it was irresistible. Just off a transatlantic plane, I followed instructions to the street, the building, and the floor. She had somehow managed to arrange a reading of *Hands of Light,* with only two days to round up actors and no rehearsals. *Hands of Light,* she informed me, had twenty-five speaking roles (which is irresponsible), but she thought I should hear it anyway (responsible). I was simply blown away by the surprise, the effort, and the generosity of the gesture. It remains as great an experience as ever I had in theater. Thank you.

Bernard Pomerance
November 2000

SUPERHIGHWAY

New York City and environs, spring 1973.

CHARACTERS

ELLA, a dying woman about 55 years old

SAM, her husband, about 62

BENJ and **JOE,** their sons, about 30 and 27

MATTY, Ella's sister

ROY, her husband

DOCTOR RALPH, the family doctor

INGA NILSON, a surgeon

MISS JOHNSON, a ward nurse

MRS. ROBERTS, a surgical nurse

BARNADINO, dying Mafia capo

CARLO, Barnadino's associate

OLD WOMAN, Barnadino's mother

RABBI, of Sam and Ella's community

ACT I

Darkness. SAM *sits at a table, four chairs in semi-light.*

SAM Not being a believer—being, to put it mildly, skeptical about prayer—I confess in all humility I am desperately unsure who or what to call on. Jehovah, this old dealer in relentlessness? The powers of creation or decay? Whatever leads the wheat from the ground and makes the generations of the leaves? Whatever burns out the stars, or makes their dark more potent than the light, or makes the new-mown hay smell sweet before it rots, or any other of those phenomenal astonishments the Bible is so fond of recounting to prove how small we are—which I have never doubted—whoever, whatever, however, I am here, in lieu of prayer, to place a fairly dismal position-wanted ad:

"Successful businessman, own business, law degree, formerly some practice, age sixty-two, two grown sons, highest references from associates, clients, friends, many interests, wishes to be allowed to exchange his life for that of his evidently dying wife. Has seen every kind of crime and corruption in lifetime. Does not pretend to understand it—under no illusion will understand it if live forever. Further history if required. Wish quickest reply."

ELLA *groans with pain.*

SAM *(cont.)* It figures.

Semi-light rises on Ella in bed in another area. DOCTOR *gives her a shot.*

9

DOCTOR Ella kid, you're going to sleep like you never slept in your life.

ELLA I'm worried about Sam. Stay with him, Ralph, till the kids arrive, or my sister.

DOCTOR Sam'll be in good hands. You get your rest.

Doctor crosses to Sam.

ELLA Colostomy. Bypass or shortcut between the mouth and anus. A kind of plastic superhighway to replace the old dirt road. The intestines are cut out, in part or whole. Yards and yards if necessary. The bloody remainder is connected to a tube. A new gate is made in the body. A hole in your side.

The plastic tube is run out. You attach a plastic bag. The bag collects the wastes of the digestive process. You change the bag regularly. A colostomy is performed in cases of cancer of the colon. A lot of people, so they say, live happy lives with one. I will not. If they had not done it to my mother—if I had not thought any life was more important and allowed them to do it—oh well, it was the best money could buy, everyone said so. The best money could buy was a superhighway to the grave. It was humiliation heaped on agony. Death came anyway. She suffered like an angel with her wings ripped off. If my colon is affected—I draw the line at this. I nightly beg Mother to forgive me and to give me strength. I am so afraid—so afraid.

Light fades from Ella. She sleeps.

Lights rise to reveal Sam and Doctor at the table. Behind all, a flat representational image of a house, it being clear that this is the house in which the action takes place, but seen from without.

SAM Ella asleep?

DOCTOR Doped up to the ears.

SAM God, I hate to see her like that.

DOCTOR Got to kill the pain to get the rest, Sam.

SAM Did she ask if Benj and Joey'd arrived yet?

DOCTOR Didn't come up. They still out grabbing a bite?

SAM Not an egg in the house. I really can't cope.

DOCTOR Leave houses to men, they'd be empty, pal. We'd still live in caves.

SAM Maybe the boys should have seen her tonight.

DOCTOR I explained to them. Surgery coming, you rest.

SAM She asked if they'd arrived yet. I lied. Said no. She asked if Matty and Roy'd come in from Washington. I said no. I felt her reading my face. Wondering why I was lying, if I was lying. (*beat*) I suppose lying badly becomes one way of telling her the truth.

DOCTOR Pal, open the brandy. Let's get the knots out of our guts.

SAM (*pours*) Here's to you Ralph. For keeping the night watch with me.

DOCTOR The boys said they'd bring us sandwiches; I hope they remember.

SAM I guess you've seen all this before.

DOCTOR I guess I have, pal.

SAM I remember in '45 when my father was dying. Drip by drip. Death of the leaky faucet variety. I couldn't conceive anything worse. I'm always making that mistake; there's always worse.

DOCTOR Yeah.

SAM You know, you're a hell of a good doctor, Ralph.

DOCTOR Pal, I didn't think you'd paid my bills these twenty years because you were infatuated with my body.

SAM Inga Nilson too. Top surgeon.

DOCTOR Any woman who gets accepted has to be twice as good. She had a time, but she's there now.

SAM You remember Ella's mother? What Nilson did?

DOCTOR Useless. But it might not have been.

SAM The old lady should've been allowed to die in peace.

DOCTOR That was a tough one.

SAM Ella says don't let it happen again.

DOCTOR No useless operations, she means?

SAM Not being reduced to a bag of bones, a howl, and a coma. For nothing.

DOCTOR No one wants to do that, Sam.

SAM Then why this surgery? Why not the truth? Why not painkillers to help her get through it? Some dignity.

DOCTOR And when the painkillers stop killing the pain? Look, pal, you've practiced law, right?

SAM Ralph, Ella's really scared. She's obsessed about it. So am I.

DOCTOR   Say you've got a court here. Say you're pretty sure this guy cancer is guilty as hell.

SAM   Which you are.

DOCTOR   So's every schmuck DA who brings a case. We're both imperfect. It's got to be proven. And that takes evidence. This cancer's a guy you don't want on the streets again, right? So you make damn sure you've got his nuts in a wringer before you indict. Well, if you had to go to court tomorrow and prove it was cancer, and fatal, you couldn't do it, pal. There's doubt. I'm a good doctor. But I'm imperfect. So I order tests to be taken. The tests are contradictory because tests are imperfect. Meanwhile, Ella gets worse. What do you do? You've got a mystery. Do you wait and let her get worse? Do you start planning a dignified death when it still might be possible to save her? No, Sam. You've got to operate. And when it's a mystery, it's not just for Ella or you or the kids. You're finding out for everyone.

SAM   Not at the cost of a colostomy.

DOCTOR   You approach the surgeon; you tell her that.

SAM   How do I put it?

DOCTOR   Say, Look Inga, if you open her up and find it's hopeless, sew her shut again.

SAM   Christ. . . .

DOCTOR   She'll understand. Surgeons are supposed to do anything necessary to preserve life, right? But that ain't because of their toilet training. It's the law. As long as there are no witnesses.

SAM   I just keep thinking—oh, hell.

13

DOCTOR   If you could plan, maybe she'd like a last picnic in the country?

SAM   Something like that.

DOCTOR   We'll see, pal.

SAM   It's like you get on a road. Years before. And you can't find a way to get off.

DOCTOR   Don't follow you, pal.

SAM   We escaped New York City more than twenty years ago. To live. Or was it? That's the mystery now. To live?

Enter BENJ *and* JOE.

BENJ   Joey, I've got a déjà vu.

JOE   I believe I've heard you say that before, man.

BENJ   The squalid scene.

JOE   An international scandal.

DOCTOR   What we need is you put-on artists.

BENJ   Coming in late. People waiting up. Bottle on table.

JOE   America's elders.

BENJ   Glasses, cigarette smoke, fearful eyes. It's the where-have-you-been-so-late family quarrel scene. Same people, same props, same hour. But no quarrel.

DOCTOR   You guys didn't bring my sandwich, you'll have a quarrel.

BENJ   He's trying to disarm us with affection.

SAM   You screwballs. I'm glad you're here.

JOE Mom sleeping?

SAM Doped up and out.

BENJ Roast beef okay? On rye. Russian, cole slaw, pickle.

He lays out food.

SAM Set 'er down. Go ahead, Ralph. I can't eat yet.

JOE (*pours drinks*) Dad says she's dying, Ralph. Cancer.

DOCTOR We'll know for sure tomorrow night.

JOE You mean nothing's certain even yet?

DOCTOR Business as usual, kid.

JOE Seventy-three years and a bit into the 20th century. A
million machines poking their noses about nature, and—
what?—you tell me.

DOCTOR People still die, and it's all systems go for the moon.

BENJ If you're shooting her up to sleep, it must hurt.

SAM It's pretty bad.

BENJ Ralph? Where is it?

SAM Let him finish his sandwich, for Christ's sake. He's been
doing double duty.

DOCTOR It's okay. I think the colon.

JOE Like Grandma?

DOCTOR I think. Could be other places. Could be kidney,
lot of pain lower left back. Little toxicity too, so the
kidney's not happy, not doing its job. Could be something
on the colon pressed up against the kidney.

SAM   He thinks the liver, too.

JOE   That's the ball game, isn't it?

SAM   Yes.

BENJ   The old seat of the soul. Salud.

DOCTOR   Trouble is when it's been visiting around, it could be anywhere. Bottoms up.

JOE   But you're not absolutely sure.

DOCTOR   I'm sure. Just not omniscient.

JOE   I mean it's not like preparing us for the worst so when it turns out—never mind.

SAM   It hits in waves. Drink up. You realize it in waves.

JOE   It seemed so abstract on the telephone. When you're far away, it's somehow abstract.

SAM   I better warn you. She's been through a lot of pain. You're going to get the shock of your life at how she looks. She's been looking forward to seeing you both. It'd be a hell of a thing if you—lost control.

JOE   Have you?

SAM   Not yet. But I'm in too deep to cheer her up. It'd be a real contribution if you tried to cheer her up.

JOE   You didn't have to ask that.

SAM   I never know.

JOE   You never know what?

SAM   What we'll be fighting about next.

JOE   I didn't come to fight. Did you come to fight, Benj?

SAM Every time we see you—well. Times change. Standards change.

BENJ Why don't we drop this?

SAM I was only going to say we never had your freedom. Our generation—

JOE Had the Depression?

SAM (*angry*) Well, it may be a joke to you.

BENJ Who was that peak I saw you with last night? That was no peak, that was my Depression.

JOE See, even he knows you had the Depression. We have freedom; you had the Depression. You were never at ease in life after that. Always looking back over your shoulder, see if the wolf's at the door yet. Is that why we fight? The Depression?

SAM If you understood, you'd know why we worry so much about you.

JOE Because I'm finishing a degree?

SAM Because you don't know the future, you don't plan practically—

JOE You worry because you don't know anything about me.

SAM Because you don't tell anything.

JOE Because you worry.

SAM Look: The fights have become so virulent, particularly with Mom, and they've hurt her a lot, Joe, so it's not unreasonable that now I'm hoping—

JOE You don't have to say it.

SAM I mean if she brings up any sore point—

JOE Ralph, you had the Depression too, interpret for me; he doesn't have to say it.

SAM That you won't make a—mess.

JOE Well, what the fuck.

BENJ Turns out he did have to say it.

DOCTOR Hey, Sam's been on the front line, okay? Where it hurts? He's just telling you what to expect.

SAM Thank you.

BENJ Right.

JOE You know what happens when you keep looking over your shoulder for wolves? You see wolves everywhere.

SAM They are everywhere. I promise you that.

JOE I guess they are. I'm going to bed. I'm wrecked.

SAM Yeah. Be fresh for the morning. You'll need it.

Joe goes.

DOCTOR How's the mother country, kid?

BENJ England? I'm just there for the beer. That's an English joke; it means you're not connected to what's happening. They're all there for the beer. Unconnected. They leave me alone. I write. When they run out of beer, I don't know what they'll do.

DOCTOR Ah, they'll all come over here, dine out on their English accents. We don't run out.

BENJ Funny about that. On the plane, they ran out of everything. American plane. Absolutely full. Ran out of food. Ran out of drink. Hardly air to breathe but'd just come out of some other guy's lungs. I was sitting next to a couple of black guys. Soldiers. They slept. There was turbulence, so we were all strapped into our seats. I kept thinking, I've been through all this before. But where? When? Like we were reenacting something but couldn't quite recall from where or when. Airless, foodless, drinkless, dark, tied down, crossing the Atlantic, packed in bodies, whizzing for the American shore.

    Then the lights came on. This steward got out in the aisle and started to speak. It came out like a marine top sergeant. I could've freaked. It wasn't like being a passenger. It was something else. He says, "All right now, I want everybody's attention. Everybody, please. I only want to say this one time." I don't know. Somebody should've told him to go fuck himself. But everyone sat there like good bunny rabbits. Then I got the déjà vu. Immigrant ship, slave ship, something like that tho' modernized. We were being told what obedience and customs would be expected of us on arrival in the new land.

SAM In the old days, the customer was treated like he was doing you a favor. I don't know what's happening.

BENJ That was only clue one. We landed. Got to customs, I mean immigration. This guy takes my passport, says, What's the purpose of your visit? I say, Hey, I'm American. It's home. He says, How long're you going to stay? I say, Well, I'm American, right? He says, Well, you live in England. I say, Well, I guess I'll stay here about as long as I please. And how long is that? he says. And I say, Well, I'll bet you'll just have to wait to find out. So he fusses, he grumbles, and finally gives the passport a whack that'd drop a mastodon in its tracks, I mean it.

I realized the whole thing then. He's like that because he knows; he has no power. Not over my life—or his own. He's in despair but going through the motions. That's what's changed: people know now, and it's killing them. Maybe you don't see it here.

SAM We see it. Every phone operator, every petty bureaucrat.

BENJ Well, I'm not just here for the beer. So I'd better get some rest. 'Night, Ralph. Dad.

SAM Hey, I'll go out, buy some breakfast in the morning.

BENJ Joey did already. Your impractical sons. Picked up eggs, bacon, coffee, bread and milk. They're in the fridge. Trust him, okay?

Benj goes.

SAM Christ knows what he does either. You know the Van Allen belt around the earth?

DOCTOR Protects us from radiation or something, right?

SAM Cosmic poisoning, right. The world's big roof. You ever wonder about it?

DOCTOR I've got to confess. Never.

SAM Every time I see the kids, I get this awful feeling.

DOCTOR It's called paternity.

SAM I think the radiation's getting through. Neither of them cares about earning. The Van Allen belt's sprung a leak.

DOCTOR Tell the White House to call his plumbers, huh?

SAM Look at that. The way people behave. The way things are going. How do you explain it?

DOCTOR What, that Watergate thing? It'll die down.

SAM No, no, no, that's—an effect, not a cause. There's something much bigger wrong. The older I get, the more I conclude we're just looking at the little effects.

DOCTOR You get enough vitamin A, Sam? Have some pills.

SAM It's like what that smoke rising from Buchenwald must have been to the villagers miles away. It sort of forms up against the back of your mind. It's like evidence pouring out of the earth. It's a shadow of a terrific master crime, which you know—but you don't.

DOCTOR Well, it's not the goddamn Van Allen belt.

SAM I just suddenly feel that the unimaginable's got one hand round my throat and the other in my pocket.

DOCTOR Ah, business as usual. Just a little rougher.

SAM I was brought up to believe there has to be justice in the universe somewhere, but I don't see it anymore.

DOCTOR Yeah, it got mugged crossing Central Park a coupla years ago. Forget it.

SAM Why is Ella dying, Ralph? (*silence*)
You think it's just an accident? It has no meaning? I don't believe that. I don't believe in accidents, I believe in reasons. I believe there's a reason every swindling kind of slimy schmuck in public life looks like he'll live and thrive and appall us all to the crack of doom, and the postman's

21

daughter—did I tell you this?—he's looking awful and I ask what's wrong, and for Christ's sake, his daughter, eight years old, she wasn't feeling well so they went to a doctor and it was leukemia; three days later she's dead. Jesus, Ralph. In this country. In our own time. Why?

DOCTOR What kind of question is that for a guy your age and experience?

SAM The one I'm asking.

DOCTOR You should have been a philosopher.

SAM Don't let Joey hear you say that.

DOCTOR It ain't an accident he's studying philosophy, Sam. It's you.

SAM A philosopher; a half-cocked playwright. I earn the dough, they plan the mind of the world. They're not like me.

DOCTOR A logical development, pal. Tough shit.

SAM You haven't answered my question. Why?

DOCTOR You mean leukemia?

SAM I mean ridiculous suffering.

DOCTOR From what point of view?

SAM Say I'm a Martian. You know, a greenie with long things sprouting here and here. You're an earthling. Explain what the hell's going on.

DOCTOR I can't answer that. Christ, I can't even ask it.

SAM Aha. Why?

DOCTOR Can't I ask?

SAM Exactly. Why?

DOCTOR Look, when we were young guys, we had the Depression. Do I have to explain the goddamn Depression or can I assume you've been briefed?

SAM My long things here and here wave; I've been briefed.

DOCTOR So you know, no food, no work, you don't ask those questions. You try and survive.

SAM After the Depression, the war.

DOCTOR I was coming to that. The war. You don't ask those absolute questions. You try and survive.

SAM The genocide. The bomb. The Cold War. The Korean War. McCarthy. The missiles. The Vietnam War.

DOCTOR You don't ask. You try and survive.

SAM So you never ask the questions.

DOCTOR Who has the time?

SAM On Mars, we call that copping a plea.

DOCTOR Look. Your family grows. Say your business has problems. All that suffering seems distant.

SAM Your job is close? It changes its nature? The market's quirky. You're scared by your experience?

DOCTOR These guys are my patients, Sam. Coronary fodder.

SAM The suffering's distant. Your own problems are close.

DOCTOR Right.

SAM Technology wasn't even a word when you were born? Now it's grown up, screwing a little with politics, whoring its ass to industry? Going from desperate need to shabby overproduction—there's cancer for you—so you worry? So you're always busy? Always on edge? You never ask the questions with any real attention? All your energies go into getting security? Right?

DOCTOR   Sounds like you goddamn Martians have a few problems.

SAM   My long things here and here wave poignantly. True.

DOCTOR   So since when's wanting security a crime?

SAM   When it's the lucky turning their backs on the unlucky, that's when. Not having time is bullshit.

DOCTOR   Why crucify yourself? It won't help Ella, pal.

SAM   Why not? There's a play that's been haunting me. It's haunting me because of this feeling that we're somehow reenacting it. A mysterious Greek play about a woman who takes her husband's place in dying.

DOCTOR   Yeah, the glory that was Greece.

SAM   Death calls him, but allows him to find someone else to die for him. His old father and mother won't do it.

DOCTOR   Yeah, those Greeks get quirky in their old age.

SAM   So she takes his place dying—his wife.

DOCTOR   Probably her first chance to get out of the house in years.

SAM   At the end, Hercules brings the wife back from the dead. In the meantime, the husband who let her do it looks not unlike the world's biggest schmuck.

DOCTOR She doesn't sound like such a great brain either.

SAM I sometimes think Ella's taking my place.

DOCTOR You're not the first to think it, pal.

SAM Who spent years of aggravation in the world? It's logical that I should be the sick one.

DOCTOR Logic-shmogic. It's her.

SAM You ever read history?

DOCTOR Me and Henry Ford agree; it's bunk.

SAM It's a record of how the strong force on the weak all the hard things they can't bear themselves. Why not disease, disorder, malfunction?

DOCTOR People aren't history, Sam. They're meat. Meat's unpredictable. Never know how long the stuff'll keep. Eat your sandwich.

SAM I will lay you odds they discover death by association before the end of the century.

DOCTOR Boy would that ever put the shit in the fan.

SAM Imagine. Everyone scrambling for partners who wouldn't give them cancer.

DOCTOR And getting heart attacks from all the goddamn anxiety. The world'd fall apart, pal.

SAM Jesus, what a life it's turned out to be.

Enter ROY *and* MATTY, *with bags.*

MATTY Hello all. We're here.

SAM Roy, Matty. I was getting worried.

ROY We didn't expect to stop for dinner, but Matty needed something to eat and—well, it's a long story.

MATTY The plate was not clean. And the second plate was worse. If there were one roadhouse between Washington and New York with clean plates, I'd be a happy woman I can tell you.

ROY Benj and Joe here yet?

SAM Sleeping. Ella too.

MATTY Ralph, since you're here, how about it?

DOCTOR Matty honey, we're waiting on surgery to know for sure. Hey Roy, a drink?

ROY Thanks.

MATTY She's my sister. I have a right to know if she has cancer.

DOCTOR You know some medicine, Matty. Things aren't always clear.

MATTY Sam?

SAM Some tests said yes, some tests said no. A drink, Matty?

MATTY No, thank you.

ROY God, I hope it's not.

SAM His brothers, Ralph. Three of them. Now what the hell is that about? It defies the laws of probability.

DOCTOR Genes. Sam's decided the Van Allen belt has come unbuckled.

ROY I'm supposed to be doing an article, Sam, an overall view of pollution. So I got to researching various areas. You wouldn't believe it. I'm a science writer; I'm supposed to be scientific. But the picture I'm getting is out of the book of Exodus. A plague. We're in a biblical state of plague.

DOCTOR Except we don't believe God sent it, nice fella that He is.

SAM Hey! Maybe what this country needs is a good oracle. How would that go down in Washington?

MATTY Ralph, about Ella—

DOCTOR Really nothing more to tell, kid, not till surgery.

ROY Ah, everyone in Washington's already a prophet full-time.

SAM We'd send a messenger: Matty. It'd be Matty. You're tenacious. We know you wouldn't leave without an answer.

MATTY What would the question be?

SAM We'd say, "What has brought this suffering upon the land?" Go on, try it.

MATTY Sam, really.

SAM Go on, Matty.

MATTY "Who's responsible for this mess?" is what I'd say.

SAM And how do we purge it, right? And this schizo in the nightdress, she'd foam at the mouth and say, "Rid the land of such and such a pollution or suffer."

MATTY Sounds like Billy Graham, if you ask me. What nerve. Let him tell his pal the president that, see where it gets him.

ROY So, Sam, what pollution would the oracle name?

MATTY I could tell her what: Nixon!

DOCTOR   Nah, it'd be the war.

ROY   May I stick in my plain old literal pollution?

SAM   You may stick your plain old literal pollution anywhere you like it.

MATTY   Sam, honest to goodness, really.

ROY   Well, come on, Sam, what's she going to name?

SAM   Oracles never name names. They let you discover for yourself.

DOCTOR   So who'd she finger?

SAM   It always turns out to be yourself.

DOCTOR   Us?

SAM   More or less.

MATTY   What do you mean, us? Not me.

SAM   The Great American Middle Class.

MATTY   Are you crazy?

SAM   I'm just guessing what we'd find.

MATTY   What a nerve. Why us?

SAM   It's just my opinion that's what she'd say.

MATTY   Oh, come on, Sam, really.

SAM   Matty, everyone's entitled to an opinion. It's the land of the free, kid. Right, Roy?

ROY   I pass.

MATTY   Are we all so bad? Are you bad? I'm not bad.

SAM   Are you sure of that?

MATTY Now, Sam, listen—

SAM Never mind, we're wonderful. We're all wonderful. I take it back.

MATTY Roy's not bad. Ella's not bad. Ralph's not bad. Uncle Herman's not bad. Aunt Lena's not bad—just because a judgment's cruel doesn't make it true, though it certainly will be fashionable. On the other hand, our president, so-called, is bad. The oracle, if I had any say about it, would absolutely agree.

SAM My own wife's sister thinking this, disturbs me.

ROY Our leader's in trouble. Matty's really got it in for him.

MATTY In Washington, he may fool people, but not me. They say he's so smart he'd never be involved in Watergate. I say he's up to his five o'clock shadow in it. I'm finished with that man.

ROY And when she finishes with 'em, they're finished.

MATTY It works out that way, doesn't it, honey? Somehow it always does.

SAM You're talking like he ruined everything using only his two little paws, for Christ's sake.

MATTY Well, *we* didn't.

SAM Look, we don't own the country.

MATTY I certainly don't.

SAM But our dough finances it.

MATTY Oh, Sam honey, I'm thrilled. Roy, Sam's going to give me another civics lesson.

SAM Our dough finances the country. Fact. Truth.

MATTY Pretty soon I'll know everything, like certain other people.

SAM Now, for this, we've been allowed to hold the lady's legs apart while the biggies, the corporations, the banks, et cetera, screw her ass off.

MATTY I really don't like to hear about unnatural acts, Sam.

ROY Yeah, why her ass?

DOCTOR Easier target.

MATTY Ralph! And you a doctor.

SAM Now, Matty, it's true we're innocent in the sense that we don't instigate.

MATTY It's the Gospel according to Sam! I should probably take notes!

SAM We're basically accomplice types. We ourselves are far too kind and good and moral ever to stick it in. We get our cookies from keeping silent, a silence which, if I may say so, has come to resemble nothing so much as stupidity. Let's at least have the dignity not to look for a scapegoat.

MATTY I wasn't looking for a scapegoat. No one's given me any cookies.

SAM Ah, you want it to be Nixon.

MATTY Sam, what did we do wrong? Just us in this room, Sam.

SAM How about: Said yes when we were asked to and shut up when we were told to. Sold our birthrights, so to speak, for a mess of blue-chip pottage.

MATTY We've had some dangerous times, in case you'd forgotten.

SAM Now it's collapsing, so we're screaming like stuck pigs.

MATTY Have a little pity for your own, Sam.

SAM I'm not the one who's screaming, "It's Nixon, he's a crazy crook!" or "It's the blacks! They're uppity! It's the kids! They're irresponsible. It's the Commies! They're conspiring!" It's this, it's that, but never us? It's us.

MATTY You're beginning to sound like you-know-what.

SAM (*furious*) Like what!

MATTY You know what.

SAM I don't know what!

MATTY You know.

SAM A disillusioned businessman?

MATTY What kind of person blames us, Sam? Ask yourself that.

SAM So don't face it. I don't care.

MATTY There is nothing to face, if you ask me.

SAM Have a scapegoat. You'll feel better.

MATTY You've turned sour, Sam, but you don't mean it, honey.

ROY The war has soured a lot of people. I have a lawyer friend who's in the Treasury, and he says when Watergate gets opened up and the shit hits the fan—

SAM It'll confirm to Matty that it's someone else's fault—and it isn't.

31

MATTY It is.

SAM It's you, kid, you, him, and him, and me and—

MATTY I'm ignoring this, Sam. It didn't happen. You're just disturbed.

SAM You're goddamned right I'm disturbed!

DOCTOR Sam.

SAM I'm sorry. It's the anxiety. The brandy.

DOCTOR Hey, Roy, so how's Washington these days?

MATTY Yes, we better change the subject. Sam's upset, aren't you?

ROY The cherry blossoms are coming out, and six Japanese tourists were each sold the Lincoln monument.

DOCTOR Ha-ha, business as usual, eh, pal?

ROY Lincoln appears to be very admired in Japan.

MATTY People are frightened in Washington, Ralph. Very.

DOCTOR Jesus, do you know what I read? His daughter, Nixon's What's-her-face? She says she's willing to die for the South Vietnamese government.

SAM So's our schmuck rabbi, if you haven't heard.

DOCTOR Ah, come on, Sam. He's against the war now.

SAM When it counted, he stood up for Johnson and shouted hosannahs. We should've known when he bought the Mercedes.

ROY Our rabbi's been against it from the start. Hard, in Washington.

SAM You, Roy, are lucky. Can you imagine what it's been like? Your spiritual leader walking around with the president's pecker nine miles up his ass, and he tells us it's good for the Jews? Anyway, like Nixon's daughter, it raised a moral question I don't think even the Talmud ever covered. Should an American Jew immolate himself in his Mercedes-Benz for the murdering Catholic president of a Buddhist noncountry? My principles took a battering on that one. But I'm a liberal guy. I'm for equal opportunity. If all those poor black kids from Alabama are allowed to die for that corrupt sonofabitch South Vietnamese government, I don't think under American law and custom we can deny the right to our rabbi, though obviously his loss would tear me up something awful.

MATTY Nice talk about a learned man. He studied hard to be a rabbi.

SAM Matty, if he was my doctor, he'd be sued for malpractice. If he was my lawyer, he'd be disbarred. If he was my stockbroker, he'd be in jail for fraud. If he was subject to law—I mean, Rockefeller you expect it from. But him?

DOCTOR Van Allen belt.

SAM Well, what is it? What is it?

MATTY Sam, honey, you're really drinking too much.

SAM I earned it the hard way, right Ralph?

DOCTOR I'm keeping an eye on him, Matty.

MATTY A slightly bloodshot eye if you ask me.

ROY I'll tell you Sam, what really frightened people was the last bombing of Hanoi, at Christmas. First he's making peace—

DOCTOR   Yeah, then Merry Christmas, Hanoi—Love, Richie.

SAM   Napalm for all the screaming kiddies. Enjoy it kids.

MATTY   Washington thought he'd gone bananas.

DOCTOR   That was one of those days, I hear the news, I want to run out on the streets and start screaming.

MATTY   A nice sight that would be: you, a mature man!

SAM   The defender of the faith has spoken.

MATTY   If you talk that way in Washington, you're a Red, I'll have you know. You'd go out of business. Internal Revenue would investigate you right out of business.

SAM   Hey, Matty, I'm honest, I'm clean.

MATTY   In Washington, that wouldn't help you.

SAM   But this is New York, okay?

ROY   They whisper in Washington. They're scared as hell. They say the same thing in whispers.

MATTY   It's awesome, honey, isn't it? It really is. People are really afraid a few nuts and bolts are missing and it's all going to shake itself to pieces.

ROY   This lawyer friend of mine at the Treasury, O'Flaherty, says the war's got to end—

SAM   Hurrah for O'Flaherty of the Treasury!

ROY   He says not only can't we afford it anymore, but if it ends tomorrow, the economy is so screwed up, no one'll know what to do. He says the Vietnamese, the Russians, and the Chinese know it. We're the only ones who don't know it.

SAM Hey, Matty, you're right. It is awesome.

MATTY Call *Time* magazine, Roy honey. I want witnesses.

SAM Fifty thousand American lives. Millions of Asian peasants. Official lying, constitutional corruption, civic disintegration, public savagery, and military barbarism, blood on the boob tube for over eight years, and the schlemiel accountants bring it grinding to a halt. Hey— this is going to give money a good name again.

DOCTOR It's got a great name with me, pal.

MATTY If you don't believe anymore, Sam honey, you shouldn't criticize.

SAM What do I have to have, wings on my prick? Don't you ever ask what's happened to us?

MATTY You're the expert. I'm not qualified.

SAM You are, you know, you really are. Think back twenty-eight years, that's all: end of the war.

MATTY I don't dare speak. I'll get a civics lesson, the thrill of it.

SAM Remember, Roy, we were all together?

ROY We went out to Times Square.

DOCTOR I was there too. Just out of the navy.

ROY It was wild: the cheering, the screaming, the crying—

DOCTOR This girl grabbed me and kissed me; she had zeppelin knockers. Every year passing, they get bigger in my mind.

MATTY Just think what they really look like twenty-eight years later.

SAM Remember, Roy, you said to me and El you were proud, remember?

ROY Sure. I'll never forget.

SAM What was it, Roy? Pride in steel mills? Pittsburgh? Aircraft production? Industrial muscle?

ROY It was moral pride.

SAM Right!

DOCTOR Some good winning out in the end for once.

SAM Christ, what a feeling. My father was on his last legs then. I went to see him, you know? To tell him the Dark Ages had passed. I wanted to thank him for getting to America: a twelve-year-old Russian kid with a sack on his back getting to this country—(*stops*)
     I don't guess Benj and Joe'll come to thank me when this war ends. I don't blame them either. O'Flaherty of the Treasury is the only one to thank. Jesus, what a shame.

ROY It was our great moment, wasn't it Sam? '45.

SAM Ah, it made us crazy, and look at us now.

MATTY Sam, let's just not continue this, if you don't mind.

SAM Roy and I used to sit around. It was after the revelations of the concentration camps. We used to wonder.

DOCTOR Ha. I still wonder.

ROY Sam means, what kind of bizarre and awful creatures the Germans must have been.

SAM What kind of pigs. Snakes. Filth. Well, do you see how it's done now?

36

MATTY Does he see what?

SAM Who the good Germans of today are.

MATTY He does not.

ROY I don't really think that way, Sam.

SAM You live in Washington. You see it, all right.

MATTY It makes me sick to hear a Jew talk this way.

SAM And it makes me sick atrocities take place in my name and I can't do a goddamn thing about it.

MATTY How dare you even imply that we're Germans.

SAM I'm not implying, that's what we are.

MATTY No! Not me! I'm not a German!

SAM A good German, Matty. There are nuances. It means you don't stoke the ovens with your own two hands.

MATTY There's no way I'm a German, do you understand?

SAM Isn't there?

MATTY Never.

SAM Would you accept another million Vietnamese dead if Ella could live?

MATTY Sam. Live?

DOCTOR Sam!

SAM Rockefeller'd do it for his sister. Come on, Madeleine, what's a million burning peasants more to you?

DOCTOR Sam!

MATTY Yes, I would! And you?

SAM Correction! The good Americans!

MATTY How dare you use my sister's—

SAM My wife's—

MATTY —life—

SAM —dying!

MATTY —as a stick to beat me with . . . ?

SAM Oh, my God.

MATTY I knew it. I just knew it.

SAM I'm sorry.

MATTY Just like Mother. I knew it. I knew it.

SAM I'm . . . I'm—grasping—at something. I can't see why.
Why we're being so punished. A case builds up. The old
reasons fall away. Lies. The old causes you think cause
things—they're just front jobs for something else. Evidence
keeps pouring in. Patterns form, then break up. New
patterns form. You can't see through; only that it's shaping
into—something terrible. Inevitable. And you grasp at it.
And it slips through your grip. A crime has been committed
somewhere. It's engulfing you. And your life is being—or it
has been—or it will be—your decent, honorable,
hardworking life—made fraudulent. Corrupted. Criminal.
And one by one—or all together—we're going to pay for it.
For whatever.

MATTY Please stop, honey.

SAM Because we never learned to say no before; because it
was a sunny day in a golden age and things seemed good,
and it didn't seem worth the trouble, and it did seem to cost

too much. So we won't be able to say it now. And it'll cost much more now: everything.

DOCTOR   Eat your sandwich, Sam. It'll raise the blood sugar.

ROY   I'm always amazed. You can say anything in New York. In Washington, you never know who's listening,

DOCTOR   Hey, Roy. Have you heard this one? What has four wings and a crooked dick?

ROY   I don't know that one. Go on.

DOCTOR   The White House!

The men laugh. Matty puts her head in her hands.

ROY   Oh, I've got to remember that one! Crooked dick!

SAM   Ho-ho, crooky dicky! We're going to—ho-ho-ho, we're . . . we're going to laugh all the way to the grave!

ROY   We better go to bed, Matty honey. We're worn out from the trip.

MATTY   Can't I see Ella?

DOCTOR   She won't wake tonight. Take these pills, get some sleep. I'll see you in the morning.

SAM   Ralph, you're a brick. I'd—I don't know what I'd do without you.

DOCTOR   See you for the move to the hospital, pal.

SAM   To bed.

MATTY   Good night, all. Sam, honey, good night.

SAM   Good night.

As they are about to go, Ella wakes up suddenly with a cry.

ELLA Sam! Sam!

SAM Jesus, don't even drugs work anymore? Doesn't anything?

Ella comes to them.

ELLA I dreamed of Mother again. She howled. I got so frightened. I—Oh. Matty. Roy. Ralph. You're all here. And that—isn't that Benj's coat? Oh, what a nice surprise. Matty, dearest.

She embraces Matty.

ELLA (*cont.*) How are you, honey?

MATTY Fine, honey. I'm just fine.

Lights fade to blackout.

Music.

ACT II

Hospital. Ella is in bed. NURSE JOHNSON *is fixing Ella's hair. In another area, curtained off, lies the gangster* BARNADINO. *Ella is trying to work on a needlepoint picture.*

NURSE JOHNSON We want to look nice, don't we?

ELLA But I'd like to finish this section before the operation.

NURSE JOHNSON Needlepoint's not going to help us look nice. If we want to look nice, we've got to hold our head still. This isn't a needlepoint center, honey. We're here to be built up. Looking nice builds up the morale.

ELLA It's my fault. I should have finished it earlier.

NURSE JOHNSON Your lovely family'll be here soon, and they'll want you looking nice.

ELLA It's why I never was an artist. There were always distractions.

NURSE JOHNSON You do want to look nice for them, don't you?

ELLA So much to take care of. Nurse Johnson—

NURSE JOHNSON I mean, if you didn't want to look nice, why'd you do your face so nice? Hold still now.

ELLA Can't I interest you in what I want to do?

NURSE JOHNSON Sure, soon's you look like you want to look.

ELLA It's supposed to be a needlepoint of western Pennsylvania—

NURSE JOHNSON Where you were born, you told me.

41

ELLA   The hills in autumn. This is the sort of view you get going back to it from New York. On the Pennsylvania Turnpike. I was born just over those hills. I grew up there. Coal-mining country. It was during the Depression. Pop had a small shop. He gave credit to everyone. He couldn't bear cruelty . . . he was a religious man. We all were then.

NURSE JOHNSON   I always say there's nothing—but nothing—like looking nice for your family.

ELLA   There's always looking lousy and being in good health.

NURSE JOHNSON   Didn't look so hot when you signed in. But we're building you up!

ELLA   Nurse Johnson, you sound like you're stuffing a Thanksgiving turkey.

NURSE JOHNSON   You're the one going to give thanks when you see the job I'm doing. They're going to think you had a professional hairdresser in, they're going to be so surprised.

ELLA   Sometimes it seems a part of yourself comes to life. A part from when you had time. To waste time you don't have anymore.

NURSE JOHNSON   I want it to look professional, know what I mean? My mother always told me, Honey, if a job don't have a heart in it, you put your heart in it; it changes everything. There is a way through the world, she used to say, a broad highway, big enough for everyone with a heart—but there is no way around it, she used to say. I feel a challenge with this hair, and I am going to dominate it, that's what. Hold still.

BARNADINO Pass the word, Carlo. It ain't nice dividin' up the kingdom before the king is dead.

CARLO What dividin'? Dividin' who?

BARNADINO Just tell 'em. I ain't fooled. I may be dying but I still got power.

CARLO *exits from Barnadino's area.*

NURSE JOHNSON That man! I need him in my ward like I need a hole in my head. Do I need a hole in my head?

ELLA You do not.

NURSE JOHNSON That's right. I don't need a hole in my head.

Enter Matty, Roy, Benj, and Joe.

NURSE JOHNSON (*cont.*) Here they are. Aren't you happy you look nice now?

ELLA I am underwhelmed.

NURSE JOHNSON You are not. You are happy.

ELLA You're very kind, Miss Johnson. Thank you.

NURSE JOHNSON I'll leave you to your family now. Doesn't she look nice?

MATTY Hi, hon. You look lovely.

Nurse Johnson goes.

ROY Ella, honey, I'm dashing in to say goodbye. I've got a few days of conferences coming up in Washington and no way out. Then I'll be right back to help Matty.

OLD WOMAN *enters Barnadino's area with huge bowl of spaghetti.*

BARNADINO Clams! Beautiful. Mama, give me a kiss.

ROY We still have the Cosa Nostra with us?

ELLA His mother brings him his favorite dishes. He wants to share with us, but—

NURSE JOHNSON Mr. Barnadino! Look at that stuff swimming in oil! You know that food's not allowed in here.

BARNADINO Have a heart, lady. My mother thinks it cures cancer.

NURSE JOHNSON Well, it doesn't.

BARNADINO Yeah? Well, neither do you. So fuck off.

Nurse Johnson goes.

MATTY They really ought to have a separate hospital for these people.

BENJ The Lucky Luciano Memorial Research Hospital.

MATTY Well, I have half a mind to complain.

JOE The other half runs the motor functions.

ELLA Sam says this is Corruption in person. But he seems very nice.

ROY Speaking of nice, kids, since I'll be away, you help Matty out if you can, okay?

MATTY They are nice, honey. They're family.

ELLA So: Tell me quickly about the house.

MATTY The shopping and cleaning have been arranged, you'll be happy to hear.

ROY The last two days since you came in qualify as the biggest organizational feat since the first day of creation.

MATTY Any fool can divide darkness from light. But try getting good help today. You're lucky your sister is the can-do type.

ELLA You're making me feel much better already.

MATTY Well, a house is such a personal thing. To arrange someone's else's is a delicate business. Honey, I step on toes, but I get it done.

ELLA The cleaning is really a problem.

MATTY For dirt it's a problem. There's not room in the same house for me and dirt.

ELLA But you can't do it alone.

MATTY Well, hon, I've gone and leaned a little bit on your friend Alice, and Alice'll lend us her girl, at least till we get one, but that might take a week, and I hate to do that to Alice. Alice is so spick and span, I hate to deprive her. But Alice says she wants you to have peace of mind. So we'll just take her girl till we get our own, and I must say your friend Alice has turned out to be a very wonderful person.

JOE Does this "girl"—I mean, does she have a choice?

MATTY She's more than willing. It's a living, you know.

ELLA Anyway, bringing her from Alice to us is practically the Emancipation Proclamation.

MATTY Maybe with you it is. I intend to see she does the work she's paid for.

ELLA Matty, hon, if anyone doesn't cooperate with you, ignore them.

MATTY   If you can't be ruthless running a house, you'll never get anything done in life; the house'll run you.

ELLA   I'll tell Sam you're in charge. It needs a woman.

MATTY   And if you kids want the maid to have dinner with you just because she's black, take her out to dinner on her day off. In the house she's getting paid to work, something you know nothing about.

JOE   I just want it clear that if she makes a break for the Canadian border, we don't go after her with the hounds, okay?

MATTY   Slavery's what your mother did. This one's getting paid a nice sum.

ROY   Hon, I'm not going to make the train if I don't leave now. Ella! I'll be back soon. I'll call tonight to see everything's okay.

ELLA   (*suddenly frightened*)   Roy. Thank you.

ROY   Believe me, I don't need thanks. It's going to be all right.

ELLA   Hurry back. Don't leave Sam alone, honey.

ROY   Yes. See you soon.

Roy kisses her goodbye.

MATTY   I'm going to the station with him, so he gets the right train. . . . I'll be back before you go in, honey.

Matty and Roy go.

ELLA   I'm glad we have some time alone. It looks like I'll be out of circulation awhile, doesn't it?

JOE   Jesus, we've been getting thirty phone calls a day about you. It's driving Dad nuts. You better hurry back.

ELLA I don't think that's going to be easy.

JOE Well, if the love of your friends'd do it, you'd be back already. You're the most popular girl in town.

ELLA Except with my sons?

JOE My friends all want to come and see you. I'm not kidding.

ELLA What about you? And you, Benj?

BENJ Hey, we're here.

ELLA Yes. I'm grateful to you both.

BENJ Grateful? What grateful.

ELLA It's made me feel I didn't completely fail. I know I haven't been the perfect mother. Please don't protest—as if I had to say it. Well. Read a thousand books on kids, decide what mistakes not to make, and you still zig when you ought to zag.

BENJ Maybe you should rest.

ELLA Oh, I'll have time to rest. Look: I'm still working at the same needlepoint.

JOE It's gotten really beautiful.

ELLA It's where I came from. You knew Grandma. I wish you'd known Pop. Whatever I had that was good was from them. They had no money, very little property really, just the house they were paying off. They had real values, though. They had beliefs. They had loyalty. They had love: for each other, for us. It was really all they had. If I could have passed that on to you, I'd be a happy woman now. Instead. . . . You've both chosen to live so far away.

47

JOE You moved to New York to live.

ELLA But I still loved them. What does family mean to you?
Oppression and embarrassment. I loved Mom and Pop. I
wrote every other day when I left. Do you write?
(*silence*) What does religion mean to you? Not a great
tradition; hypocrisy. Well, it wasn't when we struggled. I—
feel like a messenger sent to the big city who just gapes and
gapes and loses the message. And I've seen you suffer for
not having it.

BENJ You're not about to inherit what you don't live. I can't.

ELLA Some do. It's simpler. Sometimes I feel the world
spinning, quicker and quicker; I get frightened. I'd have
lived Mom and Pop's lives. Would you live Sam's and
mine? No answer needed.

BENJ Then why blame yourself?

ELLA If I go now, what would you want to keep of me, of
mine?

BENJ Times change and you change.

ELLA The desire to leave something real behind—I suddenly
understand Sam's mother, pressing her strange old objects
on people, trying to pass on something of value. I
sometimes think if I'd been tough I could have done it,
even in New York. And I sometimes think it was hopeless.
I sometimes think of the trips we took out to Pennsylvania
to see Mom when she still lived there; and Matty and Roy
did too, before they moved east and did well. That's where
it was. I so hoped mere exposure would do it. I hoped you
would see it. I hoped it would take root somehow: family.

48

Loyalty. Faith. Friendliness. Innocence, really. God, if only I'd just had one daughter.

BENJ Ah, even with daughters, times would've changed.

ELLA A daughter would know what my life has been like. I'm not a model to you. There is one thing in life you will never know: to have something different come out of your body. Something biologically different. Something to live a different life in the world. Something alien almost, yet yours, yet in an alien place you weren't born in, something you'll never be a heroine or model to. Something for which you're victim to an abject, crippling love. (beat)

  I really didn't deserve being treated like shit just because I loved you. I just want to say that once. I didn't deserve you running away, living far away, never writing, not treating me like a mother but like a strange and dangerous . . . whatever . . . creature. Ah, my God. I was never so powerful. I was never that pitiful either. You couldn't see me, and why couldn't you see me? If you could have seen me, you wouldn't have hurt me. If there'd been no Depression, if I'd taken Sam to Pennsylvania to live, if you'd grown up there, it would have been so different—so much better for us all. But that just wasn't to be, it seems.

Silence.

ELLA (*cont.*) I'm sorry. I'm not after pity. My weakness saved me, in a way. I've had a good life. I hope I'll have more. Because I gave myself to it. And I was glad. And when I feel bitterness creeping around my ankles about you two, I look down and I find I'm still glad. Abjectly proud and glad. The only regret's in what I had and failed to pass on. So—left nothing.

BENJ Who says you're going yet, for Christ's sake?

ELLA (*wry*) It's nice that as you get older you sound more and more like your father.

BARNADINO I love ya, Mama! I love ya! Tell Carmella I want stuffed clams and veal tomorrow, okay? You're my girl!

Old Woman exits from Barnadino's area.

ELLA I'm going to talk to that old woman. Maybe she'll tell me her secret.

Enter Sam.

SAM Kids, take a break if you like. Get a coffee, keep an eye out for Matty. I need to discuss some things with your mother.

Benj and Joe kiss Ella.

JOE Be back soon.

They start out.

JOE (*to Benj*) Pennsylvania. All the time I was little, they're all telling me how when I was born she nearly died—you too, you know, 'You almost killed Mommy when you were born' and now she's dying and I got to listen to how it would've been different in Pennsylvania. Well, not for me. I've been accused of attempted mamacide for too many years. That's my great heritage.

BENJ The death scene belongs to the dying. It's too late to finish the argument.

JOE   Pennsyl-fucking-vania my ass.

Exeunt Joe and Benj.

SAM   I managed to get an hour alone with Inga Nilson.

ELLA   And?

SAM   She will respect your wishes.

ELLA   Not?

SAM   Perform a colostomy. No. If it comes up.

ELLA   Was it hard?

SAM   To persuade her, you mean?

ELLA   I meant for you.

SAM   Yes.

ELLA   Could you bear it if I ended like Mother?

SAM   I think not even Dr. Nilson could bear it. She was— very emotional.

ELLA   If they had to take it all out—if they left me like Mother, I'd kill myself.

SAM   It was the clincher. I quoted that.

ELLA   What did she say?

SAM   Life isn't so fastidious.

ELLA   I am.

SAM   She was very upset how lousy you felt for the way it worked out with your mother.

ELLA   Mother had real weapons, at least. She really still believed in God. Not that He came to the rescue. Not that

He ever does. What would you do if I lived on like her? I'm so afraid of that, Sam.

SAM   Nilson says—if worst comes to worst—she can only . . . be happy—not doing it—if she's sure no one else knows.

ELLA   Is it the same as pulling the plug?

SAM   For her. So I promised her only you and I'd know. And of course, the surgical nurse.

ELLA   But if I request it?

SAM   Legally speaking, she mustn't operate then.

ELLA   She ought to be proud. People should know how good she is. And I promise you it's because she's a woman. She's had to struggle so hard and sacrifice to get where she is. She told me her life once; it's really been hard.

Enter NURSE ROBERTS.

SAM   Ella; Mrs. Roberts, the surgical nurse.

NURSE ROBERTS   Dr. Nilson'll be right along. She's talking with the anesthetist. I've just come to get the consent form signed. Here; it's the standard form for exploratory surgery.

ELLA   "Exploratory surgery" is nice. It makes me feel like a new country or something. (*reads*)   Being opened up by intrepid explorers. At my age anything like that makes you feel new is good. Excuse me, dear, but this form gives Dr. Nilson virtually carte blanche. She can do anything.

NURSE ROBERTS   It's standard. She can't operate if you don't sign.

ELLA   Sam.

SAM   That's what I meant. The law.

NURSE ROBERTS You're not to worry. It's standard.

Enter NILSON.

SAM Dr. Nilson.

NILSON Sam, we're friends, aren't we? It should be Inga by now.

ELLA Hello, Inga.

NILSON How's my girl? Looking well. Is that the consent form, Mrs. Roberts?

NURSE ROBERTS I think Ella's a little bit worried.

NILSON My dear, you are not to. You have my word. I won't do anything you don't want. Now that's enough said. Sam?

SAM We're grateful—Inga.

NILSON I've been through a lot with you, Ella. I may have made a mistake before—at least *we* may have made a mistake—but it was all I could do, my best, and I won't make the same mistake again if you don't want. But we sure can't leave you like this, can we? Now, the anesthetist is preparing. When the consent form reaches the office, I'll send for him.

ELLA Give me a pen.

NURSE ROBERTS Here.

ELLA *(signs)* I trust you. Completely.

NILSON And you have reason to. Mrs. Roberts, please witness.

Nurse Roberts signs.

NILSON (*cont.*)   Please take the form to the office.

NURSE ROBERTS (*to Ella*)   You have my admiration, if I may say so. People have to take hold of their own destinies, much as they can. It's the only way any good comes about. See you soon.

Nurse Roberts goes.

NILSON   Mrs. Roberts is very impressed. So am I. Sam, I told Ella once, I was brought up on a farm. Animals know what's right for them, what's right and what's wrong; people get so scared they forget, and more's the pity. I grew up with the idea of nature and the rhythm of life, and no matter how long you work in a great hospital, if you had it once, if you weren't city bred and born, you never lose it, do you, Ella?

ELLA   You never did.

NILSON   I should hope to God not. This needlepoint's gorgeous. My mother used to do needlepoint. It's a lovely art. I'd assumed it was lost.

ELLA   I'm hoping to finish it.

NILSON   We'll try and see you do.

ELLA   Inga: Thank you in advance—for whatever.

SAM   Yes. Thank you.

NILSON   Take some more time, you two. But the anesthetist has got to come soon.

Nilson goes.

ELLA   My God!

SAM What's wrong?

ELLA I feel a pillow's been lifted off my face. I've always been so afraid. Everything always seemed out of control, Sam. So sick as a child; you had to be careful. All those years, always careful. The stock market crashed. All over town, people were ruined. Good people and bad, it just didn't matter. Mom said to Pop, "You have to be careful." It's like an ugly refrain from my childhood; when Pop died, it went in like a knife. All I could think was, I better be careful. Find a safe place. I did find one with you; I knew I had. Then the war, and the kids being born. I never told you how frightened I was. What right did I have to give birth at that time? I was so scared I'd offended somehow. I was afraid I'd be punished for being so happy, so happy with my babies. It's worse being afraid for their lives. It gets under your skin like a tropical bug. First for your own life. Then for theirs. That they'll pay for some offense you've given. So you look for a place, another safe place. A place you don't have to move and be noticed, a place your happiness passes unnoticed; a place that fits what you have become, from terror, death, war, all that hate. A place you can pass on your fear to the kids. But they get afraid of catching your fear. I guess that's why they run away. So you find yourself . . . safe, yes, but lonely. Not too much honored. Not like I honored my mother and father. But finally, finally, finally, you do something right. Taking hold of this—terror. Turning it around. (*beat*) Sam? Thank you. For everything. (*beat*) You being cheerful would make it complete.

SAM There's only one thing'll cheer me up, Ella.

ELLA I better say it: If I die, Sam, marry again.

SAM   What, are you kidding?

ELLA   After thirty-five years, I know what you need.

SAM   I don't want to hear that kind of talk.

ELLA   Find the right woman; don't waste your life mourning.

SAM   Hey, come on, your job's not to die.

ELLA   Seriously, hon, who'll take care of you?

SAM   What am I, a basket case? This is really premature.

ELLA   Don't count on the kids, Sam. They're selfish as hell.

SAM   Ah, the great Defender's seen the light.

ELLA   Find someone mature or you'll be unhappy.

SAM   Yeah, well, I'll go check at the maturatorium, see if they've got a sale on.

ELLA   In the best of worlds, you'd be out looking already.

SAM   Who'd I meet? Some gold-digging dame?

ELLA   And if I lived, you'd come back; you'd tell me, "I looked around. There was no one like you."

SAM   I can tell you that already.

ELLA   Sam, if I die, you'll come down for breakfast, you'll sit for hours at an empty table.

SAM   Worst comes to worst, I can boil an egg.

ELLA   You hate boiled eggs.

SAM   So circumstances would give me new tastes.

ELLA   Who'll you talk to?

SAM Who'll understand me anyway?

ELLA Someone who cares; but who'll care if you don't find someone?

SAM But if I don't care, I don't care if they don't care.

ELLA You're so stubborn.

SAM What's this trying to dispose of me?

ELLA I've made my arrangements but—I'm worried for you.

SAM Jesus, you'd think tonight was your wedding or something.

ELLA Would you rather I was frightened?

SAM Christ, no, but I didn't expect this.

ELLA Remember on Crete?

SAM What on Crete?

ELLA Nothing. I just want to know you'll be all right.

SAM I'll be all right if you are, and that's that.

Enter Matty, Benj, and Joe.

MATTY Everything okay, honey? Anything you want?

ELLA No. I have what I want. Sit down all.

MATTY Guess who we just met in the corridor? The head surgeon, hon, and he knows all about you; he's a real dedicated man. Oh—it's a real red sunset. Is it in your eyes, honey? I'll shut the blinds.

ELLA Leave it. Just let me look at your faces awhile.

Enter Nurse Roberts.

NURSE ROBERTS   I'm sorry, dear, it's time. They're ready to give you your shot.

ELLA   Mrs. Roberts: my sons; my sister Matty.

NURSE ROBERTS   Nice meeting you.

SAM   Well. We'll say good night.

JOE   Good night.

Joe kisses her.

ELLA   Good night.

BENJ   Good night.

Benj kisses her.

ELLA   Good night.

MATTY   Good night, honey.

Matty kisses her.

ELLA   Don't let them stay up all night, waiting.

MATTY   I'll do what I can, hon. Just don't—worry.

ELLA   I won't. Good night, Sam.

SAM   Good night.

Sam kisses her.

ELLA   Good night. Good night.

NURSE ROBERTS   We have your number. We'll contact you as soon as it's over.

Lights fade as they go, indicating time passing. Lights up on Barnadino's area as Nurse Johnson opens his curtains.

BARNADINO Open it, open it!

NURSE JOHNSON Open what? It's open.

BARNADINO Open it, open it!

NURSE JOHNSON I better call someone. A doctor.

BARNADINO No . . . just open it.

NURSE JOHNSON Open what? I don't understand.

Exhausted, Barnadino falls back, breathing loudly.

NURSE JOHNSON (*cont.*) Mr Barnadino? I don't . . . ?

Nurse Roberts wheels Ella in on a trolley, Nilson follows. They transfer Ella to bed.

NILSON (*sits*) I better be here myself for when she wakes. Mrs. Roberts—

NURSE ROBERTS I guess so. I'm sure not going to explain it.

Nurse Roberts goes.

NURSE JOHNSON Mr. Barnadino? I'm getting someone—

BARNADINO No. Open it.

NURSE JOHNSON You're not going to last.

BARNADINO Just open it!

NURSE JOHNSON Open what, Mr Barnadino?

BARNADINO *You bitch, open it. You bitch! You bitch!*

NURSE JOHNSON I'm going for someone in charge—

BARNADINO I'm in charge. Like I always been. Open it. Open it! *Open it!*

Nurse Johnson runs out.

BARNADINO *(cont.)* *Mary Mother of God!*—Oh.

Barnadino dies.

NILSON Mrs. Roberts!

Nurse Roberts comes.

NILSON *(cont.)* It was something unexpected. The head surgeon came in to watch. I—had to do it.

NURSE ROBERTS *(angry)* Never mind it. You hear?

NILSON Mrs. Roberts. The head surgeon fought like the dickens to get me my job here. It was a men's club. When he came in to watch me work—I didn't know he was coming—I just couldn't not do it. I had no choice.

NURSE ROBERTS Her liver's riddled, she's as good as dead.

NILSON She'd have been dead in two days if I hadn't performed a—I just couldn't betray him—

NURSE ROBERTS How long?

NILSON A week. Two. A month. No, not a month. I had no choice.

NURSE ROBERTS She trusted your word. I trusted your word. What about me? And you had a choice. Because I gave you one, that's why I said it: You promised her not to! Right in the OR, and you ignored it. You promised her not to. He heard me.

NILSON I have explained why I had to—

NURSE ROBERTS Bull.

She glances at Barnadino's area.

NURSE ROBERTS (*cont.*)   You wouldn't have broken your word to that one, would you? God knows what he'd have done to you, if you had. Save that loyalty bull. It's just who you're more scared of, that's all it is. Shit-scared, that's all it is.

Nurse Roberts goes.

Nilson sits alone, grim, rigid. Ella groans. Nilson doesn't move. Ella groans. Nilson rises. Ella groans. Nilson turns to look at her. Ella groans. Nilson, uncertain, reaches out a hand—hesitates—then smooths her hair.

NILSON   My God. My God.

ACT THREE

The representation of the house is at back, the table and four chairs in front. Roy, Doctor, and Joe are at the table, Doctor reading newspapers. It is two weeks later.

DOCTOR So your youngest brother died of cancer too.

ROY Same as the others. I was—shattered. But I discovered something.

DOCTOR Market's dropping like up had disappeared. I can think of six patients who're going to have coronaries when they see the stock page today.

ROY See, Joe, you get this feeling of such—impotence.

DOCTOR (*absently*) Like being in bed with a woman you love. But.

JOE More coffee, anybody?

ROY Thanks, no. But, now, the real beauty I'm trying to describe—the flower in the dungheap, I call it—not that it cancels out the shock or pain—

DOCTOR Jesus! Here's a guy I got to show to Sam. He made a mint in pork bellies. Futures, they're called, buying pigs that aren't born yet, hoping prices'll rise. I suppose it's preferable to real live pigs in your living room. But, pal, ask yourself, is that a future? That's what it's called, a future. Ho-ho. I have seen the future and it goes *oink-oink*—oh. Sorry, Roy, go on.

ROY The beauty is how life arranges this support system around a crisis. It does it naturally, I mean. It doesn't require an authoritarian center to organize. There's sympathy in the cells, and a crisis comes, and we just get to it. Purposeless activity drops away.

DOCTOR Schmuck. He made millions in pigs that don't exist! Jesus, imagine if they'd existed! I'd like to make that money off patients who don't exist. Some doctors do.

ROY Everything humane and scientific pulls together.

JOE Be nice if we could get it on earlier, no?

DOCTOR Nah, no crisis, people say, why bother?

ROY I suppose we're incapable of stimulating the best in ourselves until it's near too late. Now look at Ella, Ralph, you'll see what I mean. She's supported by three pillars. First, whatever's in the plasma that won't give up even when she does. A kind of life force. This pillar just provides the space in which the extraordinary could take place—not saying it will.

DOCTOR It's not going to, pal.

JOE You haven't seen her in a week, Roy. She looks about ninety years old. You're going to think you walked into a concentration camp.

ROY Alive, though, Joe. Which for plasma is the point. Second pillar: Sam. And Matty. Keeping things going. Third: medicine. Trying to exploit the space the plasma is providing. I got to thinking this out last night on the train from Washington. Now, supporting Sam and Matty, there are you, Joe, Benj, all the relatives and friends, and so forth. And supporting medicine are thousands of research workers, hospital workers, laboratories, technicians, philanthropists, government agencies. You can see a kind of pyramid of life

63

support if you look at it. And that's the beauty: You can look at Ella's suffering and suffer until you can't any longer. Or you can look at the pyramid and be somewhat—consoled—at how life works. My youngest brother's death taught me that.

JOE That's what I mean. When the plasma goes, the whole fucker crumbles like a cookie.

DOCTOR Sam's going to laugh his head off when he reads this. Pig in the future's worth two in the hand! Hey, Roy, sorry, how's it going? Need anything? Traveling back and forth getting you?

ROY Write the articles on pollution. Go to the meetings. Then I could be here to help Matty out.

DOCTOR Pal, if I could, I'd do it for you, you know that.

ROY Actually, working with these environmental kids is very stimulating. Dedicated, bright, purposeful; best thing I've done in years. I keep thinking, Who knows? Maybe they'll even save us.

DOCTOR Jesus. Then what'll we do?

Enter Sam, busy with files and papers.

SAM All honor to the painkiller. Welcome.

DOCTOR How's the Van Allen belt treating you, pal?

SAM It's progressing. I figure if you've got to worry about the Van Allen belt, something even worse is probably wrong. Black holes in the sky or something, and it's already too damn late.

DOCTOR Hey, you catch the president on television last night?

SAM Hoo-hoo-hoo-hoo-hoo. And read what *The Times* says.

DOCTOR Hah, I'm hung up on this guy, a story you'll love, guy made millions out of nonexistent pigs.

SAM Futures. Anyone can make millions out of nonexistent pigs. Know why?

DOCTOR Why?

SAM Costs nothing to feed nonexistent pigs.

DOCTOR Oh, I got to remember that one! We'll all be rich, oink oink.

SAM Listen, there's a guy on the phone. I've got to run along. If I don't get this paperwork out of the way, I'm going to have some trouble with some very real pigs.

DOCTOR I'll be giving Ella her shot in a while, okay?

SAM We'll have a drink. You'll need it if she's like yesterday.

DOCTOR Yeah.

Sam goes.

ROY I thought there was a cobalt treatment this morning. Shouldn't the ambulance be here?

DOCTOR We've canceled. It was hurting her, and the liver wasn't responding. The guy said, Forget it.

ROY Two weeks—for nothing.

JOE There's pillar three of the pyramid. They've given up.

ROY I didn't know.

JOE It's just us and the plasma now. And time. Which is where we began, I guess.

Enter Matty.

MATTY Hello all.

DOCTOR How're you doing, kid? Ella awake?

MATTY Benj is with her. Joe: You haven't been talking to Ralph about the surgeon, I hope.

DOCTOR No, he hasn't.

JOE He knows what I think.

MATTY I'm sure he does. We all do.

DOCTOR Kid, I understand both sides. There was a real problem. Nilson gave under the weight.

JOE That, Ralph, is—the kind of statement that gives cowardice a bad name.

MATTY Oh, you and Benj and Sam upset me so much.

ROY Matty, honey, don't provoke it.

MATTY They provoke, they provoke.

JOE You're not the primary concern around here. Just leave off the mind-control stuff, that we should all believe what you believe, and we'll be okay.

MATTY The surgeon was right. She was absolutely right. To preserve life. Not to break the law. She was right, life is sacred.

JOE You call that living in there?

MATTY You don't know what life is, even if you are my nephew.

JOE Christ, Matty—first she does it to your mother, then she does it to your sister, and you admire her principles. Whose side are you on?

MATTY This whole family, I just don't understand you. It's what modern education does, I guess. It makes everything okay. Everything is not okay.

ROY Relax, Matty, hon. Sit down.

JOE You're waiting for the miracle, aren't you, Matty?

MATTY Yes! And I'll tell you something else. I'm praying. And why aren't you? And why isn't Benj? Why isn't everybody?

JOE Pillar number two is crumbling.

Enter Benj with electric toothbrush buzzing.

BENJ Hey, one of you with fingernails. I knocked it on the floor in her bathroom, some plastic doodad broke off. I can't stop the bastard.

MATTY (*tries*) This is supposed to be really good for the gums.

BENJ It's trying to tell us something. No one can stop it. It's the last message of four hundred years.

MATTY Damn. I broke a nail.

She hands it to Joe.

BENJ I am your son, I am your daughter, your mourner. Therefore send not to know for whom the electric toothbrush buzzes, my brethren; it buzzes for thee.

JOE (*pulling it apart*) You've cleaned your last molar, friend.

MATTY   What were you doing in Ella's bathroom, if I may ask?

BENJ   I had to take her there to empty the bag. It's like carrying a broken kitten.

JOE   I had to do that yesterday.

ROY   How is she today, Benj?

BENJ   She can't walk anymore.

ROY   I know.

BENJ   Hardly talks; too weak. When she does, it's like a junkie.

MATTY   Very nice, your own mother: "like a junkie."

BENJ   I was reminded. Junkies get strung out. Have this obsessive single focus. Can't stop talking about that one thing. An endless chain of half sentences about that one thing. In her case, shame and betrayal. Betrayal and shame. Self-disgust, self-loathing, shame, betrayal. And the imagined smell of excrement. She hopes for help and no help comes, only more shame and the smell of excrement. She asked to see you in a few minutes, Matty.

ROY   Just like Mother all over again.

BENJ   Right.

ROY   I've spent my adult life watching my most loved family crucified on lingering illnesses and I'm stumped. I feel like an Ishmael. I feel I should do something. Or say something. But I don't know what. Maybe I'm too passive. But my actions just seem so foolish when confronted with this astounding malignancy I witness, and witness again, and come to terms with, and then lose the terms of. I don't know. Maybe I'll think of something.

MATTY It was the cobalt treatments! It never should have been cobalt. I'm sorry, Ralph, I even tried to warn Sam, but would he listen? No.

DOCTOR Kid, it was the only thing that might've been a stopper.

MATTY It should've been chemotherapy.

JOE Are we going to go through this again?

MATTY I always said it should have been chemotherapy. But who listens? No one, that's who. It couldn't have been worse than it has been.

DOCTOR Sure it could. Two weeks of vomiting and nausea on top of the rest.

MATTY I just think the doctors were wrong.

ROY Matty, honey, please.

MATTY Not that anyone listens to me, but they never should have followed up with cobalt, no matter what anyone says, anyone.

DOCTOR Matty, you know a lot about medicine. But this time, believe me, kid, you're wrong.

MATTY Oh, Ralph, doctors always say that.

JOE Will you shut the fuck up! Will you stop it and shut the fuck up for a change? Shut up. Go home. Get out of here.

Joe goes.

MATTY Well! Some people may want me to go, but as long as I am useful here, I'll stay.

DOCTOR Come on, kid. No one wants you to go. Relax.

MATTY It's been grueling, Ralph, but as long as Ella needs me—she does, doesn't she, Benj? Even if you and Sam and Joey think—

The doorbell rings.

BENJ Matty, you're being a brick. But sometimes you drive people nuts. Excuse me.

He goes.

MATTY Not that some people have very far to be driven. You can see I'm not the most popular girl in town, Ralph.

ROY I just don't understand it.

DOCTOR Getting a little rough, eh?

ROY She cries on the telephone to me.

MATTY Only once, honey. Don't exaggerate.

ROY The treatment from the kids—you just saw some of it— is really shocking.

MATTY Well, they are in a state of shock, honey. It's not important.

ROY It's important if it upsets you, hon.

MATTY I don't mind, really. It's all in the family. Well. I better go see Ella now, see what she wants.

She goes.

DOCTOR I'll be in, give her her shot in a minute.

ROY I worry about her. She's doing everything she can. She says Sam can barely talk to her.

DOCTOR Uh-huh. Well.

ROY And the kids. My God.

DOCTOR Look, pal, what's a man's life? He usually works at something that doesn't exactly give him a hard-on, right? He marries. Sometimes he has kids, hoping they'll take care of him in his old age. I hear all that's changing, but that's the way it used to be, before the age of the nonexistent future pig, right? So: He loves his wife, he loves his kids. This is assuming there are no monsters involved.

ROY But we love the kids too. As if they were ours.

DOCTOR Let me finish. The wife loves the husband, loves the kids; the kids love them, et cetera. And they also occasionally hate each other, if you hadn't noticed. Complicated, a family, right? Now: Comes a time for dying, pal, the love comes up, the hate's stowed in the closet. Well. Hate don't like closets, right? So you sock it to someone else. Scapegoat. Load the sins on some poor schmuck's back, a boot in the fanny, and drive them into the wilderness. Feels real good.

ROY Why should Matty be the scapegoat?

DOCTOR Why not? Maybe she does it for love, protect Ella. It's got to be somebody. Seen it a hundred times, pal.

ROY What do you mean? If Matty's a scapegoat, who're they attacking?

DOCTOR You know who.

71

ROY   You mean they're really attacking Ella?

DOCTOR   Proud of you, pal, got it first time.

ROY   For heaven's sake. Attacking her for what?

DOCTOR   Probably for dying. All I'm saying is, Roy, don't scratch it. Give it time, it won't get infected, okay?

ROY   Ralph, as an old friend, I want to ask you a simple question.

DOCTOR   Oops. Got a déjà vu.

ROY   I want to know why you just can't end it with a shot. This is purposeless suffering.

DOCTOR   Roy, suppose I was a gambler. Suppose I lost everything. And I come to you, and I say, Roy, embezzle from your boss. Cheat on your taxes. Steal from your neighbor. But get me the dough because if I don't pay these guys, they're going to rub me out.

ROY   I'd help you borrow it from a bank.

DOCTOR   There's your answer.

ROY   I don't see it, Ralph.

DOCTOR   You'd stick within the law. Why not me?

ROY   I'm sorry.

DOCTOR   I'm a simple guy, Roy. You have respect for the law, I have respect for the law. I decided it a long time ago. We've all seen crooks get away with murder. We've all seen officials be corrupt. I just decided that the law's still a good thing. It's a good thing even if it's slow to catch up with people's needs—even if it helps the real schmucks thrive—

72

for me it's still good. It's the north star, pal, can't navigate
so good without it. Shit. I know what I know. But I just
decided that none of those bastards, no matter what they
did, could take that away from me. My belief that it's good.
I know there are higher considerations sometimes. I know
there's unbearable pain. I just decided I'm a limited guy. I
signed on to relieve pain in every way I can. That's all I do.
People want me to do otherwise—I figure they're hoping
the courage'll come from the outside, pal. But it can't. That
I promise you. Call it mercy killing. Call it anything. The
courage can't come from the outside, pal.

ROY Look: Come in there with me, Ralph. I hate for Matty
to shoulder it alone. But I'll be a mess without some
support.

DOCTOR It's almost time for her dope, anyway.

Doctor and Roy go. Enter Benj, Joe and the RABBI.

BENJ Dad's actually pretty busy, Rabbi.

JOE He says hold on, he'll be with you in a minute.

RABBI Do you think there's any way I can help?

BENJ Well. Care to have a try at making a new mommy?

RABBI Perhaps spiritual support. I think I have some idea of
what the family's going through.

JOE None of us have been to temple in years, you know.

RABBI Why, there was the service for your mother's mother
not two years ago.

BENJ Well, one swallow doesn't make a spring.

RABBI I—that is—I really only came to offer help.

BENJ Just stand right there. Don't touch anything with that—uh, y'know, Vietnamese blood on your hands, okay? I'll see if I can hurry Dad along.

Exit Benj.

RABBI Oh dear. Well. (*silence*)   President Johnson was a more impressive man than you'd suppose. (*silence*)

A man of tragic error, however; but his sheer force—I—well, it was like straying into a magnetic field. Even with profound doubts, you—went along. Were carried along. He had such an open special fondness for Jews. He seemed so hurt that so many were opposing the war—him. I suppose I wanted to redress the balance. Magnetic, magnetic man. And was sucked in, I confess, way over my head. Better than me were.

Enter Benj and Sam, carrying papers.

SAM Rabbi, what can I do for you?

RABBI The question is really what I can do for you.

SAM Right now I don't think anything, thank you.

RABBI My first wife passed away of cancer, as you probably remember.

SAM Of course.

RABBI Well. If and when you feel the need—as a man, as a husband, as a Jew, in any way—please call on me. I will be there. I know how difficult it is.

SAM Yes. Well.

RABBI It is hell. Well. I'll be going. Joseph. Benjamin.

SAM Is that your car? Isn't it a new car?

RABBI The Mercedes-Benz caused too much comment, I'm afraid. I suppose it was insensitive of me to buy it. But when she . . . passed away—my wife—I don't know what happened. A man loses his footing sometimes. I did things, I said things which I'm sure you know—I have grave doubts about now.

I wish the Mercedes was the worst of them. The damnedest thing is it's the only good car I've ever owned. My fate in cars is strictly lemons. You simply wouldn't believe what goes wrong. Don't see me out. You're busy. Call on me.

Rabbi goes. Sam lays out papers and works.

BENJ Prick.

JOE Is there going to have to be a service?

SAM Yup. And—here, Joe, sign this—Christ, you guys'd really relieve my mind if you'd grow up a little. First of all, if at your age you don't know the difference between a prick and a whore, then Christ what *do* you know? Second, he's suffered for his mistakes. You were looking at a shell back there. He didn't even try and hit me for the contribution I don't make anymore. Anyway, he's paid for his mistakes. It's about time we forgot it. Besides, it could've happened to anyone. Benj, sign this.

JOE Could it have happened to you?

SAM In his position? I can be flattered. Hey, I'll bet he knows a good estate lawyer. Maybe I will go see him. Make a note here.

BENJ What happened yesterday?

SAM When?

BENJ Evening. When you were talking with Mom.

SAM Sign this, please.

BENJ You looked like a ghost.

SAM It's harder sometimes than others.

BENJ Then you started to work like a madman.

SAM Oh. Well, you can't imagine the problems with estates. Taxes. I was supposed to die first. Now everything's screwy.

JOE Is that what you're doing now, for Christ's sake?

SAM I have no choice.

JOE You have a choice. Put it off.

SAM If you hadn't utterly turned your back on practical life experience, you'd know I can't.

JOE She's not dead yet.

SAM Oho. Has the time come, when I'm down, you're going to stick the knife in?

BENJ Hey, that's not it at all.

SAM The hell it isn't.

BENJ Did she say something? Why are you mad?

SAM Why do you think?

JOE I wasn't sticking the knife in.

SAM Then sign this. Because I do not propose to let the tax man get one penny more than he's entitled to.

JOE Fuck him. Forget him.

SAM This is for your sakes, not mine.

JOE Not for mine, it isn't.

SAM You don't know law. You don't know business. You don't know money. So who's going to protect you? Sign this, please.

JOE No. It's not right.

SAM Look. I'm going to have a few years left. That's time enough to grieve. But if those Internal Revenue vultures catch you grieving and not minding the shop, they'll cut your nuts off. They're heartless, kiddie, and there's nothing you can do about it afterward.

JOE Well, you're a very practical man.

SAM You better thank your stars there's one in the family.

JOE You talk like this was sharper-than-a-serpent's-tooth-ville.

SAM Isn't it?

JOE Have you seen her today?

SAM Every day. And in my sleep.

JOE Are you asking her to sign things too?

BENJ Take it easy.

JOE She's in some kind of private Auschwitz and you're doing the taxes?

SAM Will you sign it, Joe?

JOE Sure, let's have the surgeon to dinner too. I mean there used to be—frameworks for these occasions. Proper frameworks. You could hang your feelings on them. You knew what to do, what to say. There was respect for the occasion. It was okay, somehow. I mean, what are you doing? What the hell is this?

SAM I am surrounded all day long by people waiting for me to break down. Waiting in order that they can give vent to this unbearable grief freely and not—upset me. I have been trying to explain that I cannot afford to. Break down. I am hard pressed, however, to keep my nose above water. I'm trying to for your sakes. Because since neither of you, nor anyone you know, is capable of making these obscenely materialistic arrangements, I must do it. Now, I do not—I have never—begrudged you the freedom you've had. Just once—now—remember that I paid for it with forty years of sweat and allow me, I'm begging you humbly, to continue. Now will you sign?

JOE I wasn't sticking a knife in.

SAM You were. And I am bleeding.

JOE Benj?

BENJ It's not going to save her, to sign or not to.

JOE That isn't the point. You got to respect the occasion. I mean Death, Death is the Man, right? The Big One.

BENJ Yeah, with a cock like a donkey.

JOE I mean, be serious!

BENJ Not signing's not going to make up for—whatever.

78

JOE Is that all you can say?

BENJ I don't even think it's going to provide fuck-all.

SAM Well, thank you very much, my sons.

BENJ Neither do you. Not really.

SAM There appears the slightest chance our world will not disappear in the next fifty years. I am trying to provide for that chance. I am also trying to keep my mind busy for reasons I would've thought I didn't have to explain. If not for your own sake, then sign to help me, Joe.

JOE On the flight here, I thought I'd been kidding myself.

SAM If you mean your concern for your mother's happiness could have begun earlier, I agree.

JOE I meant the feeling that I'm not just me. I'm so much her idea of me. The shaping hands, all that stuff. Then the thought that it might be about to disappear. I mean, maybe the shaping hands are all that's holding you together. . . .
It was like the airport you're headed for won't be there. So where do you land then? What's your course? The old control towers are abandoned. The radar's off, the machinery's rusted. The runways've buckled and grass grows in the cracks. The scenery, the hills, the fields keep passing beneath. But reference points are missing. What's your location? How'll you find out while you still have fuel? Then you don't have fuel. The gauge reads empty. The red lights flash. The engines sputter, and then they cut. You go into a glide, over unknown territory. You glide for miles and miles, I guess. Nothing's familiar.
There's this silence in gliding, which begins to take over. Then the sea comes up in the distance. It's a beautiful day of

spring blue and gold. And water's rushing away beneath
you. This blue rushing silence, except for a little hum of the
wind. You can't maintain height. Unnoticed, you hit. Big
white plumes of spray explode up. Plane busts like an egg.
In a while you sink, leaving nary a trace. Do you know
what I mean?

Sam works.

SAM After thirty-five years with her, don't I?

JOE Give me the paper.

He signs.

SAM When you live so long with someone, who are you
without them? . . . Funny. I tried to pray a while back.
Sort of.

BENJ At the operation?

SAM Before. I was pretty sure then. I wanted to take her
place. I asked to. I was afraid what it would be like, after so
long, being alone. What part of myself'd disappear. Now
it's over. That fear. The worst we tried to avoid's pretty
much happened.

JOE Things haven't worked out the way I expected.

SAM It's going to take a thousand years to explain.

JOE There must have been control of the situation at some
point. How did we lose it?

SAM The old usual dream we'll control our lives. The mirage
that keeps you going in the desert.

JOE I'm—disappointed somehow.

SAM In me?

JOE No. I mean I thought when we faced this kind of problem, we were somehow better equipped. Any Eskimo?—Amazon Indian?—New Guinea mudman?—any of them would've put together a better package than we got.

SAM Jesus, what romantics you are.

JOE I'm trying to say I thought we were different.

SAM You may as well learn it now: There's one thing no one's different in and that's in getting screwed. Anyhow, I'm not letting the tax man screw me too. There are some things after sixty years in this world I know how to do right and still keep honest, by the way.

BENJ You mean screwed because of not telling her the truth before the operation?

SAM What truth?

BENJ That it was one in a thousand, her chances.

SAM One in a thousand, she'd take it. Even so, she said: No colostomy. Even so, they went ahead and did it. How do you stop the bastards? That's the mystery. Sign here please, Benj.

JOE She should've stopped the head surgeon. She shouldn't have let him stick his nose in.

SAM (*continues working*) It's not the medicos. I finally know what it is. Too late, as usual. It's because no one's got any sense of—what? Honor? Quality in life? I don't know if it's got a name. It used to. We've lost it. Today, no matter what the menu describes, no matter what you sit down and order, you get the shabby bargain instead. The easy way.

The short cut. The shabby no-blame botch-up. The all-holy all-embracing bargain. Value for money. It's the real black hole in the sky, I promise you, kiddie. The meat shredder of human meat: value for money. It's our obsession. It's what we worship. It's what we've got.

JOE Amen.

SAM (*continues working*) Even the law's built on it. To give the bargain. The deal. So what's the law? The rich don't have to obey it. The poor can't afford to obey it. Jesus, I think the middle class was invented for the sole purpose of having someone to obey the law. That's a joke, too. I've seen in my lifetime every middle class in the West wiped out. For worshiping the bargain, the deal. And they still worship the bargain. We're so stupid you can sell us anything as long as you tell us it's value for money. If it actually has any value, the rules are changed from above. Otherwise: It's the shoddy tin-can car. Corrupted elections. Rotten politicians, without an idea in their heads or a scruple in their hearts. Bogus nothing education. Watered-down religion. So-called judges screwing justice; lawyers like parasites on all human weakness. Big banks speculating with your hard-earned dough; unions speculating with their pension funds or selling out their members' jobs. It can be overvalued pumped-up stock pushed at you by the pillars of the community. It can be lousy ignorant medical care; phony building programs full of graft; social schemes that take a situation from horrible to even worse—graft, bribes, kickbacks, murders, blackmail, thievery, prostitution, you name it. Silence as the price of the good life. The good life itself. We'll buy it if it's value for money.

★ ★ ★

It can be a cheap easily winnable war in Southeast Asia. It can be an America-loving tyrant in Greece, a thieving murderer in South America backed by our dough. It can be hiring experts to smooth death over. It hardly matters. One thing is for sure: You'll get too much sand in your cement every time. And every time when it collapses, you'll scream. And next time, you'll nibble at the next bargain again. The next easy way. The next wonder solution. The next shortcut. Trouble is, where there is no value, no real value at the center of things, there can be no value for money. No bargain. And there isn't. There is only painted whoring greed. Vanity. Me-me-me-ism. It's high-placed pimps. It's low executioners. And brother—end of sermon—they gobble us like peanuts and wash us down with the law. (*beat*) I was walking the streets after the operation. I couldn't really believe what had happened. I didn't see it then. I was like a sleepwalker. I was actually stumbling, out of focus. Then these spring sales signs caught my eye. And it all came into focus. See, there were all these women striding along Fifth Avenue, dressed to kill—and where were they going? Going to their miserable churches. Going to Temple Beth Bloomingdale's Department Store. Going to Macy's of the Sacred Heart. To Saks Fifth Avenue the Divine. Going shopping. Looking for what? For the bargain that this whole wide world tells them exists. That's when I saw it. Before they know what hit them, they'll be shredded meat too, like your mother. I felt such pity and such contempt for us all. Shredded meat, and who'll know why? Will you?

Benj—sign this please.

BENJ (*signs*) Our Bargain, which art in heaven, hallowed be thy name.

SAM You ain't just whistling Dixie either. And here.

BENJ (*signs*) Thy Bargain come, thy will be done, on earth as it is in heaven.

SAM You know what I'm afraid they'll finally sell us, of course? I had this dream of it last night. There was this nuclear war.

JOE Je-sus.

SAM Yeah, I mean it. Bombs, rockets, screaming through a monster hole in the universe. Everything went. Not a stick left. Whole planet like a sea of smooth glass. Cold. A round cold glass ball. Joe? Here. This one.

JOE (*signs*) Hey. How about, "Give us this day our daily Bargain."

BENJ And get me a good deal concerning my trespasses, for which I'll be willing to overlook certain other individuals' trespasses.

SAM Another one, Joe. Here.

JOE (*signs*) For thine is the Bargain and the power and the glory for ever and ever, amen.

SAM It really was the most awful dream of my life. I was blinded by the first blast. There wasn't pain, though—oh, damn it to hell, the stupid bank forgot to—well, it's their problem. No, goddamn it, it isn't. It's mine, as usual. Benj, sign here; I'll work it out later.

BENJ (*signs*) Fourscore and seven years ago, our fathers brought forth on this continent a New Bargain, conceived in liberty and dedicated to the proposition that all men are created equal.

SAM You know what it was? In the dream? It was more like
being invaded by light. Very gentle—and very terrifying. I
thought, Uh-oh, they've blown up the world—first telling
us why, of course. I actually started laughing then. I
thought, Well, fellows, it wasn't much, but at least it was
ours. In the dream, it seemed very witty. I woke up
specifically to tell Ella. But of course she wasn't next to me.
I guess there'll be a lot of that in the future. What a life.
Last one, Joey. Another power of attorney to me.

JOE (*signs*) As the consumer consumes the great Bargain, so
shall he—she—be consumed by it utterly. . . . Hey, what in
hell are we talking about?

BENJ Just tossing images around to fill the void.

SAM Yeah? Well, ask yourself if that's a fit activity for a
grown man.

BENJ Imponderable, given what grown men do.

SAM I suppose. Christ, I used to think maturity was being
married, earning a living, having children. Now I'm happy
if I can shave without cutting myself and get my cock back
in my pants without the last drops making a surprise raid
down my leg. That's maturity. The care that goes into
simple things.

BENJ Doesn't leave a whole lot of mature people, and most
of them are women.

SAM Yeah. Well, I have my doubts about them, too.

JOE You may not have noticed, but you're not leaving much
to look forward to.

SAM It's—I don't know—you know what she said to me? Your mother? Yesterday? Last night? She held my hands tight as she could, told me she wished she hadn't been born. Is that like her? A couple of hours of surgery, a couple more of cobalt treatment, but mainly heartless treachery—betrayal—and so many years of happy life, or anyway life we used to call happy, wiped off the slate like yesterday's dust. Her. Your mother. My wife. Wishing never to have been born. I don't know anyone who loved life more. She was always giving. To others. They revere her even. And there it was. Eyes shut. This ravaged, skeletal, ancient, skullish face. My—wife? My *wife?* Tears streaming out. My Ella? Is this my Ella? Your mother. Is this Ella? She wished she hadn't been born. And when she—when she—when she said it—I wished I hadn't either. Been born. I—oh, Christ—I've, I've, I've, I've, I've, I've—I can't cope. I worry so much about you. I—oh. Oh, oh, for Christ's sake, I'm crying. I'm sorry. I'm sorry. I just can't help it. I'm sorry, I'm so sorry.

JOE I'll get you a drink.

SAM You think you'll change anything? There's more muscle in this world than you ever dreamed. It's coming down the road to crush you. I can't stop it. I don't think anyone can.

JOE Drink up.

SAM I'm so worried all day long, all day long.

BENJ Hey, what's to worry? I always figured, with any luck at all, why, we'll have our genitals cut off, stuffed in our gaping mouths, our throats slit, and then'll be left wide-eyed, bloody, and grotesquely sprawled by the side of the road as an example.

86

SAM (*changing to laughter*)   Jesus! Example of what?

BENJ   Yeah. That's the mystery.

Enter Doctor.

BENJ (*cont.*)   Hey, Ralph, Dad was just saying someday all this will be ours. (*they laugh*)   Of course, he adds it ain't worth having now that he's done with it. (*they laugh*)   Because— because—hey, because— (*they laugh*)   What is it this week, Van Allen belts? Black holes? (*they laugh*)   Because of black holes!

They laugh. Enter Matty in tears.

DOCTOR   Sam. Kids. You better come quick.

They go. Sounds of death-rattle howl. Silence. House opens to reveal Ella on a haystack doing needlepoint alone.

ELLA   Pennsylvania hills. Western Pennsylvania. A small town. No place you'd know. Wonderful trips Sam, the kids, and I made back there after the war. In September, we used to come to the rolling western hills turning red and gold. The old small towns, still-cobbled rural streets, the horse troughs and the hand pumps. Rural America. The world's hope of the future once. A delusion I seem to cling to. When we'd gotten that far, I'd turn to the kids in the back of the car and say, "We're almost home." Not home, of course, but where I was born. It was a long trip in those days, and roads weren't as good or cars nearly as comfortable. But how wonderful it was. First we'd head south through the awful stench of New Jersey. Then we'd head west onto the Pennsylvania Turnpike. The seven black tunnels of the Pennsy Turnpike. In you go, and when'll you come out? A real superhighway in its day. In the sun it looked like a silver thread, it really did, a thread to guide you through the hills and then back to your origins. We used to stop for lunch and break the trip. This was in Amish and Mennonite country, those strange people who came to America to flee oppression and never ever gave up their ways. This was literally in the middle of the alien corn; for there were bright green and yellow cornfields as far as you could see and, in the middle, the big red barns with hex signs on them to ward evil off.

Then there'd be the farmhouse restaurants on old dirt roads you'd follow a handpainted sign to get to. Inside there'd be the family and other travelers, and vast wooden tables laid with homemade sausages, roast chickens, eggs, creamed corn, corn on the cob, tomatoes, mashed potatoes, gravies, a thousand fresh home-grown vegetables, sauces, pies, biscuits, breads, cakes, all home-baked. And the nicest people. And home-brewed apple cider, too, and wine, if you knew to ask. The children had eyes bigger than their stomachs and ate too much. But it wasn't embarrassing with these people; there was plenty, and they'd smile. When we finished lunch, the sun would be at its height. We'd get back on the highway then, we'd continue west, to the town where I was born, grew up in, and left for New York so long before. There they were waiting, my mother, and at the time my sister and her husband, waiting with open arms to see us again. The hills I am sure are still there. The rest, I suppose, is gone. I wonder: Who will ever know? Who'll ever know what a pleasure it was in those days, in that place, right after World War Two, when we were happy, healthy, and good?

Oh. The needle. Damn. I've lost the needle. I've lost the thread.

Lights fade out. Ella disappears. House closes.

Enter Sam and the rest as mourners. They shake hands or embrace, slowly, silently. They depart, leaving Sam alone.

SAM Behind this veil of daily, busy, busy-ness, there seems to be an interlinkedness—of things—in which you are imprisoned. If you look for causes, you find other causes. Look further, you find they multiply, in a kind of fan shape out toward infinity: a kind of malignancy of things causing malignant things. It is still not clear if this strange cage against which we like to think we beat, even as it closes in, still not altogether clear if it's some unfortunate and abysmal fraud; or a mystery, perhaps, in which nothing turns out expected but an occasional good gets its way. I find this lack of knowledge the real baggage I've got to lug with me toward old age: that for all my efforts, I'm going with no more protection than I had when I came, a voice to cry for help with, which I doubt will come—and a few square feet of human skin. That—the best and the worst being over—the rest is just the rest.

Darkness. Music.

Sam goes.

QUANTRILL
IN
LAWRENCE

Lawrence, Kansas, and environs. August 1863.

CHARACTERS

JOHN CANE, Mayor of Lawrence

SARA CANE, German immigrant married to Cane

GILLIE, their daughter

JUDGE CHARLES JENNISON, a Kansas leader of retaliatory raids on Missouri

MAY JENNISON, his wife

JENNY, their daughter

ANDERSON, a big farmer

BELLE, his daughter

SHERIFF STONE

DEPUTY

TOWNSPEOPLE

GENERAL THOMAS EWING, Commander Union Forces Kansas, Military Governor Missouri

MAJOR BLOOD, his adjutant, a cavalry officer

LIEUTENANT TERREL, an officer

SOLDIERS

WILLIAM CLARKE QUANTRILL, guerrilla raider in Kansas

COLE YOUNGER

JIM YOUNGER

JESSE JAMES

This is a rewrite of a text performed at the ICA Theatre in London in late spring 1980.

MAJOR BLOOD *is reading a letter.* GENERAL EWING *opposite, confers with* LIEUTENANT TERREL.

BLOOD   Mine eyes have seen the glory, dear sweet wife. News we have won at Gettysburg has come. Tell our little boy that surely now this cruelest of all wars, civil war, is won for our sweet Union. Our cause, and the whole earth's dream of freedom, has sizzled in the most dire jeopardy; now, to destiny. We will unify the country. We will knife to the Pacific. A continent tamed. Savagery subdued. And empire: American empire. I am more than ever certain the tactics we prove here in Bleeding Kansas, as they call it, will be a model to tame continents. Your loving husband, Hal, who fixes his eyes on the future.

Terrel salutes Ewing, goes to Blood. Terrel and Blood confer. Ewing reads:

EWING   August 17th, 1863. From General Thomas Ewing, Commander Union Forces Kansas, Military Governor of Occupied Missouri. To John Cane, Mayor of Lawrence.
   Sir: I write to you as the foremost man in Kansas, indeed as the father of the state. The growing audacity of the Confederate guerrilla raider William Clarke Quantrill has troubled you, I know. It is with deep regret I report the following.

   A deserter from Quantrill's Raiders, with unimpeachable evidence, has sworn your own daughter and some other girls, whose names are included here, sneak out at night to the bushwhackers' camp or sites near Lawrence; has sworn in fact they are widely known as Quantrill's whores; and further, raised the possibility that they are carrying reports of our strength and deployment to the enemy. I know you will find this as intolerable a breach of our security as I do and will wish to clean your house immediately.

Terrel returns to Ewing. Blood, in shock, follows.

EWING Major Blood, I am so sorry about your son.

BLOOD No, my son is not—he was fine on Friday. A fever is just. Heat. Nothing.

EWING I am releasing you for the funeral. In the circumstances, this letter best go Lawrence via the lieutenant.

BLOOD It was my prisoner. My interrogation. I will go to Lawrence.

EWING Hal.

BLOOD No. Sir. I. There is a wonderful surgeon there, though I forget his, his name. He will save the child, I am sure.

TERREL (*to Ewing*) The doc worked all last night. The boy died 5 this morning.

BLOOD You have got that wrong, Lieutenant. Look: I just wrote him the good news. My wife is doubtless hysterical.

EWING Lieutenant.

Terrel goes aside to wait.

EWING (*cont.*) The funeral is tomorrow. Your wife expects you.

BLOOD My father was a soldier; and I am. What do I have to do with funerals—if indeed he, he has not got it wrong.

EWING Hal, your father was my best friend. I urge you, go. Be with your wife.

BLOOD Sir, excuse me. My duty is in Lawrence. I love my son. But. She will—weaken—me. My wife. You know how they are. I—out there—there—is what I have been bred for. Fixed my sights on. Quantrill. Destiny.

EWING Terrel.

Terrel comes back.

EWING (*cont.*) The major will go to Lawrence.

BLOOD I am adding a postscript to my wife. Now. If you will carry it to her.

TERREL Yes, sir.

Terrel salutes; Blood salutes. Terrel goes.

BLOOD She is still young. There is still time.

EWING Major: Report when all's in order.

BLOOD If John Cane will not put Lawrence in order, be assured I will.

They salute. Blood goes.

Blackout.   Pentheus ← we seen Pen in him

SCENE 2

Lawrence at night, 17 August. Enter JENNISON *and* ANDERSON.

JENNISON My daughter gone? And yours?

ANDERSON And Cane's.

JENNISON Damn, Anderson, this is a sorry state. And I'll tell you why: mercy. Softness. That General Ewing!—giving those Missouri bastards amnesties last year. First thing they did was join Quantrill. Amnesty? Reprisals is all they understand. Be merciless with terror. Herd those Missouri scumheads into camps, guard them till the war is over, and hope they starve. The world's degenerating, you ask me; getting soft and womany, Anderson.

ANDERSON Judge, our reprisals only make it (*stops*) I mean, Osceola, Palmyra, Harrisonville—if we're going to be barbaric like that, I just don't know.

JENNISON Ought to kill them all. What in hell's war for?

Enter DEPUTY with torch.

JENNISON (*cont.*) I demand to know what Mayor Cane will do.

DEPUTY Judge Jennison, he's coming.

JENNISON Sara Cane. Oh, Sara.

Enter SARA CANE. She has a slight German accent.

ANDERSON The search all over, Mrs. Cane?

SARA All over, yes, all over.

ANDERSON Didn't find the girls?

JENNISON The girls ran, Anderson. What about a garrison here?

SARA If we don't cease the traffic with the enemy, yes, a garrison.

ANDERSON Your city or your daughter.

JENNISON Garrisoned. Us. Us!

ANDERSON Mayor, Mayor Cane.

Enter JOHN CANE, *Blood,* TOWNSMEN *with torches.*

CANE Mind those torches, do you hear? All we need to cap the night is Lawrence up in flames by accident. Major: Ten years we've spilled our blood. Kansas is a free state. We showed Missouri who'll control our borders.
     If we've got to show who'll control our women, we'll do that too. Girls or not—I've sent some men out with Mr. Stone. They will bring the girls back.

ANDERSON Someone is going to get hurt that way.

CANE Then someone will get hurt. I, John Cane, made Kansas. I brought ex-slaves to our army. I fought, I lobbied, I won Kansas for us, Anderson. They will be brought back and punished.

ANDERSON Sir, my girl's fifteen—what if there's a fight out there?

CANE Fight? Not Quantrill, not after dark. Major, tell them what you told me.

BLOOD Fight? He is too drunk. When the sun sets, according to my interrogation, he sets his corner of the earth to the wildest carousals. They perpetrate things, like animals. Lewd things. Disgusting things. In front of others. He mixes opiates and belladonna with the whiskey; they just down it all night long. If you'd heard what I have, it'd turn your guts, the vices, the lewd practices; this enemy you have not taken the measure of, not yet. The South itself disowns his loyalties. They refused him a commission. Even to our foe,

99

his travesty of war is all too horrible. This vicious barbarous turncoat is conducting dregs of your defeated neighbors into the smeariest revenge he can make up against you. Oh, I think if you'd heard what I have, and imagined your own children in the midst of it, you'd die to wipe it off the earth.

CANE I propose a special jail—

JENNISON —A jail's too good!

OTHERS —Traitors! Traitors!—

CANE Order here! Not in front of—you don't show Kansas at its worst in front of me.

I believe in justice. I believe in law and in God's morality. Let the jail be a symbol of all that. Let people say we cared enough. If this stable was converted, how'd that suit you?

JENNISON They like filth, let them live in it.

CANE Prepare this place.

SARA That stable was abandoned.

CANE Sara, hush.

SARA It was unfit for horses then.

CANE I know what I'm doing.

SARA Against nature, doing this, they'll say.

CANE Damn nature. We have a city and we know what's right. We are in a nightmare old as man is. To wake, we must shake ourselves and plainly say: Enough. Enough disorder here without obscenity.

JENNISON Hip-hip. Hip-hip. Hip-hip.

OTHERS Hurrah! Hurrah! Hurrah!

CANE I acknowledge the fault in my own household. Therefore, for all the work done here, let me John Cane pay.

Off, a cry. Enter GILLIE, *nightgowned, followed by* SHERIFF STONE.

GILLIE Mama.

SARA Gillie. Come.

SHERIFF The way in, she broke loose. We caught them by the old woods, miles out. I'm sorry her gown got tore; they fought. We didn't want to wait around out there.

CANE I think I speak for everyone. Thank you, Mr. Stone.

GILLIE Mama. Look.

SARA They beat her, John.

CANE Righteousness goes armed.

GILLIE Mama, I'm afraid.

CANE Now that you're home? Afraid?!

GILLIE He said we'd go to jail.

CANE Are you a whore?

GILLIE Are you a whore's father?

CANE Are you a spy?

GILLIE Do you tell strangers, "Beat my daughter?"

CANE Who's the stranger here! We who rode together and sacked Osceola, we're not the strangers here. What do you say to that?

GILLIE I can't talk when you're so angry.

CANE I gave you everything. Life, a father's love, a home, a growing place you'd be proud of, and you've made me so ashamed I wish you were dead. You betray everything—but say nothing.

GILLIE I can't.

CANE Just one sign you're sorry.

GILLIE No.

CANE Repentance for the pain you caused. Help me; help yourself.

GILLIE I didn't carry information, I swear it.

CANE We have evidence.

GILLIE It isn't true.

CANE Prove it.

GILLIE Prove it?

CANE Lure him here.

GILLIE Lure who?

CANE You know who.

GILLIE Quantrill?

CANE Send word you need help.

GILLIE You're asking me to whore for you?

CANE I'm asking you to show you are my loyal little girl again.

GILLIE I can't do that.

CANE I will believe you. I want to.

GILLIE I can't.

CANE Did you hear me? I said I want to.

GILLIE He wouldn't come for me.

CANE I said, I want—

GILLIE What you want is impossible. What you've always wanted is impossible, a world as pure as sugar is.

CANE (*to Sheriff*) The others.

JENNY *and* BELLE *are brought in.*

CANE (*cont.*) You will rot in here or you'll repent and show it. Take them to the jail. Take them in, lest all the lessons they were taught at home, lest we ourselves, are mocked.

GILLIE Mama: Aren't we proud of Daddy now? And his wife.

Sheriff takes the girls away.

BLOOD Sir, you've done justice to your reputation. Mrs. Cane.

SARA I know your kind. From Germany.

CANE Excuse my wife. We two are of a piece; the Union be preserved by us. All of you, now, go home and pray. Women, to your hearts. Look in, look deep: You brought them up. Now, stop gaping. No talking with them yet. Go on.

Come, Sara. It is done. Someone lead the way. A torch! Let's have some light.

They go.

SCENE 3

Near dawn. QUANTRILL *waits, wrapped in a blanket.* COLE, JIM, *and* JESSE *enter. They bring Major Blood: He is gagged, wrapped, hooded. They force Blood onto his knees. Quantrill sends Cole off. Quantrill uncovers Blood's face. Hums or whistles a few bars of "Rally Round the Flag, Boys" and covers it again. Nods to Jim. Jim and Jesse remove Blood.*

Quantrill hums again, briefly. Withdraws as he hears voices. Enter Sara. Enter MAY JENNISON, *face bruised.*

MAY   Sara?

SARA   May. Not sleeping?

MAY   And you?

SARA   I think my insomnia is going to be old enough to vote soon. Your face—?

MAY   Charles.

SARA   Again?

MAY   And him a judge, him a judge.

SARA   Poor May.

MAY   He accused me. Making Jenny a whore. By how I raised her.

SARA There, there. Don't cry.

MAY That word. For our girl.

SARA There, there.

MAY I didn't argue back. I sat down. I played my piano. Wasn't that okay? Charles flew at me. Screaming.

SARA There, there.

MAY He used to like piano so much.

SARA May.

MAY I want my little girl. I don't care what Jenny's done. I wish I was a man. Some man Judge Charles Jennison was just scared to hell of. I'd stab him, Sara. I'd drink his blood.

SARA Calm. Calm.

MAY I wish I had your dignity. I just know Charles wouldn't beat me if I did.

Enter Sheriff, Jennison.

JENNISON The hotel. Wake the major. Post guards.

Sheriff goes.

JENNISON (*cont.*) Girls: We have a—situation. William Quantrill is here in Lawrence. I just got an emissary. Cane did too. Quantrill's here; he knows.

MAY About our girls?

JENNISON The girls, the jail, all of it. Must've been in the woods last night.

why is he here?

. . . hey come to talk . . . some kind of deal.

. . . ney, I just don't know what's going to happen. I just
. . . you home safe, before I meet with the mayor. Please,
. . .

MAY I'll be home, Charles. You'll find me there, I'll make
coffee. Sara, you best go too.

May goes.

JENNISON She's right, Sara.

SARA In Göttingen, where I was born, they save the bruises
for Saturday. It makes repentance more real the next day.

JENNISON Order begins at home. The Bible teaches what, if
it doesn't. First woman, the first outlaw.

SARA Oh? Satan?

JENNISON Eve, Sara. Come on. First civil war, between her
sons. Greatest warrior was Samson, undone by the same
twitty malice that every lady thinks makes her an exception
to every law. Remember Samson?

SARA Perhaps Delilah found the jawbone of an ass is a tiring
instrument to be courted with.

JENNISON God, I sometimes think we'd be better off without
women altogether. Keep away from my wife. Leave May
alone.

Jennison goes.

SARA Just seventeen, my father sent me here. "Better there,"
he said. "Dear, dear God, save my girl from this."

SCENE 4

Quantrill emerges, wrapped in blanket.

QUANTRILL   May well storm today, Miss Sara. Clouds coiling up there, in the west.

SARA   Who's that?

QUANTRILL   People said, two years ago about, that the kindly woman known to me only as Miss Sara had inquired where the teacher Charley Hart had got to.

SARA   Charley? Charley Hart, is it you, really?

QUANTRILL   See for yourself.

SARA   From the grade school. From Wichita. Good to see you again.

QUANTRILL   Likewise.

SARA   What has it been, two years?

QUANTRILL   I guess.

SARA   You have a way of disappearing and appearing, I must say that. Why are you here?

QUANTRILL   I was just about to ask you.

SARA   But I live here. I am Sara Cane.

QUANTRILL   John Cane—your man?

SARA   You didn't know?

QUANTRILL   You're just Miss Sara. Looks in, sees the school's okay, kids are learning something.

SARA   You were our best teacher, Charley. Your father was a teacher too, no? In Ohio, was it?

QUANTRILL What a memory.

SARA Oh, Charley. For you? You—look much older. From the fighting?

Silence.

QUANTRILL Well. You still like walking out on the prairie?

SARA I am not allowed.

QUANTRILL I still do.

Go out, listen to the corn gossip: Heard about the wheat, what a scandal. Rats nibble. Quail squeak. Beats town life. No hypocrisy. Just prairie. Humps. Coos. Grows. Multiplies. Flowers up. Dies. Lives again. . . . My pa, you know? Poor bastard. Spent years whipping Latin into me. Greek. Can't recall a word. I walk and walk out there. No need for words. Just dream and watch the buffalo butting skulls.

SARA Are you ill? The blanket.

QUANTRILL No. Just not to scare you.

He drops the blanket. He is wearing a Confederate officer's uniform.

SARA Their uniform? Charley?

Silence.

QUANTRILL Do you know what I think about, Miss Sara?

SARA Charley, how can you? You are one of us.

QUANTRILL Well. Anyhow. I was so pleased when I heard you asked about me.

SARA Go on. What do you think about?

108

QUANTRILL Well . . . I . . . Miss Sara, is it your opinion that if trouble be following you long enough, it's telling you to lead it? I have grown sure it is so.

SARA What has become of you? I remember a passionate idealist. Twenty-two or -three. Came all the way from Ohio to teach Kansas children. About freedom, Charley. For a pittance. They worshiped you. Charley, what's happened?

QUANTRILL "Charley." Miss Sara, Charley Hart was just a fellow I'd been to prison with. I'm not really him.

SARA Prison?

QUANTRILL I shot—it was this Utah man. Back then.

SARA You borrowed someone's name? What was wrong with your own?

QUANTRILL Belonged to a jailbird.

SARA Start again. Tell me what to call you now. Your name.

QUANTRILL I am William Clarke Quantrill. That's my born name.

Silence.

SARA I see.

QUANTRILL Anyhow. I heard you'd asked—

SARA Of course I asked. A Monday morning came. Charley Hart did not arrive. The children waited at their desks. It was after some reprisal raid, Osceola. I asked, had anyone seen you. Someone said you had gone the Wednesday earlier. Returned Sunday night late. Monday you were gone.

QUANTRILL So funny . . . her your daughter. What a funny thing.

SARA I still want to know what happened.

QUANTRILL Oh. I rode. All Wednesday and all Thursday. To Missouri. Osceola.

SARA You went to see it?

QUANTRILL Oh, sure. I admired John Cane so much then. I just wanted to see the glorious thing he'd done to Osceola. Friday morning is when I got there. At dawn.

SARA John said it got out of hand. He lost control of his men.

QUANTRILL Sure. I could see that.

Quantrill regresses to visit at Osceola.

Saw this black elm tree. With a necklace of women and children hanging. Jennison had hung them. Not slavers. Not owners. He was forcing them to say where their men were at. They were—their necks were terrible long. . . . And broken, like dog's legs. Their eyes, hooded, empty . . . Saw men's limbs scattered around. Like a box of spilled matches, rotting. I saw: all kinds of faces and bodies that time spent so much time fashioning nicely all unbuttoned by gun wounds. And green fields were black. Smoke, still rising.

I saw: this town. Been all painted so carefully white—not just happy to leave it wood but bringing whitewash a thousand miles, all the way, to paint it like a nice lived-in place. Saw white churches—Baptist, Congregationalist— places men spent a month putting a steeple up to show where they aspired to, and not just splashing the paint on but stroking it carefully on each long plank, more careful than their homes I'll bet, and putting a nicely made black iron rooster on top of the steeple for telling wind direction . . . I saw all that charred black; and collapsed into ruins; still had these women bawling and weeping over the bodies; telling anyone who'd listen how our Kansas horsemen had been howling around, glorying in all this vengeful destruction; and I said to myself: My Lord—why?

I never lived rightly. I don't claim that. But I believed in man, that God made him the best creature on earth. To prevail and get himself more perfect and grow in liberty. Like I was teaching Kansas kids. And here it was. What Cane and Jennison did. Behind my back. Osceola.

Saturday, Sunday, I rode back to Kansas. A pair of lips, kind of; teeth; a tongue; a voice, kind of; hurt in my mind while I rode back. One day, it said, one day. Cane. Let him beg forgiveness. Started praying for it. Let him beg forgiveness. Here is how I pray, Miss Sara. (*kneels suddenly*)
Dear God—or Satan, if there is a difference! Whoever you are who for fire, and our good times, hoots *I am!*—This dawn I call to you from Lawrence where I am you know well why, to see what price this man will pay, who born of woman now locks up woman born of him.

Bring me John Cane. I want him.

SARA My God.

Enter Cane, Jennison, Cole, Sheriff Stone, Deputy, Anderson, and others.

III

SCENE 5

CANE Sara? For the love of—get home! This is twice you have embarrassed me. Think how people look at me when you do this, for God's sake. Go.

SARA What will you do with him?

CANE Sara.

Sara goes.

CANE (*cont.*) Are you William Quantrill? Mr. Younger: Is he?

Cole nods yes.

CANE (*cont.*) Seize him.

Men seize Quantrill.

COLE You agreed to talk. We came to parley.

CANE Amnesty breakers like yourself, Mr. Younger, and men who raise the black flag to signify they obey no rules of war, like him, are not entitled to the rights of parley. Where is Major Blood? I asked for him.

JENNISON He wasn't at his hotel.

CANE We'll proceed without him. (*to Quantrill*) You know who I am. You came to laugh at me. Laugh.

Silence.

CANE (*cont.*) A rope around his neck.

Deputy does.

CANE (*cont.*) You were in the woods last night; your man here says you have objections to our new prison.
Is he mute?

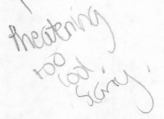

112

COLE   Probably just doesn't care for the unfriendly hands.

CANE   You came to add insult to injury. What did you expect?

COLE   We came to talk. A deal.

CANE   Deal.
I want you all to hear this. On the 21st of August, in three days, the Confederacy—who disowns and scorns you, sir—has called for their forces to observe a day of prayer and mourning for the dead. Mr. Younger?

COLE   Yes, sir. That's right.

CANE   He says: Release the girls by that date, or else.

COLE   Well, no, sir.

CANE   No?

COLE   No, sir. That's not it.

CANE   Am I a liar?

COLE   You're angry.

CANE   Am I a liar?

COLE   No, sir. Not a liar.

CANE   Well, then?

COLE   Quantrill says he won't obey it. The day of mourning. If honoring the dead means ignoring friends locked up to get at him.

CANE   To get at him?

COLE   What I said, he said, is if you will amnesty the girls, we'll exchange the courtesy.

CANE In twenty years of political life, I've never heard such neck. Amnesties, anyone?

JENNISON/OTHERS Never, never, we'll never.

CANE You heard. Put him on the stool.

Men lift Quantrill onto stool to hang.

COLE Quantrill?

CANE Five hundred men out there might make you safe, out there. In Lawrence, my friend, it's another story.

COLE Mr. Cane, don't do this.

CANE Let him ask me not to.

COLE Mr. Cane, I swear to God. We didn't come provoking. Quantrill: Please say something. Will you come on?

QUANTRILL (*to Cane*) In Egypt once, an angel of the Lord on slaying business overpassed the dwellings of the Israelites; they sacrificed to show goodwill. Your sacrifice is free my friends. I will replace your girl with someone you love better.

CANE You heard? You all heard?

No, sir! No deal. Not with traitors. Not with turncoats. Not for my daughter. Not in two years, two whole years, have you dared attack us. Because you know men here. You know me. And still you came.

They're not going to dare without him what they didn't dare with him. Judge, proceed.

JENNISON William Clarke Quantrill: For a multitude of crimes, well attested to by many witnesses, in Kansas and states bordering—aforesaid crimes including anarchy and its advocacy by flying the black flag; treason to the Union; multiple attested-to instances of murder, arson, theft; attempts to stir up Cherokees in the Territory; extortion of monies in three states; and violation of the rules of war—by the Emergency Powers vested in me by General Thomas Ewing, I sentence you to be hung by the neck until dead.

COLE Quantrill.

CANE (*to Quantrill*) Any last words? You've turned your back on civilization. We allow you your last words, however.

QUANTRILL If it is of interest: I William Clarke Quantrill, a Northerner like you, born in Ohio of good Christians, turn my last look to the prairie where I seek eternal life and from whence salvation comes. I saw lots of real good hunting there. I'd see hounds knife through the sweetgrass. And cornflowers wave and part. And hares kick up their heels and flee. And quail hide, and snakes, all kinds, coil up above their eggs and wait to strike. You'd see the quail scatter, and the guinea fowl sort of flutter up and spray the blue with little cries; and baby quail'd follow on with tiny little squeaks. And same time you'd see the hunters' guns poke up and holler out. You know the good spring day I mean, the kind you get about mid-May when the elk'd come down to the river to drink.

And, so happy were the hunters, and so intent, and the hounds, and so furious yelping and barking they'd be, they'd miss it, spinning up behind them: old prairie twister. Gunbarrel black, a mile high, mindless whipped-up pipe of blind chance—tornado—which'd suck them all up, hunters, hounds, guns, fury, all, and hurl them far away. With little squeaks. And cries . . . All is vanity, Ecclesiastes says.

JENNISON (*disgusted*) The man's gonna die drunk.

COLE Bring Major Blood!

Enter Jim and Jesse with Major Blood. He is gagged, bound, near naked, breasts drawn on his chest, perhaps rouged, gun to his head.

JENNISON Major?

ANDERSON More of them, sir, more of them.

CANE What is this?

QUANTRILL We had made you a new daughter you'd like better. All you had to do was trade.

CANE My God, what kind of man are you?

COLE It ain't too late.

QUANTRILL No trades now.

COLE You said we were coming to deal, come on.

QUANTRILL I want John Cane.

COLE Aw come on!

QUANTRILL (*to Cane*) If I do not have you, nothing will. Dingus, Jimmy—the third time Quantrill stamps, make the major's brains fly off like quail.

JESSE (*to Blood*) Grunt goodbye, you bastard.

CANE Don't anyone give an inch! Take aim.

ANDERSON Mr. Cane, please.

QUANTRILL If they don't give in, blow Cane to jelly.

ANDERSON For God's sake.

QUANTRILL Hey, fly quail fly, Quantrill will not die!

Stamps.

JENNISON Mr. Cane?

CANE Stick it out, you stick it out.

QUANTRILL Hey, fly quail fly, Quantrill cannot die!

Stamps.

ANDERSON No. No.

CANE Don't give in, you hear me?

QUANTRILL Fly quail fly, Quantrill cannot die! (*Stamps*)
That's three. Do it.

ANDERSON No! Were not moving.

JENNISON Don't shoot him! Don't shoot him!

ANDERSON Don't for God's sake, don't.

JENNISON Not moving, not moving, look.

CANE You've given me to them. No. Ah, my God, you've
given me to them.

Cole seizes Cane.

QUANTRILL Dingus. Tie Cane up. Gag him.

*Jesse takes rope from Quantrill and gag from Major Blood, puts them
on Cane.*

JENNISON Help, help!

Exit Jennison.

BLOOD You—

QUANTRILL Hold your peace. (*to Jesse*) Take Cane to the
woods. There's a clearing, you know it, full of ferns, a

natural one. Where we entertain dear Lawrence friends. We'll have to improvise. Hey, don't get lost. Being August, it'll smell of mint and wild sage.

JESSE I know where it is.

COLE The army. Ewing.

QUANTRILL (*baring Cane's throat*) See this? Here is the throat which uttered the word, which was in the beginning, which drew everyone of you—and others too—to Kansas. If Ewing and the army will forbear pursuit, this soft thing is safe in my keeping. (*to Cane*) When you return to Lawrence, if you return to Lawrence, they will disown you too. Shift him.

Jesse drags Cane away.

ANDERSON My Lord. Dragged like an ox.

JIM Shift out. All of you. Move it.

Exeunt Townspeople.

COLE Major Blood.

QUANTRILL Hal? I have heard of you. And what a dandy you are, sir. Brave, smart, and relentless. Would you care to join us?

JIM Quantrill!

BLOOD Join you?

COLE That's the belladonna talking. Come on.

QUANTRILL Some men are fortunate and given many virtues. Some are poor and only get one. You have many; I have only one: just loyalty to my own. Now, if you with your many virtues were one of us, you would have that loyalty, and we'd be a damn sight richer. Hal, I ask you a second time: Will you turn coat and join us?

BLOOD   I am a soldier of the Union. It has all my loyalty. / *wants to remain an outsider*

QUANTRILL   You always wanted to see our camp.

BLOOD   My duty has been to find you and destroy you. You know that.

QUANTRILL   That just makes you a bigger prize, sir. I ask you a third time: Join us.

BLOOD   Your war is lost. You've lost Gettysburg; *it's lost.*

QUANTRILL   Billy Gem is all I've lost recently.

BLOOD   What?

QUANTRILL   Sixteen-year-old half-wit? Billy Gem? Liked to dance a lot. Nice boy, made grieving men laugh.

BLOOD   I don't understand what you're talking about.

QUANTRILL   William P. Diamond?

BLOOD   Oh. You mean the one who deserted you.

QUANTRILL   Half-wit en route to his sister Helen's wedding in St. Joe. Ran into an army patrol. Billy didn't desert.

BLOOD   You know very well we are here to pacify irregular elements in the state and—

QUANTRILL   You are the Major Blood who questioned him?

BLOOD   I did my duty.

QUANTRILL   Believed the wild stories of a half-wit?

BLOOD   I did my duty!

QUANTRILL Begged him to see. "Oh, take me to the camp alone at night, if that is true, and let me look."

BLOOD My God. Who told you that?

QUANTRILL Found Billy dying, by a stream. "Billy-boy," I said, "what has happened to you? Must've been some wedding, child." He pointed down. To where you'd sliced his soles clean off. The bottom half-inch of his feet.

BLOOD You never meant me to join you.

QUANTRILL Three times Quantrill asked; three times you said no.

BLOOD What's gone on in Kansas, this new warfare with no rules, the army has had to feel its way, adjusting to it. It was in the course of duty that William Diamond, who you call Billy Gem—it was after three days and nights of questioning, I lost patience. He was an imbecile! I warned him to walk me toward your camp, or he'd never walk again. (*laughs*) By God, he was the dumbest reb I've ever seen. He was like a newborn buffalo, he was so stupid.

QUANTRILL (*sings*)

Where has my Billy gone?
Far far away.
When shall we meet again?
On another—(*stops*)

BLOOD I accept that I am a prisoner of war. Just remember. It's a war you've lost; your behavior will be held to account.

QUANTRILL This man of many virtues has a passion. <u>He wants to see what he won't join.</u> Cole, take him to our

120

camp. Show him anything. Whatever. Then grapple your
hands up, sort of. Like claws.
      Blind him.

COLE I can't do that.

QUANTRILL Find someone who will. Jimmy, linger here.
Keep the rest dispersed.

BLOOD Quantrill! It's lost! What's the point?

QUANTRILL Quantrill's business now is in the woods.

Exeunt.

SCENE 6

At the jail. Gillie sings.

GILLIE The wide Missouri has to flow
           Down from the snow to some blue sea
           Along its banks blackbirds crow
           "Where'll you go, what will you be?"
           I won't be going anywhere
           I don't know why it's so, it's so.
           I won't put flowers in my hair
           Or Spanish comb, or bow, or bow.

Enter Sara.

           A wind is coming up somewhere
           Honeybees fly home, fly home
           August storms will split the air
           Your honey will be gone, be gone.

SARA Gillie? Hello? Gillie.

GILLIE Go away.

SARA I want to see you.

GILLIE I don't want to see you.

SARA I want to talk to you.

GILLIE I don't want to talk to you. Go away.

SARA Gillie.

GILLIE Guards! No one's supposed to.

SARA I need your help.

GILLIE I sure don't need yours. Guards!

SARA There are no guards. (*silence*) William Quantrill came. Your father tried to hang him. Now no one wants to be caught guarding this place. Did you hear me?

GILLIE I hear.

SARA They took your father away: Quantrill; men. To the woods I think.

GILLIE He came here?

SARA Yes.

GILLIE On our account?

SARA You were the excuse; anyway.

GILLIE No, wasn't any excuse.

SARA I don't understand.

GILLIE He don't need excuses; you need excuses.

SARA I—?

GILLIE People going to die, they make excuses. Excuse for this, excuse for that. He can't ever die. You understand? He don't need excuses.

SARA Who can't die?

GILLIE Quantrill can't! Can't die till he brings the sun up in the west at night. An old Injun lady prophesied it. All the boys know that.

SARA Do they.

GILLIE And since no one can bring the sun up in the west at night, he going to live forever, and everybody just do what they like.

SARA Does my own girl believe that?

GILLIE I'm not talking to you! I'm not going to argue with you about something you are ignorant and stupid about, and is true. Why didn't you stand up for me? Why didn't you?

SARA I couldn't. I wanted to.

GILLIE Don't act beaten. It makes me want to scream.

SARA Maybe I am beaten.

GILLIE You were so strong. If you're beaten, I'm whipped before I start. I got to do something; I got to break loose, got to break loose; loose. That's all I could think, last couple of years. If she's whipped, what chance for me?

SARA Oh Gillie.

GILLIE Stop it, or I'll scream the sky down!

SARA It's no use. I won't get help here.

GILLIE Help from us? For who? Look at us.

SARA I must go find them. In the woods.

GILLIE Why?

SARA He is your father.

GILLIE He is my jailor, he is my warden.

SARA If anything happens, I'll never be able to face the rest of my life. Help me. Please. Then I can free you.

GILLIE Free yourself.

SARA What?

GILLIE He's a mountain on your head. Just shake him off.

SARA You don't know what twenty married years do.

GILLIE Only what they did to you.

SARA You may not judge me. No.

GILLIE You don't remember what you were.

SARA A foreign woman. An immigrant. An impractical one. I remember, thank you.

GILLIE A goddess, Mama.

SARA A what?

GILLIE Someone from a fairy tale. From far away . . . My mother. Funny accent. Holding me. Telling me what you did as a girl. Different . . . somehow. When I bawled, you knew why. When I laughed, you also knew why. Like magic.

SARA Some things—some things I don't expect . . . that you will understand.

A sense of powerless in her character ↓ restricting Freedom

GILLIE   I worshiped you. Somewhere along the line, I got turned over to him. The great man.

SARA   If things had worked out, they'd explain themselves. They didn't. Why. Us. Here. What we hoped. I will try.
   We had a belief. A cause. Freedom. Or we thought so. We compromised to avoid what was mad. But the mad became very usual anyhow. Then everyday. Then powerful. Liberty for all, we intended. Then, maybe you might say, war courted us. We were excited; we were flattered. Such a power, to court us. We accepted. To please him, told lies. Shed blood. (*silence*)
   I shut my eyes sometimes. I see two fast black trains crumple into each other. The engineers' faces. Frozen in madness. They knew they'd hit. Drown us in blood. But first in lies.

GILLIE   Mama—

SARA   Twisted. Monstrous. Wreckage. The shrieks from Kansas; from Missouri. The innocent voices calling, There has been a terrible accident. But we know it was no accident. It was hate. It was lust for power finally. It just happened . . . another lie.
   I withdrew myself. I put everything I had into you. Perhaps that is what seemed to be magic. For you. For me—us—total defeat.

GILLIE   Mama.

SARA   I was no goddess, of any kind. Your father was my husband; I was his wife; you were ours. As long as you exist, I am bound to him. Not by him, or you; by myself. It doesn't matter if I like it. It matters if I honor obligations I

125

make. Free, you say. Free yourself. I could have throttled you as an infant. Yes, then I would be free. Or dead. Yes, then I would be free or dead. But, this—this bloodied sack where defeat stuffs the losers like us—like me—this loss I am feeling about everything I hoped—I tried—thank God at least there is love. Not free. But . . . love, greater than all pains put together. Love, which I had for you. Preserver of life.

Silence.

GILLIE Go find Quantrill. I'll help you.

SARA What?

GILLIE Go to the woods. Isn't that what you wanted? Take a witness.

SARA Yes?

GILLIE Just say not to punish Daddy.

SARA He hates your father for other reasons.

GILLIE I'm telling you how, Mama. Listen to me.

SARA But will he believe me?

GILLIE I don't know. That's up to you.

SARA Will he trust I come from you?

GILLIE Take my bracelet. Take it.

SARA You'd do that for me?

GILLIE Being a bad daughter to some people seems inevitable. How can I to you?

SARA Thank you.

GILLIE It's probably better anyhow. You think?

SARA   Not if you owe him something.

GILLIE   It's not like that with us.

SARA   Gillie? You didn't spy?

GILLIE   No. (*pause*)   I think Jenny did.

SARA   Why didn't you say?

GILLIE   Doesn't matter: I'm with them. We're with each other. That's what matters. Anyhow, there's nothing to tell. Jenny's just a girl likes to play up to boys. Everybody in Kansas knows where the army got its camps and troops. Oh, Mama, I'm sorry. I'm sorry.

SARA   My big and little girl. So old; still so young.

GILLIE   Mama, how am I ever going to be free?

SARA   For sure, we will get you out now.

GILLIE   I mean, how, if I'm not free of you?

SARA   Time, I think, will take care of that.

GILLIE   Tell them hurry. It smells of rot here, and it's awful, and I'm scared.

SARA   Keep your spirits up. This will end well. It will. It must.

GILLIE   Kiss me before you go?

SARA   Yes. . . . I have money saved. I will get you away from here. California.

GILLIE   The Pacific. Really? Can you see Japan? China? Siam? I'd love to see all that.

SARA   All. Yes. Yes.

Exit Sara. Sounds of distant storm.

GILLIE (*sings*)

> I will not be what I'll be
> I don't know why it's so
> The world is shaking at my feet
> Dear world, don't let me go.

Fade-out.

SCENE 7

In the woods. Jesse enters, dragging Cane, bound and gagged, and removes gag.

JESSE Now, set you down. Yell your little heart out.

CANE Boy, untie me. I'll make sure you are rewarded.

JESSE Don't call me boy.

CANE Dingus?

JESSE He call me that, not you. My name is Jesse Woodson James.

CANE Jesse, how would you like five dollars?

JESSE Better than four. Not so much as six.

CANE Untie me, son. It'll be worth it.

JESSE I'm not your son. Just give up, will you?

CANE How old are you?

JESSE Near seventeen.

CANE   You don't know what you're doing. I didn't, at seventeen. This war makes it worse. Twenty years on, this whole period won't make the sense you think it makes.

JESSE   Don't make sense now. I ain't complaining.

CANE   Quantrill is fighting for slavery; that is a terrible evil.

JESSE   We don't own no nigras, mister. That's rich folks. Quantrill, he even freed some. Ran 'em to safety in Kansas, 'cause he hated the owner. Owner got humble, Quantrill pretend he'll sell 'em back. Takes cash, then he rattlesnakes on the owner, shot his head off anyhow. He says it's all lies. You just want 'em free for your army! Fight for you, or something. Say you abolitionists all biggest damn hypocrites he ever seen.

CANE   You are from Missouri. The Confederacy disowns the man. Do you know that?

JESSE   Can't disown something you never own. Anyhow, who cares?

CANE   I had not realized. What a poor school for youngsters this war makes.

JESSE   Quantrill teached me words. Multiplying. He teached me and Frank—that's my brother?—the names of some stars even, and constellations, and how to get about if you follow 'em. He promise we'll kill all the fiends in Kansas. Just like they kill us.

CANE   A maniac. And you ape him.

JESSE   Leave off him, or I'll punch your teeth out.

Jesse goes.

CANE Bugs. Everywhere. Crawling. Shadows. Damn. Heat stops at the treetops. Spiders. Keep calm. Centipedes. Spiders: Damn. What was God reaching for when He came up with this skittering black bastard! Gone. . . .

If I lacked proof the decent world I thought I'd know at seventeen—things having their rightful names and in their proper places; that it can all dissolve like sugar—the proof is here. Hello! I think there's a spider on my neck! Hello!

Enter Quantrill and Jesse.

QUANTRILL Dingus, honey, this yellow-hair wig and skirt is for you. You and Quantrill will each play parts. Here's our audience.

CANE There's a creature, a spider on my neck.

JESSE Naw. Just sweat crawling around.

Jesse puts on wig.

CANE Young man, don't dress like that. It is abhorrent; what's wrong with you? What's the meaning of this?

QUANTRILL We are going to present a happy-ending comedy. Quantrill has made a prologue so's you'll understand the purpose. Mayor Cane of Lawrence: Dr. W. C. Quantrill has diagnosed your backed-up state as the constipation known as the disease of dismay, from which folks die who cannot purge themselves.

JESSE He means you're full of shit.

QUANTRILL Dingus, honey, you get that wig on. You're in show business now. Mayor Cane of Lawrence: Your doctor has prescribed for you some good old entertainment to grease the rust that stops you up inside yourself. It will please since it's reality. And when you're pleased, and know what's real, you'll be <u>released</u> and, in turn, will release <u>others</u>—your sacrifice, which must be.

CANE   How long do you think, really think, you can hold me so outrageously?

QUANTRILL   Folly dies slowly in some men.

CANE   Why not destroy the town, kill me, if you could?

JESSE   Maybe less glory in that than you think.

QUANTRILL   Besides, it's work. We prefer to play around. Dingus: You play a girl who wanders to our camp. Quantrill will play a picket who meets her, and they speak. Leave nothing out; you know about how it is. Okay:
    "Betty's Shameful Loss," by W. C. Quantrill, starring same and Jesse James.

CANE   Don't expect applause. Your audience's captive, his hands are tied.

JESSE   If you really like it, just bang your head on the tree. We'll understand.

CANE   God made you a man, Jesse. Look what you've made yourself.

Quantrill and Jesse put on their play.

JESSE   "Oooh, my foots are tired. This Quantrill's camp? I sure hope so."

QUANTRILL   "Don't know no Quantrill here."

JESSE   "Oh." I mean, "Oh, don't be afraid, you willy. Silly!" Hey, they call you silly?

QUANTRILL   It's plausible.

JESSE   But is it true?

QUANTRILL   Will you get on with it?

JESSE   "Some of my girlfriends sneak off here." (*He attacks his lines*) "They said it's so exciting! I had to come! Life in town is awful! Susie says she'll come live with you for good! Oh, I can hardly talk. I am so thirsty! Some of the girls—!"

QUANTRILL   "There's water in the canteen there."

JESSE   "Some of the girls said they drank something else! Said they drank whiskey. Said it made them feel so fine, they said! And funny! Oh, thanks."

QUANTRILL   Dingus. See, when your lines end, Quantrill says something. Then you say your next one.

JESSE   Oh. Sure. I'll go back. "Feel so fine, they said! And funny!"

QUANTRILL   "Ever had this stuff?"

JESSE   "Oh thanks! 'Scuse my grabbing, I'd just love a snort or two! Glug-a glug." What's all that glug stuff?

QUANTRILL   You do some drinking motions.

JESSE   Oh. Sure. "Well! Mmm indeedy. Mmm, yes, well. My name is Betty Quick. I'm kind of hot. May I take off my— my—my . . . ?

QUANTRILL   Wrap.

JESSE   "Wrap! May I take off my wrap?"

CANE   Betty Quick, indeed.

QUANTRILL   "Well. The night has a sneaky chill in Kansas."

JESSE "Oh." . . . I mean, "Oh you're right: What a sneaky chill! Shiver, shiver. I'm shivering to death. Hold me!"

QUANTRILL Dingus, if you shout every line, it's not a tender love story anymore.

CANE No one ever denied there were willing sluts in Kansas. But Jesse, where's your self-respect?

JESSE Quantrill? I don't want to be a girl. Not in front of him.

He whips off the wig.

QUANTRILL It's just a play.

JESSE It's just a play, you be the girl.

QUANTRILL (*putting on wig*) You be the picket. Maybe I can please our audience here a bit more. "I . . . feel shivery. Maybe if you hold me? Oh."

CANE This is no better for you, Jesse. Look what the man is.

JESSE (*imitating Quantrill*) "Pore Betty—how old are you?"

QUANTRILL "An old maid, almost. And still don't know anything."

JESSE "Sure, you're getting ancient."

QUANTRILL "Fifteen and three-quarters. I could just cry sometimes. Oh! You know what I just remembered? I'll bet this fairly tickles you."

JESSE "Tickle up a storm."

QUANTRILL Honey.

JESSE Honey! "Tickle up a storm, honey!"

QUANTRILL "When I was three and three-quarters years old,

133

and my daddy used to ask me how old I was, you know what I used to say? I used to say, I'm a quarter to four—"

CANE   Who told you that?

QUANTRILL   "I feel so old, and don't know nothing yet. Will you show me?"

CANE   *Who told you that?*

JESSE   "You're shivering, darlin'. Now, don't be scared."

CANE   *I'll kill you! I'll kill you!*

JESSE   "Don't be afraid. There ain't nothing to fear."

QUANTRILL   "I'm so afraid. I really want to, but I don't know how. I mean, if you show me. I don't mind if it hurts a little, Quantrill."

JESSE   "I'm not Quantrill."

QUANTRILL   "Whoever. I'm not a snob."

CANE   Stop. Stop it, for God's sake.

QUANTRILL   You're going to miss the meat of the matter.

CANE   I don't want to hear any more.

QUANTRILL   Your girl is braver than you. She wanted to know everything.

CANE   Liar. Damned liar.

QUANTRILL   Know why they come to a thief? Learn how to steal. Steal their own candy you keep hidden from them.

CANE   No more.

QUANTRILL   The hell, no more. They were happier 'n little birds. "Oh what is this? What's this?"

CANE Stop it, stop!

QUANTRILL Fear? Sure. Some cried even. "Oh help; oh help, oh God help me, oh God; oh God." And got over fear. And did it.
    Locking them up was—folly. Unlock them.

CANE Ah, my God, where am I?

QUANTRILL Don't look around, Cane. My anger is here. Right here.

CANE She's mine! They're ours!

QUANTRILL Unlock them.

CANE I'll see them dead first! Dead!

QUANTRILL Come on, Jesse. Pick him up. Deeper into the woods.

They pick Cane up and drag him off.

CANE Like an ox!

SCENE 8

In the woods. Enter Sara and Anderson.

SARA Mr. Anderson, where are we? Do you know?

ANDERSON Nor where we're going.

SARA Don't sit—I'm sorry.

ANDERSON It's my leg. (*sits*) Piece of the Mexican War. Just give it a moment.

SARA Yes. It was good of you to come with me.

ANDERSON (*rubbing leg*) Exploding shell. San Jacinto. Lucky, too. Didn't lose the leg.

Tennessee boy next to me, he was gutted. Never forget it. Right in the soft place. Hinge of life. One moment his knees were bent. He was looking amazed. Down at his wound. Holding himself. Then at me. Gaping. He says, Mexico. That's all. Mexico. Then some big invisible fist tapped him. Down he went. Crash in the dust. His equipment clattered, making a racket. Eyes gazing at forgetfulness.

Just—how things suddenly—collapse. Never forgot it: Mexico. . . .

SARA I need to rest too. I hear blood in my ears.

ANDERSON Mrs. Cane.

SARA Yes?

ANDERSON We will find him.

SARA Yes.

ANDERSON I am proud. That you trusted me. I mean, asked me to come with you.

SARA I didn't know who to ask.

ANDERSON Well, I feel fine about it.

SARA Your wife, is she dead?

ANDERSON No, ma'am. She ran off.

SARA I see.

ANDERSON Not that I blame her.

SARA What did you do before?

ANDERSON Failed, I guess.

SARA Failed?

ANDERSON The word don't say it.

SARA Excuse me?

ANDERSON What a crime it feels like. Failing.

SARA But what did you do?

ANDERSON Printing. Selling glass. Tried lots of things. Warehousing. Warehousing was in Cincinnati. Farming. San Antonio.

SARA You don't fail here. The opposite.

ANDERSON Soil's too good to fail here. Five, six feet down black and loamy. It's why everybody wants it so bad. Place you can't fail. Place, even if you do, they don't notice. You're just a dot on a tide. Killers. Scum of all kinds. Crackpots. Confidence men. Opportunistic fellas. Washing west. Starting new. Till they find a place they succeed—or die. Paradise.

SARA Is that what we are?

ANDERSON It's what I am. (*pause*) Cane would've been fine back east too.

SARA Why did you say that?

ANDERSON He led us through the fire. He is why we are still here.

SARA You know those roads to Texas. Rutted mud, where wagons pass.

ANDERSON Yes, ma'am.

SARA   You see miserable Osage or Shawnee by the side sometimes. Pushed out. But not gone yet.

ANDERSON   Shawnee. . . . I saw Tecumseh once. As a child. Grand he was, too, grand. (*stops*)   Yes, ma'am? You were saying?

SARA   Sometimes a woman here can feel like such a road. Rutted by heavy loads. Watched. By misery. By hate—you are embarrassed.

ANDERSON   We best keep moving, Mrs. Cane. My leg is telling me it's going to really storm.

Enter Major Blood, blind.

ANDERSON (*cont.*)   Oh my lord. Oh my lord, my lord.

SARA   What's wrong with his face? Oh no, oh God, no.

BLOOD   Help me. Oh, help me. Quantrill's men left me to bang myself to death against the trees.

ANDERSON   You shouldn't have ever come to Lawrence.

BLOOD   My God, help me.

SARA   I don't—

She ties scarf around his eyes.

SARA (*cont.*)   I am not sure this helps. My husband. What will they do to him? We must hurry.

BLOOD   Mrs. Cane, is that you?

SARA   Yes.

BLOOD   Your accent. I knew it.

SARA   You must rest here.

BLOOD   For God's sake, don't leave me. I can help you. The mayor must be near.

SARA   How do you know?

BLOOD   I can smell mint. I smell sage. I think they took him to a place, he said it smelled of mint and sage.

SARA   We must take him. Help him.

ANDERSON   My arm, Major. It's Anderson.

BLOOD   Anderson. Oh, Anderson.

SARA   Hurry. Please. As best you can.

ANDERSON   Ma'am, you got a case here of blind leading the lame. I guess hurry ain't our forte.

BLOOD   That rumbling. Is it thunder?

ANDERSON   Wind's up. Yes. Come on, we best move.

Exeunt.

SCENE 9

In the woods. Enter Quantrill and Jesse, dragging Cane.

JESSE (*to Quantrill*)   Hey. You can really make the sun rise west at night, let's do it tonight. Show Cane who's who.

QUANTRILL   Honey, you forgot the second part. Shortly after, Quantrill's got to die; after messing with Mr. Sol—or so the old Indian lady said.

JESSE   "Old Injun lady said." Quantrill, you ain't never going to die. Anyhow, I'm tired dragging his municipal ass. You can make the sun rise in the west at night, how come you can't even make this sumbitch say yes?

139

QUANTRILL He will. Let him down here.

JESSE Let's just cut pieces of his face off till he says yes.

QUANTRILL Dingus, honey, you go on. Join Jimmy in town. See if Cole came yet. Cane just needs some—reflection time.

Exit Jesse.

CANE Old Indian woman. Ho-ho. Well, well: You bring the sun up in the west at night, and then ask Lawrence to punk for you. And your old Indian woman.

QUANTRILL There is no Injun woman. That story's just made up.

CANE I'll be damned. You admit you're a liar.

QUANTRILL Just giving the boys something special. They never had anything. They're mostly ignorant and poor. Tromped on as most coloreds but dumber, 'cause they don't know it. You try controlling five hundred dumb, poor, armed men, grieving for their families and their land.

CANE The magician shows his trickery. What next?

QUANTRILL Sure they believe in Quantrill. He can't ever die till he makes the sun rise in the west at night. They know it isn't true. But they also know it is; which is more than you.

CANE Treacherous cynical opportunist and thief. Jailbird, liar, pervert, and killer. Lawless. Homeless. Faithless. Savage. Ho. Wouldn't be surprised if you had a bit of Indian in you.

QUANTRILL You're shivering.

CANE Just the wind.

QUANTRILL Got a bottle of warmth right here.

CANE Oh, no. I'm not one of your girls.

Quantrill drinks.

CANE (*cont.*) I begin to see we can do a deal. You know: save face. Both of us. Work something reasonable out. Money could even change hands.

QUANTRILL Quantrill don't deal with someone who don't drink with him. (*drinks*) Warmth.

CANE A man would lack moral imagination to hear an arsonist say warmth and not shiver.

QUANTRILL No blame here, for being merely flesh. Teeth are chattering.

CANE Not fear. Cold.
    Well. Give me one sip. Just one.

QUANTRILL You're not one of Quantrill's girls.

CANE No one is around to see and misinterpret.

Quantrill holds bottle, Cane drinks.

CANE (*cont.*) You laughing at me?

QUANTRILL Is it good?

CANE Whiskey? I don't drink much. I don't need to. Can calm myself without it. Enjoy myself plenty too.
    Why are you smiling like that?

QUANTRILL The left side of Quantrill's mouth has one reason. The right side, quite another.

CANE You think I can't hold my drink. I can hold my drink as well as any man. Any man.

QUANTRILL Your strength impresses; it always did.

141

CANE   Those girls are staying in that cage. They behaved like animals. If that's folly, I say let it increase.

QUANTRILL   It will.

CANE   What's that mean?

QUANTRILL   Folly will increase.

CANE   It's right.
I'm cold again. May I have another sip? It's not as good as sleep in one's own bed, but under the circumstances— (*drinks*) F-feel better. Now. (*stops*) Now, about a deal. Don't want gifts. (*drinks*) Just to be free, which is my right. My whole life's fight in Kansas. (*pause*) My whole life . . .

Quantrill takes out knife.

CANE (*cont.*)   What are you doing?

QUANTRILL   Free you.

CANE   You're twisting words. You mean dead when you say free.

QUANTRILL   To cut your ropes. Free your limbs.

CANE   Aha. You've seen. I'm not bending to you. Quantrill. This means we make a deal, doesn't it?

QUANTRILL   Deals galore, once you're free.

CANE   My God. Your reputation. What lies. They say you burnt an outpost once where a blacksmith wouldn't shoe your horse. And killed him. But you are just a pussycat. I— (*becoming disoriented*) Funny, these words. Seem funny. I— I demand you return me to Lawrence.

QUANTRILL   If Pussy can come with you.

142

CANE Superstitious bastard. Why are you smiling like that?

QUANTRILL Your return to Lawrence will be a triumph.

CANE Oh. Yes. Happy endings. To the comedy. My eyes. I can't—I can't—seem to—focus—my eyes. Sooner or later, right wins. I will be—what?—what? Vindicate— vindiwhat?

I remember. I promise nothing in return except that I, John Cane, will see you—will see you—locked up! I—as sure as I'd put fire in a fireplace and keep it in there.

QUANTRILL Ever notice how hard it gets to be talking sometimes?

CANE We'll build the cage to hold you too, we'll—my words. I hear echoes, do you? In my head.

QUANTRILL Men who think they can cage fire think they can cage anything.

CANE Why are you watching me? Cut me loose, I—oh. Oh. I—oh. What's happening to me?

QUANTRILL It's caught you by the hair.

CANE Oh. Like cold bees. In my skull. *Zzzz. Ezz.* I'm going mad.

QUANTRILL Fly like a bird. Look down. See how far to the ground.

CANE Ohh! My eyes. The light. Oceans, too much light. Light's smashing my eyes, help me, my eyes.

QUANTRILL Fly, dog who makes cages, fly.

CANE The whiskey.

QUANTRILL Be where things are and have no reasons.

CANE   What was in the whiskey? Oh! Oh, no no no no. Oh, no no no no no no no! Catch that boy, the one with the string!

QUANTRILL   Hm?

CANE   Little bastard. Stop whirling my mind. Gimme that string. Stop, ah, stop it, stop stop stop stop stop stop stop! Please, please stop, help, kill him, kill him, kill kill kill kill kill! I can't bear it anymore!

QUANTRILL   Nothing there, Cane. Look: just quail taking cover. Prairie dogs diving for burrows. Snakes whip and slither to tunnels. Storm is just about here.

Quantrill cuts Cane's ankle ropes.

CANE   My heart. Is turning. To stone. Oh, hope, help, hope. Beat-clump. Beat-clump. Beat-clump. Oh, oh, oh, I-I-I-I—you—as—eee—oh! Oh! *Oh!* Look!

Quantrill cuts Cane's wrist bonds.

CANE (*cont.*)   Light! Look! How beautiful!

Cane slumps into glaze-eyed narcotic nod.

SCENE 10

Same.

QUANTRILL   Want your ankles rubbed?

CANE   I—*mmpf*—thank you.

QUANTRILL   Off with your. Boots.

CANE   Thank. You.

Quantrill rubs Cane's ankles.

QUANTRILL   Your wrists hurt?

CANE   Yes.

QUANTRILL   Like them rubbed?

CANE   I—pl-please.

Quantrill rubs Cane's wrists.

CANE (*cont.*)   Urc. A.

QUANTRILL   What?

CANE   Urca. Unca. Urk. Words. (*giggles*)   Eega. Eeega-teega.
Ooog oog ooga. Mur-flip. (*giggles*)   Flip! Titititititi. Br—
owwn. Murflip? Fleeglats? Girty girty girty girty girty girty.
Urk. (*giggles*)   Urga urga urga. (*satisfied*)   Fleeglats.

QUANTRILL   Fleeglats.

CANE   Ho! Fleeglats? Oho, fleeglats. Hiya huya hiya hiya.
Urcup!

QUANTRILL   Feel okay? You in there? Cane?

CANE   Prairie. Prairie.

QUANTRILL   Prairie. Storm? Inside?

CANE   I—oh. Calm. No—words.

QUANTRILL   Now: You were saying. About a deal.

CANE   Oh—I—all—ssstrange. Look. King-doms. In-leaves.
Wor-worlds. Worlds. Em-pires. Look.

QUANTRILL   Worlds.

CANE   Yes.

QUANTRILL Very good little worlds.

CANE Empires.

QUANTRILL (*giggling*) You got a deal.

CANE Deal.

QUANTRILL Trade you. Let's see. For those two leaves—empires—

CANE Empires. Mine.

QUANTRILL This here spider. This nice lady centipede.

CANE Divinities.

QUANTRILL Trade you.

CANE Trade.

QUANTRILL You drive a hard bargain.

CANE Why—laugh?

QUANTRILL You are really shrewd.

CANE Am. A man.

QUANTRILL I end up with two leaves. Whereas you got yourself two real nice little bugs there.

CANE Bugs? Bugs!

QUANTRILL This leaf's some amazing world. Look. . . .

CANE Bugs? Cheated. Oh. I—words, *mmpf, mmpf?* See—everything. I—oh, oh—afraid. Afraid.

QUANTRILL Sssh. Hear crickets?

CANE Ah. Not—afraid. They go: rehearse, rehearse, rehearse. Oh! Other voice? Behind their voices.

QUANTRILL   You hear it.

CANE   Oh—saw—awful thing. Of light. Before.

QUANTRILL   Sssh. Listen.

CANE   Listen. Music! Is he playing? Yes. With crickets. Music-playing. Oh. Marvelous. Wish. Quantrill—wish— wish. Hear more. If. Had. Other. Drink.

QUANTRILL   Would you like another drink?

CANE   Oh. Would. I. Yes.

QUANTRILL   You got your trousers on.

CANE   Wrong? Wrong?

QUANTRILL   There isn't anymore to drink—for a man with trousers on.

CANE   My hat in church. Off. Off, pants, off. (*He takes trousers off*) There.

QUANTRILL   Drink up.

Cane drinks. Quantrill hides pants, boots. Quantrill drinks.

CANE   Ah. Wonder—ous. Thank. Why? Are you so? Good to me?

QUANTRILL   We're returning soon. To Lawrence.

CANE   Like this. No pants?

QUANTRILL   You dress worse than a Baptist preacher. Put on this pretty skirt. Take the fashion lead in Lawrence. Latest thing from Paris.

CANE   No. No, no, can't. But. Cane can't. No pants. So sad. Can't return—like this. So sad. So sad.

147

Cane wanders away.

QUANTRILL Do it for Quantrill. For lots of good deals ahead.

CANE Help. Mind wanders. Out. Come back. Come back, come back, come back.

QUANTRILL Don't grab after what's already gone. You're in the mansion of here-and-now. Everything you need is in it. Why—what's this here?

CANE Skirt.

QUANTRILL What a lovely skirt, John. Try it.

CANE *(putting on skirt)* I will be discredited.

QUANTRILL Can't have that.

CANE Can't have that.

QUANTRILL So, disguise yourself. Put on this yellow-hair wig, and no will know you.

CANE If Sara sees me—my wife—

QUANTRILL She's going to want to sew one for herself.

CANE Latest from Paris: Look, girls! Oh. Sara. I didn't mean it. I didn't mean it. *(weeps)* Where is she? Sara? Sara?

QUANTRILL Likely with your daughter. Gillie.

CANE Ah . . .

QUANTRILL You'll have to return to say how much you always loved her.

CANE Ah! The girls?

QUANTRILL We come to the biggest deal of all.

CANE Gillie. Jenny. Belle. I wonder what they do alone. They say about young girls alone. How licentious, how perverse. Oh. Just once. Just to see them once, deliciously wrapped around each other. Oh . . .

QUANTRILL You'd set them free.

CANE Yes. Just the thought of it.

QUANTRILL Quantrill takes you back to Lawrence, you release his friends. Deal?

CANE What's a jail to me? I promise.

QUANTRILL Say yes.

CANE Yes. Let's go.

QUANTRILL Quantrill wants a bigger yes.

CANE Yes! Can we hurry now?

QUANTRILL Bigger.

CANE *Ye-es!*

QUANTRILL No.

CANE No?

QUANTRILL You're not flying really. You don't like being dressed up so pretty?

CANE I do so.

QUANTRILL What you need is the Prairie Twister.

CANE Tornado? Tornadoes hurt.

QUANTRILL When I was teaching school—over to Wichita? Grades one to ten, in one room, you know?

CANE How come?

QUANTRILL   Oh, 'cause in this jailbird's ear that word *freedom* was so sweet, I didn't know you didn't mean it—but that's a whole other story. Anyhow, we used to all cut school sometimes. Whole class and me. Go out on the prairie, roll up, lie back, and smoke.

And one day, we're lying there, smoking, and crazy turkeys started bursting out of the tall grass, and you'd've thought their mamas told 'em about Thanksgiving and the Puritans, they were so excited.

CANE   Gobble gobble.

QUANTRILL   Then we saw this huge swaying snake of a twister gliding up the horizon. So there was this kid Boardman. He was always picking his snout in class. Well, Boardman starts crying and saying, Tornado!—It's cause we're smoking: We'll be punished! Tornado coming! And the other kids staring paralyzed, thinking like it's the devil's horse howling up the prairie to grab them. So I was thinking they'd scatter, and I didn't want that, so I did—this.

He suddenly seizes Cane in a fireman's carry, over his shoulders, and begins to turn and stomp.

QUANTRILL (*cont.*)   Prairie twister got you, Boardman.

CANE   Oh!

QUANTRILL   Now you're going to fly, you're going to fly and die, die and fly, here we go, stompety-stomp—

CANE   Ah, you'll make me sick, I'll puke. I'll puke, I'll puke!

QUANTRILL (*spinning faster*)   Tornado yes, fly and die!

CANE   Oh, aw, oh! (*beginning to laugh*)   Oh, ha ha!

150

QUANTRILL   Tornado yes! Tornado yes! Tornado yes!

CANE   Tornado yes! Yes! Ye-ess!

QUANTRILL   Say yes. Say yes!

CANE   Ye-esss! Ye-essss!

Quantrill throws him down.

CANE (*cont.*)   Want more!

QUANTRILL   Time to go home.

CANE   Dizzy. Dizzy.

QUANTRILL   This way. Don't wander off.

CANE   Lawrence? This way? Lawrence?

QUANTRILL   Best take Quantrill's hand. Come on.

CANE   Did this hand touch my daughter?

QUANTRILL   Do you mind?

CANE   I—I?—I—no. Feel free. Oh, the wind is so nice in my nice blond hair. Look how it flies and flies. Lead on. Cane comes.

Quantrill laughs. They go. Enter Cole, Jim, and Jesse.

COLE   Not here.

JESSE   He was.

COLE   Come on.

JESSE   Quantrill? Quantrill? Whole damn thing's gone wrong. Quantrill!

Exeunt.

Scene 11

In the woods. Enter Major Blood, Sara, and Anderson.

ANDERSON I was sure I heard bells.

SARA The wind is playing tricks.

ANDERSON There. Listen.

BLOOD Mint. Sage. Smell it?

SARA In circles. We're going in circles.

ANDERSON I hear shouts.

SARA Shouts?

ANDERSON There.

SARA Bells.

BLOOD Mint. Sage. Smell it? Smell it?

SARA You smell it everywhere. It's the wind.

BLOOD You are right. *(falls)* Ah.

SARA Get him up.

BLOOD No, I am beaten. I give up.

ANDERSON We can't stop now.

BLOOD I am whipped. Leave me.

ANDERSON You know we can't. Get up.

BLOOD No. My son is dead.
  I have not said the words before. I willed it to be untrue.
It is true.

SARA What son?

BLOOD   A dead one. I cannot even weep. I am helpless. All
my life has been willed. Every moment of his four years, I
willed him to be a soldier. It's over. He is dead. I am
helpless. Blind. Still, the will goes on. I feel ridden like a
horse to death. It is over! I give up!
  What does it want from me? Pain doesn't matter to it.
Grief grief grief, what does grief matter? It pushes. It pushes.
I want it to go away. I want to lie here and dissolve. I want
to be free of it, to be at peace, to die.

ANDERSON   Mrs. Cane?

BLOOD   All this, for a half-wit. Eeee. Eeee.

SARA   Has he a fever?

BLOOD   No, I do not have a fever.

SARA   Then come. Get up now. Come. Please.

BLOOD   No, leave me.

Enter Cole, Jim, and Jesse, on the run.

COLE   The major.

BLOOD   Who's that?

JIM   He's got some bounce in him, being here.

ANDERSON   Cole and Jimmy Younger and some punk.

BLOOD   Kill me. Please. That's what he wants me to say. I am
saying it: Kill me.

JIM   Nobody wants you, Major. Let's go.

SARA   Wait. We're looking for Mr. Quantrill. We'll release
the girls.

COLE Too late for that.

JIM Cole, she don't know. Come on.

SARA Wait. At least tell us: Is the mayor back yet?

COLE No.

ANDERSON We heard an uproar—

JIM Yeah. Come on, Jesse. Cole?

JESSE (*to Anderson*) I'll remember "punk," mister.

Jim and Jesse go.

COLE Town is that way, two miles, about. Look for an Indian track, little path, follow it left each time.

SARA But

COLE Don't ask nothing. Get on back.

SARA It's good news. The girls are free. The bells and shouts you heard. They're celebrating.

ANDERSON But if the mayor's not back?

SARA Too late to free them, he said. People there must have done it. Decided it was mad and—that will mean the army in Lawrence. That's why he hurries so to tell Quantrill.

COLE Cane's jail collapsed. The stable.

SARA It what? It—*what?*

COLE There's this big wind coming when I get back there. I hear this screaming. Jesse says, It's from Cane's jail, Cole. Run. So we—we meet Jim, he's running too. Everyone. We get to the stable; it's swaying, kind of. Then it leans, kind of. No one had time to do nothing. Big gust come up.

One side wall caved in. Screaming like you never heard.
"Help, help, oh, God, help me!" We run forward, but I
seen the roof sag. Then a second wall give. Drag the roof
crashing down with it. All this time this "Help, help, oh,
God, help me!" Then just silence. Just wind swirling dust
up around. Dust blowing. Somebody weeping. Look like
after one of Jennison's raids. Only a stone chimney left. Half
one wall, that's all that held up. Just busted-up bones of a
place and dust blowing. Where people lived.

Enter Jim.

JIM   They ain't our people. Come on.

SARA   You saw my daughter.

COLE   Roof beam crushed her, Mrs. Cane. All of them.
They're dead. I'm sorry.

Exeunt Jim and Cole.

BLOOD   Younger? Please. Kill me.

SARA   Mr. Anderson. We must return.

Blood crawls off.

BLOOD   Oh, please. Someone. Please.

ANDERSON   Major.

SARA   Mr. Anderson?

ANDERSON   We won't be any use there.

SARA   I will be with my daughter.

ANDERSON   She's not in danger now. Your husband is in
more than ever.

SARA I do not care about him anymore.

Sara goes.

ANDERSON Mrs. Cane. Mrs. Cane!

Anderson follows.

SCENE 12

In the woods. Enter Quantrill, with Cane laughing.

CANE Haw-haw-haw.

QUANTRILL Well, I told him. Child, I said, every time you pick your nose, you got more brains on the tip of your pinky than your father in his whole head. Don't eat it.

CANE Aw haw, aw haw, aw haw: It's wondrous. To have comradeship, fraternity, and trust in such fratricidal times. You know what fratricidal means.

QUANTRILL Cain and Abel.

CANE Sure wouldn't be Cain if I was still Abel! Haw. Oh, get me a horse, I think I'll ride with you. Get me a horse.

QUANTRILL Let's draw one on the ground here.

CANE A big one. A big horsie. With a big thing on it, this big, this big. Bigger! Bigger! Giddyap, giddyap! Glory be! No longer a thing half mayor and half man. I'm born again, haw! The preacher'll love it. Born again! My father was a preacher in Medford. Got dandruff, haw, haw! Yours?

QUANTRILL School principal.

CANE How like father like son the world goes.

156

QUANTRILL Someone over there.

CANE Oh. My hair. I'm not really ready yet. Help me, my hair's a scandal. I better hide. I'm scared. I'm scared.

He hides.

QUANTRILL No need. Just hush.

Enter Major Blood. He searches around, finds branch.

QUANTRILL Christ almighty, look at you.

BLOOD Who's there? Where are you?

QUANTRILL Who did that to you?

BLOOD A man. Don't know. Will you help me?

QUANTRILL Who ordered it done?

BLOOD Is it you?

QUANTRILL Say the name. Remember the name.

BLOOD Quantrill?

QUANTRILL William Clarke Quantrill, son of Tom Henry and Carrie Clarke. Remember it.

BLOOD You.

QUANTRILL How on earth did you get here?

BLOOD Kill me. Do it. *(flailing branch)* You. *(flails)* You. Kill me, or I'll kill you, you, you.

QUANTRILL Appears wisdom doesn't necessarily come to the suffering.

CANE *(peeks out)* Oh, my lord. Major. Major. Oh, my lord. It is John Cane.

BLOOD Cane? Where is he? Point me, point me!

CANE We are going to Lawrence.

BLOOD Don't allow him in Lawrence. Or, you're dead.

CANE But me and him are together.

BLOOD See what he's done to me? Ah!

Removes bandage.

CANE You're frightening me.

QUANTRILL Old sockets here has scared his last half-wit. Haven't you?

BLOOD You're frightened—aren't you? To kill me.

QUANTRILL (*pause*) No one will ever say lack of daring was your sin.

BLOOD Oh, yes. You are. You're spooked now, aren't you? You know I know. You know—I know.

QUANTRILL Know?

BLOOD You just don't know what. That's why you don't kill me. Well, here's what: You will go too far, much too far somehow. And your boys won't look up to you, you were never one of them, they will desert you. Your name, it will be in the mud. Oh, yes.

    I see one night, one midnight. It will come. In a barn somewhere you'll be asleep. No human roof'll cover you.

    In a barn like a beast you'll be asleep. One midnight, rain beating on the roof. Just a handful left loyal to you, all asleep. And blue troops all around, blue troops closing in on you. And time, time running out on you. And as you sleep, someone calls your name: Quantrill? And calls your name again: Quantrill? And you're half awake and listening. And now you're up. You're leaping to your horse—but you won't escape this time—

QUANTRILL   What are you jabbering about?

BLOOD   I was told about your horse. Billy Gem said when it dies, you die too, and so it dies, it is shot from under you, your horse is shot from under you. Horse kicking, flailing, screaming in the mud. Run, boy, run. You splash through mud and dark. Run, boy, run, you're the blind one now, blind with fear. *Wait!* you cry. A mounted friend wheels around and races back. Your arm—you throw up an arm, it's grabbed, you throw yourself up behind a friend; you turn, you fire to cover your retreat. A sheet of flame answers you. A volley roars. A rifle ball speeds to you. *Ahhh!* (*sobs with joy*)   Your spine. They've shot your back in two, your back is broke. You cry out, you howl. You fall and twist, and fall and twist, it takes so long, four thousand years, you splash, paralyzed, face down, sucking mud. As you die there, so young, so astonished in that rainy slime, remember this name: Hal Blood. Now you know. Kill me. (*nothing moves*)   Ahh! (*flails with branch*)

QUANTRILL   You won't see it.

Quantrill kicks him.

BLOOD   Kick me? Kill me! Kill me!

QUANTRILL   Everywhere you pick your way, tell them Quantrill did it to you because he does not forget his friends.

BLOOD   Kill me or I'll kill you. Where? Where are you?

Exit Major Blood.

CANE Have some pity, for the love of God.

QUANTRILL Of whores? Thieves? Children? The kind your kind makes footprints of.

CANE Not for me? Or the major?

QUANTRILL Blood owed a bill. He paid it.

CANE You men. Something must be done about you men. And pity.

QUANTRILL What you did at Osceola. (*silence*) Who's hurt you for that? And Jennison at Harrisonville. And reprisals at Palmyra: ten innocent men, chose at random—lined up in front of empty coffins, their families looking on—shot by your authorities. Anyone hurt you for that? Quantrill? Quantrill just gives you fun. Doesn't that beat pity?

CANE Yes. Thank you.

QUANTRILL At the day's end, pity comes. Redemption, is it not promised?

CANE Yes.

QUANTRILL Then it will come. Meanwhile, have fun.

CANE Yes. Thank you.

QUANTRILL Then let's be on to Lawrence, see the girls; just being there will pay whatever debt you owe.

CANE Yes. Oh, yes. Oh, yes.

Cane goes, led by Quantrill.

Lawrence. Off, someone picks at a piano. Enter Sara, dazed.

SARA *(singing)*   A wind is coming up somewhere . . .
Honeybees fly home, fly home . . .
August storms will split the air . . .
Your honey will be—

Deputy and Sheriff Stone carry on three open coffins and go. The Sheriff returns with sheet, covers coffins. Piano stops. Enter Anderson.

SHERIFF   It's just temporary. Tod is seeing to the lids being made right now.

ANDERSON   Her limbs. They weren't laid out right. Weren't straight.

SHERIFF   It would have meant setting all the bones. Best not think about it.

ANDERSON   I—don't understand.

SHERIFF   Best—not think about it. Come away, sir. Come away. You can do no good here.

Anderson goes. Jennison hurries on.

JENNISON   Mr. Stone, leave that. We have a job. Cane is back. Wait till you see.

Jennison takes Sheriff off. Piano stops and starts and stops.

SARA   A wind is coming up somewhere. Your honey will. Be gone. Yes.

Enter Quantrill and Cane.

CANE   My wife.

QUANTRILL   Just Miss Sara. Go on.

CANE   Sara. Look. I am a new man. Look: Poor little kitten has lost his mittens, I have lost my boots and don't know where to find them. Sara? It's me, Jack. Speak to me.

Sara draws back sheet from bodies in coffins.

CANE   Awh. Awh.

QUANTRILL   Pulped.

CANE   Awh. Oh. Sara?

SARA   It collapsed. The stable.

CANE   Oh. Oh. Poor little kitten. Oh, oh.
Oh, Sara. Oh, Sara.
Oh, oh, oh, my kitten, my kitten.

SARA   It was rotten. It collapsed. While you wasted time, time ran out.

CANE   Oh, kitten, kitten, kitten.

SARA   What have you done to me? Oh, what have you done?

Enter Sheriff, Deputy, Anderson, and Jennison.

JENNISON   Disarm that one.

Quantrill is taken and disarmed.

JENNISON (*cont.*)   Tod. Deal with him.

Deputy takes Quantrill off.

JENNISON (*cont.*)   Well, well. The man who got us into this. How do you like it? My girl lies dead there. He puts on a dress and mocks I don't even know what. Get that dress off him.

SARA What are you doing?

JENNISON Get it off.

CANE Oh, Gillie. Don't hit me, please, Charlie.

JENNISON Take him.

CANE Leave me. My arms. You're tearing my arms out; leave me.

SHERIFF Wait, Anderson. Not here.

ANDERSON Sir! Mr. Cane. I know she was plain. But a flower can be plain. And still very perfect. Well. I mean, she was the best girl in the world. The best girl in the whole world. And look, look here, she's here, look. Well. How am I going to—to live? Heart feels like a loaded train . . . trying to puff upgrade. I swear it's going to break, Mr. Cane. Mr. Cane: How do you like that?

Anderson thumps Cane to the ground.

SARA Oh don't. Don't do that.

Men drag Cane away. Sara follows.

VOICES How's that! How's that! How's that!

Enter Quantrill, bleeding at mouth. Crawls under sheet. Deputy runs on, holding hurt face.

DEPUTY Sumbitch! Sumbitch!

VOICES You like that? How's that? You like it?

CANE Help, help, oh, God, help me.

Deputy runs off.

CANE (*cont.*) Aaeehuh.

Cane, naked, staggers in, is caught, dragged back.

CANE *(cont.)* Aaeehuh!

Silence. Enter Jennison and Sheriff Stone.

JENNISON Forget about Quantrill. Little nothing to start with, he's learned his lesson. As for Cane, just carry him to the fields. Feed the rats.

Sheriff goes. Returns with Deputy carrying Cane out alive. Piano starts. Jennison listens. It stops. He goes. Quantrill emerges. Enter Cole and Jim.

QUANTRILL Just been with our friends. Accuse me . . .

Cole and Jim lift him up.

QUANTRILL *(cont.)* Forgetting them. No, child, no, I say. I don't. I don't.

They help him off.

SCENE 14

Outside Lawrence. Four o'clock in the morning. Anderson sits alone, playing music. Enter Lieutenant Terrel.

TERREL Mister?
    Lieutenant Andrew Terrel, General Ewing's headquarters. I'm embarrassed to say I lost my way by dark. I'm looking for Lawrence.

ANDERSON Lose your troops too?

TERREL They're about a day from here. I'm alone.

ANDERSON Lawrence is over a couple of miles around that rise. Or go that way. Follow the Kaw River.

TERREL You from there?

ANDERSON Yes.

TERREL I've been sent to scout some information further. Major Blood? Still missing?

ANDERSON Yes.

TERREL Is it—true?

ANDERSON They blinded him. You mean that?

TERREL Good God. I'm half hoping I don't find him. His wife's left, gone home east; I don't know how I'll tell him. How come you're here?

ANDERSON Watching out for—someone.

TERREL The mayor?

ANDERSON The mayor.

TERREL We heard he was driven out.

ANDERSON Things got a little crazy.

TERREL What happened here anyhow? Lawrence used to seem pretty sound and orderly.

ANDERSON Let us know when you find out. We were here. We still don't know what happened.

Enter Cane, covered in mud, half naked.

TERREL A runaway slave. You. You're in Kansas now. Safe. Free territory.

CANE No such thing. Just hell, this hell, hell, hell, hell, hell.

TERREL (*to Anderson*) You'd think fighting a war for them'd be enough. Listen to me! I'm an officer in the Union army.

165

Maybe you heard rumors we make you join this army. It's
not true. War does make men, by God, though. We'd
welcome you.

CANE   Hypocrite. Kills 'em.

ANDERSON   Don't sound like he's fooled.

TERREL   You ungrateful—get out here! Now!

ANDERSON   Hold on. I don't know who you are, or where
you been. That's not how we deal, here. You understand
me? Back off. (*going to Cane*)   You must've had a long trip.
You're safe now, come on in, it's okay. (*recognizing
Cane*)   Mayor? Is that you?

CANE   Do you pity me? I pity you.

TERREL   Cane? It can't be.

ANDERSON   It's him.

CANE   Pity, man. If I had any. And you. And you. You two
and I make three. I have been thinking. About these civic
matters some. Three. Almost a settlement: seed of a town. If
you two save up pity for me and each other—and me for
you—if we pool it, I believe we then will make a true
community. Damn me if we won't. Except.
   Except. It will not grow. Do you know why?

ANDERSON   Don't be frightened. Come rest yourself.

CANE   We lack women.

ANDERSON   Mayor.

CANE   Anderson. Help me. Look how miserable.

ANDERSON   Come rest.

CANE (*confused*) You are a friend?

ANDERSON Yes, sir.

CANE You want to take another whack?

ANDERSON That—beating, that was a mistake. Give me your hand.

CANE I suffer. I am—I don't know what . . .

He takes hand and holds on.

ANDERSON We lost our heads. I'm sorry.

CANE Each bruise has been a great relief. Every ache I give thanks for. Pain clouds the conscience. When it lifts, then— then, Anderson—I am so miserable, so sorry, so sorry.

ANDERSON Mr. Cane, we want you back.

CANE Give back your hand. I need it.

TERREL Mayor? Not hardly a man.

CANE A child needs to clutch. Remember? Are you glad not to be me?

TERREL I couldn't even imagine it.

ANDERSON Sir, yesterday afternoon they buried the girls.

CANE Time means nothing to me.

ANDERSON You've been gone two—two days and a half, about.

CANE That little? (*confused*) That little?

ANDERSON Anyhow, that was when I decided to come out here. Look for you. Keep an eye out. See, no man could look another in the eye. At the service. We all knew; we

167

put the girls in that place. It wasn't just you. After, we talked. I volunteered. Mr. Cane, we're still a city. You're still—

CANE No.

ANDERSON —Mayor. There are others to think of besides yourself.

CANE I've served.

ANDERSON I'll help you up. Clean your face. Here.

Anderson cleans his face.

CANE Why? What's there? Beneath.

ANDERSON The same man.

CANE Am I? Still?

ANDERSON You walk like one. You suffer like one. Not much else to go on.

CANE So. You want me back.

ANDERSON You lost what we lost.

CANE So. You want to give me strength.

ANDERSON There's no one understands us better.

CANE I don't want strength.

ANDERSON Stop wanting strength, you hang yourself.

CANE Not without pants, you don't.

ANDERSON I brought some clothes of yours. Here.

CANE So. . . . You would like me to dress.

ANDERSON Yes.

CANE (*pulling pants on*)   Be mayor.

ANDERSON   Get clothes on your back, you'll see what a difference.

CANE (*putting on shirt*)   Clothes make the man. I can't.

ANDERSON   Put on your coat.

CANE   You can't build a being with these materials. I am so wretched; look how wretched.

ANDERSON   Easy does it. Put it on.

CANE (*putting on coat*)   Will I have Sara? Do I?

ANDERSON   Sara.

CANE   I had a wife.

ANDERSON   Yes.

CANE   Do I?

ANDERSON   Maybe when she sees you again.

CANE   Maybe.

ANDERSON   Sara's not spoke to any of us. Maybe when she sees you again.

CANE   Oh. Maybe.

ANDERSON   You shared a lot.

CANE   Once, you mean.

ANDERSON   Share a grief, you share a forgiveness. Maybe.

CANE   Oh. Maybe yes. Maybe no. Maybe things—are not the same. Is that not the raw truth of it?

ANDERSON   You're looking better, dressed.

CANE   I feel more myself, I admit. Anderson—William Quantrill escaped?

ANDERSON   Yes, he did.

CANE   Not been seen?

ANDERSON   Thinking like yourself again, there you are.

CANE   Then he hasn't.

ANDERSON   No.

TERREL   No sightings anywhere. It's like the ground opened and swallowed them.

ANDERSON   He's not going to show up in Lawrence again, that's for sure. Lieutenant, are you coming with us?

TERREL   I'll follow. I have some notes to make. Do you know the date, by the way?

ANDERSON   Twentieth. No, August twenty-first, in fact. Come on. The sun'll be up real soon.

CANE   When. When it is over. The barbarism. Theirs. Our own. When the war is over. When this infernal hate—of poor beings I call enemy—is over. When forgiveness for this—terrible, terrible destruction—has been reached for, and grasped somehow. Then—then: If there are not changes, Anderson, what are we? Just this, this— miserable?—puff of breath surrounded by no proof at all. For the body of poor beings, I will see enough food and warmth and work. For the spirit, enough community. For the mind, enough schools. To bring clarity. Light. If I am still able.

Cane and Anderson go.

TERREL Join you soon, gentlemen.

Terrel makes notes. Light rises.

TERREL (*cont.*) August 21, 1863. Certain to need a garrison now. (*stops*) Dawn? Already? (*checks watch*) Only four. Watch's stopped? No. . . . Four-oh-eight A.M. Hold on. I came from the northeast. Back there. Then to my right ought to be due west. West? Sunrise in the west? I must have it wrong—what's that?

Distant rumbling. Terrel sweeps horizon with binoculars. Enter behind him Quantrill in battle dress, wrapped in a cloak.

TERREL (*looking outward*) Horsemen. And more horsemen.

QUANTRILL Would you care to join us, soldier boy?

TERREL Good Christ. Who are you?

QUANTRILL I am William Clarke Quantrill. Perhaps the name is known to you. I have undertaken vengeance.

TERREL Oh, my lord.

Terrel backs, then rushes off. Quantrill drinks. Cole enters opposite.

COLE There you are. (*silence*) I wondered. (*silence*)
  The column's reached the top of the ridge. It's just down from there and across the Kaw. (*silence*) Quantrill, you should've seen: One rider lit his torch and rode up and down the ranks; just touch it to the others; pitch took fire; flames blaze up; you could almost hear the cheers wanting to rise out of their hearts. But they held back. For Osceola now. For Palmyra. For Harrisonville. For our girls killed.

QUANTRILL Major Blood is right. (*drinks*) War's lost. It's all pointless.

171

COLE Osceola, I said. Osceola. Palmyra. Harrisonville. Our girls! Our friends. Osceola. Palmyra. Harrisonville. Our girls. Our friends. Osceola. Palmyra. Harrisonville.

QUANTRILL None of us going to make old bones, will we? (*drinks*)

COLE They're just waiting for you to be leading them in.

QUANTRILL I know.

Quantrill goes. Cole waits. Suddenly a howl rises, becoming louder, louder. Cole goes. Then rumbling rises. Then light.

SCENE 15

In Lawrence. Off, sounds and light rising. Enter Anderson. Enter Deputy in nightgown.

ANDERSON Tod.

DEPUTY Anderson. I just woke. What is it?

ANDERSON We're being attacked. Wake everyone.

Enter Jennison.

DEPUTY My God in heaven. What'll we do——?

JENNISON Anderson——

DEPUTY We're being attacked. We got to arm.

Deputy goes.

JENNISON Attacked?

ANDERSON Lord, all in your nightgowns.

JENNISON Did he say attacked?

172

ANDERSON Our girls were in their nightgowns too.

Enter Sheriff Stone in nightgown, trousers.

SHERIFF Five hundred horsemen with torches! They're pouring over the ridge of the hill. Quantrill's leading them in to burn us! Everyone up! Wake up! Arm yourselves!

ANDERSON Wake up! Wake up!

They go, shouting. Light flickers into flame. Howling and rumbling grow louder, as hundreds of horses plow up the streets. Enter May Jennison.

MAY JENNISON Where's the judge? Where is he? Someone's got to help me, the piano, I got to save the piano, the house is burning. My piano, my piano!

Exit May. Enter Deputy, running. Enter with torches, Cole, Jesse, and Jim; they hold him. Enter Quantrill.

DEPUTY No.

COLE Stone's deputy. He's on the death list.

DEPUTY You'll be hunted down. You'll be run down, if you do. Like a hare. By men with hounds and guns and drums.

JESSE Don't waste your breath. Quantrill don't never die till he brings the sun up in the west.

DEPUTY Sun up? Quantrill, let me live. I'll tell you something you want to know.

QUANTRILL Maybe you will live, Tod.

DEPUTY When you brought your boys over the hill—with torches, flaming?—it looked just like the sun at dawn, just like when it rises up.

JIM It's night, too.

QUANTRILL Look like what?

DEPUTY That's what I'm saying. That hill is to the west.

JESSE Quantrill?

DEPUTY Ransom me. I'll pay.

QUANTRILL You should've cut your tongue out first.

Quantrill shoots him.

DEPUTY In the name of God, mercy.

Quantrill shoots him again. Deputy dies.

QUANTRILL Better men than you have died. Better yet will follow you.

COLE Everyone on the list?

JIM Quantrill? The list?

QUANTRILL Forget the list. (*crumples paper*) Every male of Lawrence must die. Burn everything they made to the ground.

They go. Shots, cries, sounds offstage. Enter May Jennison.

MAY My piano! Please, someone!

Enter Jennison, pursued by Jim.

MAY (*cont.*) No. No, no. (*attacking Jim*) You mustn't. I won't let you. You'll have to kill me too.

Enter Quantrill.

JIM (*to Quantrill*) She won't let go, what'm I going to do?

QUANTRILL Your piano's safe, ma'am.

MAY   Keep back. You'll have to kill me too.

QUANTRILL   No, ma'am.

Quantrill thrusts knife between couple, rips upward.

JENNISON   Oh. Mama, he's killed me. He's killed me.

Jennison stumbles away. May pursues. Jim follows. A shot. A scream. Enter Cane. Quantrill holds up bloody hands.

CANE   Enough, enough, stop it.

QUANTRILL   On the streets again? And wearing pants. This is twice you have embarrassed me. Why, think how people look at me when you do this. Go home.
      Look: blood of your justice. Jennison.

CANE   Stop the destruction, there are women and children—

QUANTRILL   Still? Orders are that women are exempt. Penalty of death. Nothing in a skirt'll be touched. Best you be on home, get the skirt back on, and run. What Quantrill means is save your skin as a woman or cash in.

Enter Sara.

SARA   Oh, my God. Please stop it.

QUANTRILL   (*tastes blood on hand*)   Too late now. They're about out of control.

SARA   If anything would restore them, do you think I wouldn't do it? Try. Please try. I beg you.

CANE   I forbid you to beg him. I'll stop you! I'll stop you!

Exit Cane, pulling Sara.

QUANTRILL   Slap water. The King of Persia did.

Quantrill goes. Enter Jesse. Enter Anderson opposite.

JESSE Punk? Punk? What's your name?

ANDERSON Anderson was my name. Go on, shoot. It don't matter now.

Enter May Jennison; she attacks Jesse.

MAY Jimmy Younger, you bastard—

JESSE Lady—

MAY I knew your ma, good girlhood friends!

JESSE Lady—

MAY I held you as a baby, you bastard—

JESSE I ain't Jimmy—damnit!

Anderson escapes. Jesse pursues. May follows.

MAY I got no one left, I got no one left, no one!

Enter Quantrill. Enter Sheriff Stone, behind.

SHERIFF Halt! Bloodthirsty scum—

Off, a shot: Sheriff falls.

SHERIFF (*cont.*) My back. I can't move.

Sheriff dies. Enter Cole.

QUANTRILL Lord, what a bust back does. Not much to look forward to, as futures go.

COLE Quantrill—enough. Let's go.

QUANTRILL We're gone already; just don't know it. (*kneels*) Future ain't ahead of us, Cole. It's always behind, creeping

up. To chop your cord. Lord, for what we are about to
receive, most humble thanks.

COLE Quantrill?

QUANTRILL From judgment gutted, from the busted back of
the law—life. Sure I'll drink your fucking blood. (*drinks from
Sheriff's death wound*)

COLE Don't be doing that. For the love of—you're crazy!
Come on. Lawrence is all in flames!

QUANTRILL Do what you like.

Cole goes. Quantrill drinks from flask.

QUANTRILL (*singing*) Oh, where has my Billy gone?
Far far away.
When will we meet again?
On another day.
Hope it's by a cooling stream,
Rinse this fevered brow,
And not in hell where devils scream
And this sinner burns—

He holds up his empty flask.

QUANTRILL (*cont.*) All out.

Cane enters, armed.

CANE Woman, eh?

Quantrill turns, shoots Cane down. Cane dies.

QUANTRILL Dummy. Farewell. If it's cold in heaven,
Quantrill will come with warm torches. Or maybe buy you
an ice cream in hell. Fool.

Offstage, cries and commotion get louder. Someone bangs a piano. The burning grows brighter. Quantrill rises, turning and raising both arms.

QUANTRILL *(cont.)*   Ye–essss!

Blackout. Silence.

Scene 16

Next day. A ruined street, Lawrence. Enter Anderson, Lieutenant Terrel, General Thomas Ewing, May Jennison, Soldiers, a few Townswomen.

TERREL   Five hundred horsemen maybe, General. It went on about four hours.

EWING   Terrible. Just pitiable.

MAY   I want to tell you something.
    Quantrill seized men in their nightgowns and fell on them like death. He slit their bellies; he slit their throats. He looked at me. Up went his hands. His hands—before my eyes—turned into roses, dripping red. I ran. I ran. The streets, they opened like a mouth to scream. His horsemen missed me twice. Their hooves were grinding men's bodies right into our roads. Pulping them right into mud. That's what I hoped to tell you: mud. The original thing. Mud.

ANDERSON   Come on, May. *(to Ewing)*   She's a little unstrung, but she's not wrong.

EWING   Mr. Anderson: The act of city killing is more heinous than mere murder. A city is the greater life of man, and a righteous city is his righteous life. Quantrill has doomed himself this time.

Enter Sara.

EWING (*cont.*)   Is this Mrs. Cane?

SARA   You asked for me.

EWING   My deepest condolences. If I can do anything at all for you, say so.

SARA (*thinks*)   Such as?

EWING   Why—anything. What will you do?

SARA   I? Oh . . . I will leave. I am not sure for where. Somewhere no one has heard of Kansas, or at least of Lawrence. I can cook. I can sew. I can work for my money. I hope to find a little white room. Not much. A peaceful view, perhaps an orchard. I have always liked orchards.
   I have some pictures of my daughter. I can look at them. Perhaps Oregon. Perhaps I won't make it. I don't really know. What should I have here? Not much, eh? Maybe just my little white American room of my own; for my grave. Is that what you wanted to know?

EWING   Mrs. Cane, I would like you to know the measures we will take.

SARA   I do not think I care to. These ones who are staying, I am sure they will want to hear. I hope you help them. However, my hopes have not ever meant very much. If you will excuse me.

Exit Sara.

EWING   We won't let this tragedy pass without redress.
   You people: Today I have issued order number eleven in the state of Missouri, where I am military governor. Its

179

purpose is even today being carried out. All counties bordering on Kansas, in particular notorious Clay and Johnson counties, will be emptied. Not one more man or boy will they provide to harry honest Kansas.

Their entire populations, down to the least infant at its teat, will be marched into camps, enclosed, guarded by our troops, and made to pay for this atrocity. Not one woman, not one child, will be exempt. Not one cheer will be raised, not one amnesty will be granted in those camps. We will pay back your blood with blood, and fire with fire. What I see here I vow is the future of many. Many.

For yourselves, ask our help. Rebuild. Put this from your memories as quickly as you're able. Let us begin again. I believe that is our way. Forget—rebuild. Some say hope is blind. I say it is our heritage and destiny.

Enter Major Blood.

TERREL   General.

EWING   Hal.

BLOOD   General. Sir. One hundred and eighty-two men slaughtered here, they say.

EWING   It's not your worry. Lieutenant—

BLOOD   Sir! I don't know anything else; just soldiering. I wanted to die. But then—I survived William Quantrill. I can still be useful. I can smell bodies that are still missing. Use me. . . . Take me on the pursuit of Quantrill. Please, General. I am ready to go.

EWING   Hal, I'm sorry. Lieutenant, get him attention.

BLOOD   Did he hear? I'm ready to go. Did he hear?

Lieutenant Terrel leads Major Blood away.

EWING See to the wounded where we find them. Get the
grave detail to work! They need help; we're here to give it.
  To the citizens of Lawrence: I, Thomas Ewing, vow we
will pursue and we will catch and we will kill Quantrill.
  Now, come: Show me the damage you've suffered here.

*Exeunt. As they leave, Sara enters to deliver the epilogue. A mime of
Quantrill's death is enacted.*

SARA There was that Lawrence, Kansas.
    But, not exactly this one. No Mayor
    Cane existed there; but, someone not
    unlike. There was a William Clarke Quantrill.

TERREL Quantrill! You in there? Surround the barn.

SARA On August 21st, 1863, for young women
    killed in a building's crash; for raids
    made on Missouri by irregulars
    of the Union, themselves brutally
    raided, Quantrill put Lawrence and
    its men to the fire, knife, and gun.

SOLDIER Captain Terrel, the barn's surrounded. Maybe he's
not inside—oh, there, there—!

TERREL Fire!

Quantrill attempts escape. He is shot down silently.

SARA Less than two years later,
    twenty-eight years old, Quantrill, trapped
    at midnight in Kentucky, wrapped his
    spine around a rifle ball. It snapped.
    He shortly died. Of course: not
    exactly this Quantrill.
    Not exactly these young girls.

TERREL Ride to General Ewing. Tell him William Clarke
Quantrill is dead.

Exeunt Soldiers with body.

SARA In 1863, in Kansas and Missouri,
many people knew the right
better than they knew themselves.
Or any force that moved them silently.
Right eluded them. And came catastrophe.

MELONS

A melon patch. New Mexico. Late September 1906.

CHARACTERS

CARLOS MONTEZUMA

MIKE STOLSKY

CARACOL

EDNA BRIGHTMAN

CARTER HARTMAN, geologist

GEORGE FLEMING, geologist

GEORGIA TOLSON

YOUNG MAN who is hanged

MARSHAL JOHN TOLSON

ARTHUR TRUEBORN

NOTE

As this is a storytelling session, it is essential that the production embody the listeners. To see storytelling properly you must see who is listening.

On a proscenium stage, for example, it might be a good idea if all the actors were always onstage; when in character, in character; when not, as listeners. Seeing others listen is a good example; it opens up one's own listening.

In a theater in the round, there is another possibility: to let the narrator, Montezuma, carry bits of his telling to individuals of the audience, people in the first row. But, the principle ought to be embodied somehow. Unless the characters are telling their own tales, it is essential, for clarity, that the framework tale be made the center of attention.

Melons are beautiful. I like to see as many as possible onstage, commensurate with staging the action. The mask used at the end may be a variation of a sacred mask, but it should under no circumstances be a copy. It should be appropriate.

Carlos Montezuma is the one historic person in the play. He is substantially fictionalized.

I want to thank Scott Momaday for encouragement, for hospitality, for his acute criticism and great tactfulness or, perhaps in a word, his confidence. This text owes him. However, liberties taken here, or errors, don't lie with him, but with myself.

I am talking about fruit

—A traditional conclusion to certain Apache stories designed to appease, or deceive, spirits described in the stories who might possibly be offended.

ACT I

Acoma mesa, background. CARLOS MONTEZUMA, *foreground.* CARACOL, STOLSKY *behind. Caracol, a strong man in his seventies, wears a dark jacket, not unlike Stolsky's but shabbier, over a collarless shirt worn out, light cotton pants, and legging moccasins, and uses a cane. His hair is long, gray, fastened in back in a ponytail.*

MONTEZUMA Here are the melons. This is where they meet. That handsome tabletop rock to the west is the sacred mesa of the Acomas. This is Hopaho Pueblo land. By that you know we are in New Mexico.
It is late September 1906.
I am Carlos Montezuma. I've been in Arizona, visiting Yavapai relatives. I was returning to Chicago. A white family in Chicago adopted me as an orphan. I live there now and write an Indian newspaper. Rumors of a story made me stop here in Pueblo country. But more about me later. It was an amazing story, even by Indian standards, perhaps.

STOLSKY (*to Caracol*) The army reported Caracol dead. The Old Terror. The Apache Napoleon, General Crook once called you. He thought you were dead. I thought. We all thought. Back in '94. In some—trying to escape—San Carlos reservation. What I mean is—I don't know what—what you're even doing alive. Here. In New Mexico. Being what? Pueblo medicine man? You? Caracol? Apache warhorse. At graze with the pacifists? Dry-farming . . . melons. (*beat*)

189

★ ★ ★

I—looked in on your Apaches. Ten years back maybe.
Your Chiricahuas. At Fort Sill. Just after they'd been resettled
there. After Florida . . . the prison camps. Old Nana, he was
still living. Still wouldn't talk to whites. But Kayateneh told
me: Nana believed you were dead. Geronimo said he'd heard
it too. Daklugie told me Geronimo didn't believe it. But
Loco did; Daklugie did; Chihuahua did. That you were—
(*beat*)   See, what I don't get—if you're hiding—why ask to
see me again? I'm one White Eyes who'd know you for sure.
Doesn't make sense. (*beat*)

You surrendered your bunch to me . . . twenty-five years
ago. Well I was fair; or as fair as possible to your kind of
hostile. But I got no illusions Apaches liked me for it.
Twenty years of bloodbath, Arizona's ours; you're not
about to like me for that.
    Old men stir trouble for one reason: vanity. I figure,
Caracol, you're real safe here. But no one knows you
anymore; not like me. Mangas Coloradas, Juh, Cochise,
Nana, Victorio, Lozen, the great witnesses to whom you
used to be—all dead. So there's only me. (*beat*)   Is that why
you got me here? (*beat*)

Well, no one knows me either. Old age is—well, like a
reservation. It's just old Mike Stolsky. Hopaho Oil. Vice
president for Tribal Affairs sounds good; they just kick old
Indian fighters upstairs. We don't get tribal problems
anymore. Until you. And our geologists coming on the
pueblo here.

So you heard my name. You—just—you had to have
your little surprise. Okay. I'm surprised. I'm here. But you

took some risk—I hope to hell you're not sorry for it. It's not Major Stolsky, 6th U.S. cavalry, now. I represent Hopaho Oil and Hopaho Oil is a whole other thing.

CARACOL   Arizona was a better place. I was not so cripple up. It is good seeing you.

They shake hands.

STOLSKY   Well! Caracol? Or they call you John Lame Eagle here—so, Mr. John Lame Eagle, I'm glad too. To see you farming, at peace, alive.

MONTEZUMA   A molecule perhaps—no more—unlocks in the old war chief: what to tell first, what not to. *Cuidado.* Caution. Think some more.

CARACOL   I have been watching those two redtails there.

STOLSKY   Hawks?

Puts on glasses.

CARACOL   Come from Laguna. There. Every day. Can't find him. Big jackrabbit.

STOLSKY   Where?

CARACOL   Down along there. Just sits there. Bet a dollar they miss him.

STOLSKY   I can't bet on what I can't see.

CARACOL   (*chin nods*)   Along down there.

MONTEZUMA   They watch. Amber light preserves the moment. It may be the only one they ever really share.

STOLSKY   My eyes haven't improved.

MONTEZUMA   Grandfather, it's getting late.

Silence.

CARACOL   Thought sure I was dead one time. Been San
Carlos. You was gone I guess then already. Well. Not much
to do there. I got drinking some. New horse-soldier boy he
come up, say: So! This is war chief Caracol. White people
dumb to be scared; I ain't scared. Could see he was, though.
Paid no attention. Then he push me over, trip me. Why
push me down?! I say. Don't do that! So I get up. Then that
boy scared. Bang my head, rifle butt. Well. Down I go
then, maybe dead I guess. 'Cause I wake up off San Carlos,
back home.

   This cave I wake up at, it's a cave I know. Canyon I
know; back home where the Gila River start talking. I
know I am at the entrance to the Spirit Land and I got to
go, so I try to enter. But this guard jump out. Says, Halt,
you! His face been bloody and no lips or eyelids. I didn't
have no fear. So he see me, he smile. Caracol, he say. Pass
on! So I do.

   Down the cave. Goes lower and lower. But 'stead of
darker it's getting light as day in there. So I am following,
and I come out in this new canyon. This place had narrow
passes to get by. Each time I'd come on one, a pair of
creatures would be blocking the pass. Two huge big
serpents. Two tall bears. Two mountain cats crouched
down, watching. I have never see creatures that big in this
world. But I didn't have no fear. So they move back quiet,
like inviting me, Pass; so I pass right on to be dead.
   Canyon open out to a piñon forest. I follow this arroyo
west. Then I come into this valley. I see streams
everywhere—and the water cool and good water. I see

192

game all around, and birds of all kinds. It was a fine place. I was glad to be dead then; it was a place I like. So I bend to put my face in the water, but that's when I see them; people coming towards me; hear my own name then. And I see: It's all the people I been knowing this world: Gopi. And Niyokohe. Sanza. And Kladetohe. Taza, Juh, Victorio. Mangas Coloradas, Cochise. My parents and my first wife, my babies too. Mexicano soldiers kill them, but there they are. Behind them I see Apache wickiups, and the people like they are before. All this I am seeing, them coming to greet me.

Well. I try to say something. No sound comes out. Victorio he goes to my wife then; he looks to me. Then she comes; she takes my arms real soft in her hands. She says, Victorio says to tell you this that you will not be able to speak this time. Because this time you cannot you must not stay here. But when you return to that world, carry our names. Our people do not say the names of the dead. You alone my brother may speak the names of the Apache dead. No evil will come to you or no ghost sickness.

Then Victorio turn back. Cochise comes up then; nods to my wife. She says to me, Cochise says, Oh my friend! I see you are sad. For you cannot stay with the people who are happy here. This time you cannot. This time you were only brought to see for yourself that we are well; it is good. See how we are. It is good.

Then Cochise turn back. Mangas Coloradas my uncle comes up. Well. I am seeing then. My wife too. No death wounds on 'em. My uncle has his head. Head you told me army sent to those Smithsonian men. Cut it off, you said. But that head is there, right back it is. And my wife, babies, them not rip up neither. Just like if, if them Mexican soldiers never rip them. No death wounds, no blood.

Then my wife says, Mangas Coloradas says to you: What the others say, nephew, I also say. You were brought here this time only to see. It is a holy place, and sacred. See it is good. See we are well. Go back, speak our names, do not be sad. There is something you must do in that other place. Then you will see us again.

Then my uncle draws back; and the three chiefs stand together and sink into the earth. My wife brought my parents and babies up then. She says, See how well. See how happy. We are living the old way. See the bad wounds are gone. My husband, listen to what the chiefs say. My husband, remember it carefully. My husband, something is speaking through them, and it is far greater than they are. My husband it is saying, When you have done what is to be done in that world, this is just some shadow of how we will welcome you here.

He stops.

STOLSKY   Caracol?

CARACOL   Guess that was all. Just wake up then. Head beat up, bleeding. Dirt floor, guardhouse, prison, San Carlos. . . . Every day for a week I guess, I just groan to be dead again.

MONTEZUMA   The moment is holding. Corn-smoke haze circles Acoma like skirts. Crows and sparrow hawks field-hop. Hawks weave and shuttle. A rabbit blinks. Light's golden. Stolsky, uneasy perhaps. The old slow Indian world again. He probes: to break the moment.

STOLSKY Mangas Colorado. Twenty years of war—for one old chief's head cut off.

MONTEZUMA The moment has gathered breath. It holds.

STOLSKY Shameful. Well we all paid.

MONTEZUMA And it holds. Stolsky probes.

STOLSKY Seeing you really brings it back. The old roll call. Caracol, Cochise, Victorio. Nana, Juh, Geronimo. Naiche, Loco, Chihuahua, Jolsanny. Mangus, Delshay, Diablo, Chatto. (*silence*) By God. Those days in Apacheland. By God!

MONTEZUMA The moment doesn't break, it swells. The war's appalling bloodiness bleaches in the golden light. Causes, losses, griefs, the twin spiral of mutual atrocities begun by, Stolsky knows, but hopes it doesn't still matter—not still?—his own people.

STOLSKY By God, weren't they something?

CARACOL There—look.

MONTEZUMA He has just told Stolsky everything—why here—why now—the mission, the thing yet to be done—he understood nothing. Show him something he understands. Hold the moment.

CARACOL Old rabbit. Missed him.

MONTEZUMA Northwest, hawks tilt; return to base.

STOLSKY Oh. I see him now.

MONTEZUMA Stolsky's unease. The realization: Caracol. Holding the moment. The old *diyinn* addicted to a harmony too often missing now. Too Indian for Stolsky perhaps.

STOLSKY Well, speaking of San Carlos. I didn't know how bad it was when I sent your bunch there.

CARACOL It was Arizona, anyhow.

STOLSKY It wasn't me who broke all the promises.

CARACOL General Miles.

STOLSKY General Miles. You were starving, beat. I figured a reservation, San Carlos, it'd be a holiday, practically.

MONTEZUMA And the moment slips a notch.

STOLSKY No more us chasing you, Mexican troops coming up from the south.

MONTEZUMA Another notch.

STOLSKY They didn't tell me they'd cram you all together.

MONTEZUMA Another—it's going, the moment; the world around.

STOLSKY Hell, when I heard, heard about breaking off San Carlos, I was in Oklahoma already. I told one and all I'm not surprised.

CARACOL (*waving memory away*) Been no use.

STOLSKY You can't cram different tribes and bands of Apaches all squashed together. I warned the general.

MONTEZUMA Grandfather, let it go now.

STOLSKY Recipe for trouble, I said.

MONTEZUMA He will take it just like Arizona if you don't.

STOLSKY I was right, wasn't I?

MONTEZUMA Tell him: no freedom and too little food.

STOLSKY Not that they listened.

MONTEZUMA Tell: new peyote cults to bring close good divinity you aren't free to travel to.

STOLSKY Not that they ever listened to us in the field.

MONTEZUMA Idleness, bad farming lands, promises Monday broken Tuesday, and too much too much drink; tell how then the old war chiefs, bitter and hungover glowed angrily; like radium. Enough. To horse. To Mexico. Go.

CARACOL Mexico.

STOLSKY Caracol, when the army finally brought you back from Mexico—

MONTEZUMA Say how Nana looked; Geronimo agreed: What was Apache, it's over.

STOLSKY Why weren't you deported to Florida? Prison. With the others?

CARACOL Luck, maybe. That boy rifle-butt me. Day before leaving. Thought I was dead. (*silence*) You know . . . a day like this I get marry again. On San Carlos. That was a nice day I remember.

STOLSKY We were talking about the breakout—

CARACOL Mescalero girl. Oh that was a good day on San Carlos.

MONTEZUMA Holds the moment longer, thus. Has found the way, miraculously.

CARACOL Oh she was something. Beautiful she was. We had these two little girls. Had hands this small, and pretty. Just this small. Looked like hers.

STOLSKY   Bet you were glad they didn't look like you.

CARACOL   I been forgetting how that was. Home and babies. You know Indians and families, I guess. Hands this small.

MONTEZUMA   Still holds the moment. Yet it goes, it's decaying, crows lift and go—look.

CARACOL   They was making me so happy.

MONTEZUMA   And the corn-smoke haze thins around Acoma—it goes.

STOLSKY   Well, I'm glad San Carlos wasn't all bad.

MONTEZUMA   And Stolsky remembers; rumors—married— yes—conversion! That's it. He became Christian, yes— then—? Yes. The Old Terror drinking himself to violent oblivion—

CARACOL   Too much drinking there. Keep people drunk, got no memory I guess. No memory, no destiny.

STOLSKY   Be glad you didn't die there, my friend.

MONTEZUMA   The army reports—the winter night—the old war chief drunk in some obscure Apache fury—dropping disks of alcoholic blood—ran off—

STOLSKY   Your escape made headlines everywhere. Caracol loose again. Army frantic, panic on the telegraph, searching the mountains, doubling back, bringing reinforcements in. Went on a month.

MONTEZUMA   The great blizzard of '94 shut the door. Winds hurled about, snow covered all.

STOLSKY   They thought you couldn't survive, that you died.

MONTEZUMA   December 30, 1894. Last wire to San Carlos. Finale to an era: No sign of fugitive. Impossible survive blizzard. Sending Indian trackers home. Inform Washington war dept: Presume Old Terror dead.

STOLSKY Caracol?

CARACOL Never had no luck with children.

STOLSKY But they didn't find a body.

CARACOL Wasn't dead. That's why.

MONTEZUMA The moment's gone. That world, dissolved. How long you held it, reckless to the cost, is why it may survive. Perhaps.

STOLSKY Well. To business.

MONTEZUMA You know what he wants: same crazy *pahana* question as always.

STOLSKY So, how come you're here? My geologists sent for me, but they sure didn't know it was you giving them grief. I mean, what's going on this Pueblo with you?

Enter EDNA BRIGHTMAN, *an Acoma woman.*

SCENE 2

EDNA *Guwatzi.*

CARACOL *Da-waa'eh. Guwatzi.*

EDNA *Da-waa'eh.* (*to Stolsky*) *Buenas tardes.* (*to Caracol*) Okala-homa?

CARACOL I forgot. She was coming from Acoma there. She want me to ask something.

STOLSKY Doesn't she speak?

CARACOL 'Merican—not much. Spanish. I will tell you. She has these two boys. Born same time.

STOLSKY Twins.

CARACOL Well, they ask her, Can they go this school? Pueblo minister tell them, there is this school Indians go to. So she's thinking, Not so good. Too many Indians, you know, grabbed away by marshals to them schools, come back not Indians. So then you know she's thinking: Good idea, maybe. Learn to talk to you. *Pahanas.* Well, she is marry; her man don't like it, them going. He is angry. But she say yes; so they go to that school. Well, her man been so angry, he go away. Live maybe with some Zuni woman now.

EDNA *Zuni, bueno, bueno, mujer estupida, nuestra senora cabronita de Halona.*

CARACOL Well that school they go been in Oklahoma.

EDNA *La escuela Chilocco.* Oklahoma.

STOLSKY Chilocco School! Sure. Her boys there?

EDNA *¿El los conosce—Roberto, Vincente—mi hijos?*

STOLSKY No, no, I don't know your sons.

EDNA *¿No los conosce?*

CARACOL No.

STOLSKY Does she know how big Oklahoma is?

CARACOL *Oklahoma, ta mucho grande—*

EDNA *Sí, Chiesah, sí, sí. Pero, la carta. Diga.*

STOLSKY What?

CARACOL   She was having this letter. From that school at Chilocco. She can't read it. She was working that field there; it is her family's. Well this flood is coming; just sudden, no sign. Everything wash off, you know; words on that letter just gone. Minister there can't read gone words he says. I figure those boys are dead.

STOLSKY   Now hold on. No reason to think that. They're probably learning wonderful things. Whole world opening up.

EDNA   *Todo el mundo volvieran. Pero mi hijos, no. ¿Comprendes?*

STOLSKY   All the boys came back but not yours. I understand. (*to Caracol*)   Tell her this: I am looking for two young men too. (*being ultra-clear*)   My geologists. They were supposed to wait for me in Santa Fe. That is why I am here. Where are they? Out there on a survey. Tell her.

CARACOL   She knows.

STOLSKY   I suppose she knows you kicked them off too. They all do, don't they?

CARACOL   What do you want to tell her?

STOLSKY   Young men are just—crazy. They'll likely wander in. When'd she expect them?

CARACOL   Edna. *¿Quantos años?*

EDNA   *Quatorce.*

STOLSKY   For the love of—fourteen years ago?

EDNA   *Quatorce. Sí.*

CARACOL   She does not meet so many people from Oklahoma to ask.

201

STOLSKY I am sorry. *Jo no say nada. Jo no conosco.*

EDNA *Está bien . . . muchas gracias.* (to Caracol) *Gracias. ¿Se quiere comer despues . . . ?*

CARACOL *Muchas gracias . . . despues.*

EDNA *Hasta.* (to Stolsky) *Buenas tardes.*

Edna goes.

STOLSKY I forgot how hard it is to get business done in Indian country. Tell me about my geologist boys. We sent them from Tulsa, September 3. Here to the Pueblo.

Enter two geologists, HARTMAN *and* FLEMING. *They wait to hear the story told about them.*

CARACOL Well. We don't want them around here, you know. So I am hearing your name from them. It was a surprise.

HARTMAN Are you John Lame Eagle?

Caracol turns to them. Stolsky watches the story.

SCENE 3

HARTMAN Hi. Hopaho Oil Company. The geologists? That's us. We're supposed to see the headman or cacique or something, about the survey for oil sites?

FLEMING We were told Mr. Eagle speaks? You do, don't you? You are Mr. Eagle?

CARACOL Say what you came for.

HARTMAN Well, I said: We've had these drilling leases—I mean the company has—fifteen–sixteen years. We're about to survey; supposed to find possible drilling locations.

FLEMING   We were told to inform you? Before setting out? In case you see two strange whites out there.

HARTMAN   Weren't you informed we were coming?

CARACOL   Well. We have been talking. We do not want you around now.

FLEMING   Look, this is just a courtesy call. I mean, to inform you we're here. So you don't wonder who it is out there with all those strange tools and stuff.

CARACOL   We would like you to go away.

HARTMAN   We came all the way from Tulsa, Oklahoma. What do you mean, go away?

CARACOL   Maybe best you go back.

HARTMAN   The hell you say, Chief. We're not—

FLEMING   Carter! (*to Caracol*)   We do our job, that's all. No quarrel. Hopaho Oil has a tribal affairs man. We'll wire him; he will deal with you.

HARTMAN   Hell we will! Get the federal marshal, get the authorities. Right of access in those leases. He can't keep us off.

FLEMING   I am not being out there a week with only you to protect me. (*to Caracol*)   I am going to wire our vice president for Tribal Affairs today. He will take appropriate action in Tulsa or maybe come here.

HARTMAN   You're not going to get old Stolsky here?

FLEMING   Until he settles this with you, we'll hold off on the survey. Do you understand?

CARACOL Stolsky.

FLEMING Vice president for Tribal Affairs, Michael Stolsky. If necessary, he will come. (*silence*) Good day, Mr. Eagle.

CARACOL Tell—Stolsky: I will speak with him. Here. Before—you will wait.

FLEMING We will wait.

Caracol turns away.

HARTMAN (*mimics Caracol*) Before—you will wait.

FLEMING You paid to quarrel with these people?

HARTMAN I'm not even paid to talk to them.

FLEMING Me neither. Stolsky is.

Geologists go. Caracol returns to Stolsky and sits.

STOLSKY Okay. They wired me. JOHN LAME EAGLE. TROUBLE. COME SOONEST. But I don't get it. How could you get on these agency rolls? The Indians here helped you?

CARACOL Some were saying I been a medicine man for them, been away.

STOLSKY Away?

CARACOL When they take down the names. For the rolls.

STOLSKY You're not supposed to be away.

CARACOL Getting ceremony stuff was okay.

STOLSKY Before the ceremonies were banned?

CARACOL Tell the Agent I been out gathering medicine.

STOLSKY Jesus wept, who's minding the shop?

CARACOL Shop?

STOLSKY No, no, I mean—you jump San Carlos—you, Caracol—and get yourself signed up as a pueblo medicine man, and the government agent doesn't even check on you? That's not how things are supposed to work.

CARACOL Agent said to us, Well if there is another Indian, just divide it more among you, same money. You get no more from me.

STOLSKY A thief? (*silence*) A thief. So he didn't care. Okay, listen. One: Alive, you are still a fugitive and a prisoner of war. Two: No Apache has a right to represent this Pueblo and these Indians. Three: If it were known who you are, they'd deport you. Probably to Fort Sill, with the other Apaches. But—they want you here—they adopt you here—it's none of my business. Oil is. I'm putting the pieces together. You heard my name. You remembered I was fair to you before. I'm getting it.

Well, I don't think you had any right to kick the geologists off, but I'm not here to quarrel with you. I came here to make this end well. To be fair. I will tell you something that proves it.

Enter GEORGIA TOLSON *with table, chairs, coffee set, preparing for the story she will appear in. Stolsky goes toward Georgia.*

STOLSKY (*cont.*) You'll see we can settle this. I know about the Indian's mind. I even know why you kicked my men off. Or so I believe.

You see, my brother and his wife happen to live in Santa Fe. I arrived there last night.

SCENE 4

Stolsky joins Georgia. She pours coffee. Caracol watches.

GEORGIA   Your brother, honey; he caused your problems with that Pueblo. I'm his wife; I still say it. I don't blame those Indians, I blame him. Mike, he isn't aging well. I would truly hope—cream?

STOLSKY *(nods)*   What did he do this time?

GEORGIA   It's all because of last summer, Mike. The pueblo Indians are still real upset.

STOLSKY   Last summer?

GEORGIA   Your geologists being kicked off is no mystery to me, I'll tell you. These old pueblos are under such pressure—to acculturate, the Bureau calls it; become like us, seeing as how we're so glorious. Worst is the kids. They have kidnapped those kids to government schools. Religion and languages are forbidden. Kids come home, can't talk to their parents. Well, the Indian Bureau can call it acculturation, but I am a southern girl, darlin', and I know reconstruction when I see it. Anyhow. The pressure has just been splitting tribes up: traditionals so-called, so-called progressives. So they got all the dogs yapping at them, Bureau, statehouse, churches lopin' in and wolfin' down souls, getting ceremonies banned and old Indian ways, and then guess who came to dinner?

STOLSKY   My brother?

GEORGIA   Be patient, he's coming. No. Anthropologists! Anthropologists! Smithsonian anthropologists. Rush out here. Get the poop on the vanishing race before it goes *poof.*

Swarm over the confusion like weevils. Well: Some poor Tewa Indian this prying anthropologist got addled told her something he shouldn't've told. She published it. And! What a stir honey. And the traditionals decided that since they can't banish people anymore, this Tewa man had to die.

Enter YOUNG MAN *in hood and noose.*

GEORGIA (*cont.*)   Last July. That's where your brother came in, and why you're here now.

Enter MARSHAL TOLSON, *then* TRUEBORN. *They go toward man in hood and noose. Enter Edna to watch them.*

MARSHAL   They have jurisdiction, Trueborn. Tribal crimes. Of course they can hang him.

TRUEBORN   For violating tribal secrecy? Marshal Tolson, it's the twentieth century. The governor said you should stop them.

MARSHAL   They ain't in any of our centuries.
    I address myself to you elders from various pueblos gathered here near Santo Domingo. As federal marshal for Santo Domingo County, I am here to observe that this hanging be done in accordance with lawful statutes of the Department of New Mexico and nothing else. I have also been sent to ask you for mercy. Why? Because you intend to hang this man for talking about so-called secrets to some ethnographer. That was his crime. But he does not deserve to hang for that.

    What did he speak of? Anthropologist reports that some of you older people round here have a belief. That now that times are so poor for you, your savior is coming to

207

reverse them. A messiah is prophesied coming out of the desert. Old Kiva Man, returning. Some ghost warrior from the ancient race who first built around here—Anasazi, you call them, the ancient ones—or so the ethnographer says. Also this ghost messiah will bear some mark of the prophecy, and that is how you'll know him. That he has come, further, to change the worlds or to bring on the fifth world, whatever that stuff means. And that he will do this little world-switching by the revival of blood sacrifice; of another, or other, human beings.

STOLSKY You said they could've banished him.

GEORGIA The old days. The governor's scared they'll just banish each other, go wherever they please.

STOLSKY I see.

GEORGIA Oh, Mike. They've been here thousands of years; they're not going anywhere.

MARSHAL If you proceed, you will be hanging him for talking about something that's not going to happen anyhow. Hear me well: If I find any blue cornmeal spread anywhere and mumbo-jumbo drawings in it, and bloody drops spattering it, or a mutilated corpse, even of a chicken, so help me God I'll be back here and fall all over you like shit from a tall cow!

There will be no blood sacrifice, by ghost or man or otherwise. Not in my county. Not in my jurisdiction. Some of you are Christian here. You explain to those who aren't.

We also have a savior. He also came from a desert. He also promised to return and turn evil around and redeem our sins. Well, I look around me. I look at Santo Domingo County. I look at the Department of New Mexico. I think it is fair to say that our Lord, like yours, ain't in the vicinity right now. Better than waiting for either of them is to learn to live with the world as it is. Sooner or later you got to comply. You don't, someone comes and chops your feet off.

STOLSKY Chops feet off?

GEORGIA Religious rebellion three hundred years back. Spanish chopped the surviving men's right feet off.

MARSHAL I am finished. Let there be no complaints. I acknowledge your legal right to punish tribal crimes. But I ask you to forbear execution in the name of mercy and good relations between us.

YOUNG MAN I accept the cacique's decision. I just wanted them to know the worlds will change now. I have seen him, I have seen him!

TRUEBORN What's he say?

MARSHAL It's in Tewa. Don't know.

YOUNG MAN He has come! He has returned!

The Young Man is hanged.

TRUEBORN Goddamn.

MARSHAL I'm going to have to teach these bastards a lesson.

Young Man, Trueborn, Edna all go. Trueborn returns, dragging a small howitzer.

GEORGIA The furor broke. Traditionals and progressives just boiled over at each other. Tribes split. John and Trueborn returned with this cannon.

MARSHAL   I've come back to help you locate your messiah!

GEORGIA   They toured the pueblos. Caciques, clan chiefs, medicine men were forced to kneel at the cannon's eye. To be inspected as to whether they were willing to die for their people or not.

STOLSKY   John Lame Eagle too?

GEORGIA   You got it, honey.

Spot on Caracol.

MARSHAL   John Lame Eagle!

Trueborn yanks Caracol up to the cannon. Note that Caracol limps. He is forced down, head at the cannon muzzle. That is, he has been dragged into the story within the story.

MARSHAL   Is it you? I'm dying to meet this ghost messiah. This one from the old race, this Old Kiva Man. But no luck so far. He's not at Acoma, not with the Zunis; no one came forward at Santo Domingo; can't find him with the Keres; can't find him with the Tewas; he's not at Zia, not at Isleta, not at Jemez, not at San Juan; no luck at Cochiti, no luck at Tesuque, no luck at Laguna—where the hell is he?
  Mr. Trueborn, the lanyard. Isn't he supposed to lose his head? Isn't that the prophecy? Say it: You are or you aren't. We'll help you fulfill your damn prophecy.

TRUEBORN   Say it! Yes or no!

MARSHAL   You Indian brats watch.

TRUEBORN   Yes or no! Say it.

CARACOL   I am not a ghost.

MARSHAL   This one don't care to die either.

210

Trueborn replaces Caracol. Hauls cannon off.

MARSHAL (*cont.*) Not in my country! Not in my jurisdiction. Not even a chicken. You have been warned.

Marshal takes bottle out, drinks.

GEORGIA Your geologists walk in some weeks later. Lame Eagle kicks them off. QED honey, now you know. (*pours coffee*) Cream?

STOLSKY No. For Christ's sake, Georgia.

GEORGIA I told you. He's having a hard time.

STOLSKY Where is he?

GEORGIA Being angry won't help him or you.

STOLSKY He's going to help me whether he likes it or not.

GEORGIA I think, Mike . . . whatever the quarrel between you, it's time you thought about reconciling.

STOLSKY When he calls himself Caz Stolsky again.

GEORGIA Come on.

STOLSKY I don't know this John Tolson. I don't forgive him that.

GEORGIA Who's fooling whom?

STOLSKY When he changed his name to Tolson, he lost my attention.

GEORGIA There hadn't been a war between the states, you two wouldn't ever have been on the same side of anything.

STOLSKY By God, he's going to help me fix up what he messed up or I'll know the reason why!

GEORGIA Mike, listen. He changed his name only because he didn't want anyone guessing he's Catholic.

STOLSKY The hell difference.

GEORGIA Honey, this isn't Oklahoma. The only Catholics here are Mexicans and Indians. He's a federal marshal. Who do you think he's riding herd on? The statehouse would not—well, never mind. They're the only people he's comfortable with, Mexicans and Indians. And he hates them. Please help him out. He needs—something.

STOLSKY Caz.

Marshal reels in to join them.

MARSHAL Michael. The fuck've I done now? Ten years I don't see you, must be something.

GEORGIA John, honey, best you sit down.

MARSHAL Don't be embarrassing me! Hey, Major Mike, 6th U.S. Cavalry, vice president of Hopaho Oil, my long-lost hero brother. By God. Find some starving Apache war chief. Get in his way when he wants to surrender, be sure you got your photographers, you end up an Apache Wars hero. Hey. Still dining out on that?

STOLSKY Sit down.

MARSHAL I'm a federal marshal, bro. Watch it.

STOLSKY Jesus, Caz, what's happened to you? Sit down, you'll fall.

MARSHAL Already fell. It's just the goddamned legs keep going—aw, hell.

Marshal falls down.

STOLSKY Come on, Caz. Up.

MARSHAL Hey, Georgia, look. I'm the white man's burden.

GEORGIA I'll fix you some coffee.

MARSHAL Been at *Jo*-a-keen's drinking; best you don't stinge on the cream. (*to Stolsky*) Why did you come, Mike? What do you want after ten years?

SCENE 5

STOLSKY We're getting on. I wanted to see you—

MARSHAL Bullshit. Georgia, we got anything to eat?

STOLSKY Caz.

MARSHAL My name is John Tolson! That is my name. Why are you here?

STOLSKY You know why.

MARSHAL Sure, sure, Hopaho stuff. Oil!

STOLSKY Georgia was saying about last summer.

MARSHAL Musta been a big spoon stirring the clouds . . . Christ. I've never seen nothing like it. Indians haywire; governor got his head up his ass counting bribes he's held back from cronies; I'm overworked, pleasing nobody, and the Belle of the South here decides she'll help out. She writes away to join them women who want to vote.

GEORGIA Us women'll change the world.

MARSHAL Her and the Indians, all summer that talk.

GEORGIA Well, I had it in mind since Election Day 1900. I said to myself, Georgia, honey, this is the twentieth century

213

now; and you are still doing the same thing you did in the nineteenth. Well, you're getting statehood next year, Mike—I mean, Oklahoma—so I plan to disguise myself and sneak in a voting place and get me some practice.

MARSHAL   No wonder people think I can't keep my house in order.

GEORGIA   Keep what house in order? Who keeps this house in order?

STOLSKY   Caz: My business here will need your help.

MARSHAL   Get hers. She's teaching some Hop women at school, home economics.

GEORGIA   As far as I can tell, Indians are the only ones who ever made this country work.

MARSHAL   My father made this country work! Twenty-eight years at the face! You know how much coal that is? Mike, tell her; Mike knows. If he hasn't forgot.

GEORGIA   The Hopahos are some of his favorites.

MARSHAL   No favorites with me. I love 'em all.

GEORGIA   You just lump them together and call it love, John.

MARSHAL   They are lumped together; they're my jurisdiction. That is their American name. Hey, we have any peach pie left? Go on, will you, and get me some?

GEORGIA   Two ticks of a lamb's tail; be right back.

Georgia goes.

MARSHAL   I've been your brother sixty-three years. I still can't tell what you're thinking. Get to it.

STOLSKY You know John Lame Eagle? Company has a problem with him. I'm meeting him tomorrow.

MARSHAL Must be embarrassing as hell. Founder names the company after the tribe and they tell you to stick it.

STOLSKY What's he like?

MARSHAL What are they all like? Sit on their mesas like toothaches in the desert, throbbing around with witches and *brujos,* scaring the bejesus out of each other. Magic. Sorcery. Poor as dirt, snooty as deer, pray to snakes when no one is looking, and still think they make the sun rise and set.

STOLSKY You got my geologists kicked off.

MARSHAL I didn't ban the old religions. They just don't want white people on their lands anymore.

STOLSKY You and your cannon.

MARSHAL That was July. Your boys came September.

STOLSKY They couldn't be kicked off till they arrived; it was you, Caz.

MARSHAL Mike, they're talking good old Abraham–Isaac stuff. That sure gets the governor's head back in the sunshine. He don't want us New Mexicans known as your human sacrifice crowd.

STOLSKY You offended every tribe for two hundred miles.

MARSHAL You can't reason with 'em. They been here too long. All you can do is make 'em respect you.

Enter Georgia with pie.

GEORGIA You've become a parrot for the statehouse. That's a parrot for a dog.

MARSHAL Is that all the pie?

GEORGIA It was just a group of poor old Indians taking hope in old Indian stories.

MARSHAL That what the girls in Hop home ec tell you?

GEORGIA Defeat, carpetbagging, nostalgia—I grew up with it all.

MARSHAL You should've married Mike; you share a taste for heathen.

GEORGIA It's why I married you. Use your head, John.

MARSHAL I am. I'm eating.

GEORGIA I lost ten of fourteen girls in my class. In July. I was just so mad, Mike. Four finally returned. Just plunk in the middle of the home hygiene stuff. Missed the whole beginning; what good is that? They think Arthur Trueborn's the devil. You think that's respect? I think they're right.

STOLSKY Caz, you can make some amends.

MARSHAL Amends? Amends for what? I was ordered onto the pueblos, the governor sent me. We got a religious furor. Goddamned army wanted to go in, but no one here wants a massacre; we just want to keep order, okay? Governor says we got no chance at statehood if we go all mushy on Indian doings. We had to do it.

STOLSKY And you'll have to undo it.

MARSHAL For the love of—you don't—he don't understand what I said.

STOLSKY Yes, I do.

MARSHAL   I said statehood! You know how much they got tied up in statehood? What they're up to now is nothing. Statehood is the nest egg, Mike. They're not letting some bunch of Indians stand in the way of that. And they take care of me, Mike; them, not you—

STOLSKY   Here's what I want: You go find my geologists tomorrow. They broke their word to wait for me. That's how you help me.

MARSHAL   They're your employees. You go find them.

STOLSKY   I didn't lose them.

MARSHAL   I didn't either.

STOLSKY   I didn't humiliate all the caciques.

MARSHAL   You don't even live here!

STOLSKY   When you find them, you bring them to me.

MARSHAL   Where, on the Pueblo?

STOLSKY   To apologize.

MARSHAL   Apologize!

STOLSKY   It's the only way, Caz. Or you don't know Indians.

MARSHAL   To John Lame Eagle?

STOLSKY   For breaking their word.

MARSHAL   Apologize to some fucking sorcerer? What do you think that savage is?

STOLSKY   Never mind using that word to me.

MARSHAL   Never mind apologizing, not to him, not me.

STOLSKY I'm warning you, Caz, I'll go to the governor. There's a little obstacle to investment in the Santo Domingo federal marshal's office. I've never taken this from you; I'm not starting now.

MARSHAL Georgia! You want to know why we don't get together too often?

STOLSKY You helping or not, yes or no?

MARSHAL Didya hear! My own brother. We were kids in a coal mine. Wilkes-Barre, Pennsylvania. I followed him west like a puppy. Can you believe it? Didya hear him! Go to the governor?!

STOLSKY Caz—

GEORGIA Mike, stop.

MARSHAL I follow him to the army. Pennsy Fourth. He goes west, I—like a puppy, like a puppy! I don't know, am I stupid, am I that stupid!

STOLSKY I want an answer.

MARSHAL Get away from me! Pa knew how to fix you, I wish he—I wish he—

STOLSKY You couldn't stay sober enough to get to his funeral.

MARSHAL I don't answer to you!

STOLSKY You will get my geologists tomorrow. You will bring them in to apologize.

MARSHAL Caracol's dead, bub! I never surrendered to you.

STOLSKY Caz—

218

MARSHAL   I am federal marshal for Santo Domingo County! I ain't being threatened!

STOLSKY   I'm going tonight.

Gets up to go.

GEORGIA   Mike, have some pity.

STOLSKY   I feel sorry for you. Take care.

MARSHAL   Wait. (*silence*)   Okay. There is a stream. Near the mesa you're meeting Old Lame Eagle. Got willows. Tamaracks. Cottonwoods. I'll look for your geologist boys there tomorrow.

STOLSKY   Not just look. Find them.

MARSHAL   It's the only water near. They're surveying, they'd camp there.

STOLSKY   Bring them.

MARSHAL   I'll find them. (*silence*)   No more reunions, Mike.

STOLSKY   I guess not.

GEORGIA   I sometimes wonder how you northern boys won the war, the way you do go on. I thought you might love him still; like I do.

STOLSKY   I'm sorry.

GEORGIA   So cold and weak. And he's so weak and violent. . . . Weak. Cold. Violent. Careless of others. Like my father was. And his brothers. With the added imbecility of fighting for the state of Georgia. Well, they frightened me. And you frighten me too. You just make my heart pound when I hear you. I just don't think we deserve this beautiful country sometimes. John, get up. Come to bed, honey.

MARSHAL I'm sorry, Georgia. It's one life for heroes, another for the rest. Right, Mike?

STOLSKY Hero to a name-changing drunk, maybe.

MARSHAL You patronizing sonofabitch!

He seizes Stolsky.

GEORGIA John!

Marshal lets Stolsky go.

MARSHAL Won't ever know now, will you? Will you?

GEORGIA Come to bed, honey. I'll be back to see you out, Mike. Have more coffee. There's the cream.

Georgia and Marshal go. Stolsky returns to Caracol and sits.

STOLSKY It was my brother. Last summer. Marshal John Tolson. Surprised?

Caracol rises, goes to the melons. He stops, facing west, Acoma.

STOLSKY (*cont.*) You'll be the first medicine man in New Mexico history to get apologies from a couple of whites, though. They'll do it. Makes this a historic day.

Silence. Montezuma comes forward.

MONTEZUMA Indians have never done too well on "historic" days. I have known some old men to be very ironic about it. This one's silence I can guess at. But I am—a little afraid to.

CARACOL Where is your brother now?

STOLSKY Out looking for the boys. At some stream nearby. As I said.

Caracol turns to Stolsky, remembering something, furious.

STOLSKY (*cont.*)   Old friend . . . I once saw what you and
Victorio had done to a gold-mining camp in revenge for—
(*stops*)
    You don't hate mining worse than I do. My father mined
coal. He was buried in coal. Only the Civil War saved me
. . . hear me out. Oil. It's replacing coal. That is nothing but
progress. Progress makes things easier. Makes things more
fair. It's why I'm here, not in court. I came from Tulsa to
work out a deal.

CARACOL   Your men who came here.

STOLSKY   Geologists.

CARACOL   Well.

STOLSKY   No problem—they'll be brought in. They'll
apologize for not waiting. Your "honor" will be satisfied.

CARACOL   They came back.

STOLSKY   What's that mean? They just went off to survey.

CARACOL   They came back first.

Enter the two geologists. They wait.

CARACOL (*cont.*)   Brung this other Indian. College Indian, talk
for them. Raised by whites, I heard.

Geologists go to Montezuma.

HARTMAN   Carlos Montezuma? Dr. Montezuma? I'm Carter
Hartman; this is George Fleming. We're oil geologists; we
were told you might be able to help us.

MONTEZUMA   Is that Hopaho Oil?

FLEMING   You know about it already?

MONTEZUMA White people being kicked off Indian lands tends to make news in Indian country.

FLEMING I imagine.

HARTMAN It's not all that funny.

MONTEZUMA I'm laughing because I seem to be the only Indian you can find who won't send you away—but, you see, you see I don't live here.

HARTMAN We have legal leases, my friend.

FLEMING Carter—hold it. Dr. Montezuma, we just walked in blind. We didn't know about last summer. We've been hearing.

HARTMAN These Indians are pretty sore over that cannon business?

MONTEZUMA More than these.

FLEMING We had no idea 'bout the—the religious cufuffle, no offense. We walked in to survey, *boom,* kicked off.

HARTMAN See, the old man doesn't understand. Will you try and talk sense to him?

MONTEZUMA John Lame Eagle.

HARTMAN We just got nowhere.

MONTEZUMA Well. You got off pueblo lands.

FLEMING Carter, hold it. Doctor?

MONTEZUMA I'd be interested to meet him. Powerful medicine man, people say.

HARTMAN Powerful medicine man, terrific; and you're a qualified doctor?

FLEMING I'm sure you can explain our position.

MONTEZUMA One condition.

HARTMAN Such as.

MONTEZUMA Call me Carlos, or Charlie. I hardly practice medicine anymore.

FLEMING George, sir.

HARTMAN Carter, Charlie. Say, you don't talk like an Indian at all. My guess is you were brought up white.

MONTEZUMA Isn't that something? I thought the same about you.

They freeze.

STOLSKY I didn't know they came back. Caracol?

MONTEZUMA Grain by grain he must weigh it: what to tell, what first, what not to.

STOLSKY Did something happen? Did Montezuma make trouble?

HARTMAN John Lame Eagle! Where is he? We're back!

STOLSKY I say, did something happen?

HARTMAN John Lame Eagle! John Lame Eagle!

MONTEZUMA Now breath fills you, Grandfather. Breath of heaven, breath of earth, canyon's breath: the Underworld's.

FLEMING Try again.

HARTMAN Hey, we're back!

MONTEZUMA Victorio's and Lozen's breath, stuttering Juh's, murdered family's, Mangas Coloradas's—

STOLSKY Caracol, I say did something—

FLEMING Mr. Eagle!

MONTEZUMA Breath of deserts, breath of mountains.

HARTMAN The hell is he?

MONTEZUMA Breath of *ga-uhn* mountain spirits, breath of lightning, willow, rock, breath of blade swiping cleanly, breath of was it—Yusen? . . . YUSEN?

STOLSKY Caracol—?

CARACOL Yes! . . . Something happen all right.

MONTEZUMA Weighed to the grain. He will tell.

HARTMAN He's right here, Charlie. What's the matter with you? Didn't you hear me?

Caracol turns to face the geologists and Montezuma.

CARACOL We told you: Go away. Don't want you coming back. Why have you done so?

Blackout.

ACT II

Hartman and Fleming join Montezuma at one side. On the other side, Stolsky watches the story Caracol tells.

CARACOL (*to Stolsky*)   These men of yours; promise to wait for you. Then they're coming back, angry I guess. Voices ain't smooth now. They're bringing this Carlos Montezuma fella. Maybe I live nine lifetimes, I still never see a better suit on an Indian.

Caracol joins the geologists.

HARTMAN   Good melons. Be nice later, cooled in a stream.

FLEMING   Mr. Eagle, this is Carlos Montezuma. Charlie, John Lame Eagle. We want him to have a chance to reason with you.

HARTMAN   One chance.

FLEMING   We've told him we have the right to survey. Access to the tribal lands is in the leases.

HARTMAN   Read it for him, Charlie. Charlie is—what?— Mojave Apache, Yavapai. He's offered his help.

FLEMING   We're not paying him.

HARTMAN   So you pay attention there, Crazy Horse.

FLEMING   Crazy Horse! Oh, cut it out, Carter.

MONTEZUMA A good idea. (*to Caracol*)   I was around Santo Domingo Pueblo. I was also at San Ildefonso. People spoke to me about what has been happening. I write a newspaper these days. For Indians. About various problems we have. I thought maybe I could help.

CARACOL *¿Habla español?*

MONTEZUMA Understand it; can't talk it, though.

CARACOL Don't speak to me in 'Merican. I don't wish to talk in that language. Do you understand?

MONTEZUMA You are speaking Tinneah, Apache. I can still speak that, yes.

HARTMAN What are they saying?

FLEMING Give him a chance.

CARACOL Mojave Apache is not Apache, they are Yavapai people. But you speak it.

MONTEZUMA I spoke both Yuma and Apache as a child. I had to. And you?

CARACOL (*pause*) I also had to.

MONTEZUMA Your way of speaking is southern, Chihenne or Chokonen, isn't it? Or am I wrong? (*silence*)

CARACOL I guess I heard Yavapai people are kept on San Carlos. Must be a very nice reservation, if you get money for a suit like that.

MONTEZUMA I wasn't on San Carlos. The Yavapais aren't there now either.

CARACOL Were they moved even farther from their home?

MONTEZUMA No, some have been moved back, Grandfather.

CARACOL How is that?

MONTEZUMA I helped them.

CARACOL You?

MONTEZUMA I wrote letters and petitioned the government for them.

CARACOL Some people have power, they say, and don't know it. Though I myself don't know how they cannot know it.

MONTEZUMA I have persistence. The law. Friends. And luck. My own village is back home. You know where the Verde meets the Gila River? Or perhaps you don't know Arizona.

CARACOL I know where that is. How was it you were not on San Carlos?

MONTEZUMA I was kidnapped by Pimas, Grandfather. Before the move. I was sold.

CARACOL Pimas sold you?

MONTEZUMA To one white; he gave me this name. He died. I was adopted by others. They raised me in the north, Grandfather.

CARACOL You call me Grandfather. (*beat*) Have you an Indian name?

MONTEZUMA Wassaja. I am a medical doctor. After college I treated people on reservations in the north. I saw different tribes have common problems but no way to know it. So I began this newspaper. To know what problems all of us share. To forget old conflicts and fight for what is needed now.

CARACOL In their language?

227

MONTEZUMA Our problems are in their language.

CARACOL I have heard of an Indian doctor around. Goes around talking. Writing to say, Abolish the Indian Bureau, make those agents go get work.

MONTEZUMA Would you like a cigarette?

CARACOL That would be very nice.

MONTEZUMA Nearby I treated some children from a pueblo. For trachoma. Sore eye. No one in the Bureau lifted a finger. We can't be worse off without them.

HARTMAN What's going on?

FLEMING Mmm, prolonged traditional salutation stuff.

HARTMAN Oh.

FLEMING Smoking the peace Camel.

HARTMAN Peace Camel. Slip me a peace Lucky.

CARACOL Do you practice the banned ways or theirs?

MONTEZUMA I was raised as a Baptist.

CARACOL They interfered plenty. Old ceremonies and rites were banned.

MONTEZUMA That was federal and territorial doing.

CARACOL Christian.

MONTEZUMA A ban breaks the tie to valuable property. They know Indian religions are tied to the land.

CARACOL You care about that?

MONTEZUMA Yes.

CARACOL *Too bah gheesh chin' en?* (*beat*)   Are you a Child of the Waters then?

MONTEZUMA   I—am not sure what those words mean.

CARACOL   No. . . . Well—thought water was sacred to you Baptists there.

MONTEZUMA   As it is to—oh, you were joking.

CARACOL   I had a son once. He'd be near your age. I wonder if he would be like you.

MONTEZUMA   Was he taken off to some school?

CARACOL   Mexicans ripped him. With his mother. Our two girls, too.

MONTEZUMA   No other children?

CARACOL   Had two more, yes.

MONTEZUMA   I often wonder what my father was like, too.

CARACOL   You say Pimas killed them?

MONTEZUMA   My parents? Yes.

CARACOL   Those Indians work for the army. Trackers.

MONTEZUMA   To get protection from Apaches, yes. I don't blame any other Indian. All that's rubbed out. It's history now.

Caracol is silent.

HARTMAN   Indians make me nervous, you know that?

Caracol sits. He gestures to Montezuma to sit.

FLEMING   Been accepted, I guess.

HARTMAN Charlie, tell him we're not going to drill through the melons. Maybe see if Mr. Eagle'll sell a couple.

MONTEZUMA First: He speaks. Second: His name is Lame Eagle, not Eagle. Lame is not his middle name. Third: If you gentlemen want someone to haggle at a market for you, you're wasting my time.

HARTMAN "If you gentlemen." Education's a wonderful thing. Go to it, Charlie.

CARACOL Say what you came to.

MONTEZUMA I—(*to Hartman*) What was that crack?

CARACOL (*stopping him*) Ignorant. *Pindah biniedine*. Say what you came to.

MONTEZUMA I heard of fighting on the pueblos this summer. And division and trouble. I asked some friends why. They said, Best ask at Santo Domingo. At Santo Domingo an old man told me an Indian savior may be coming along here: a messiah and a new age for Indians. It has set old against young, clan against clan, and brother against brother the whole summer.

CARACOL Old farts love their stories. You know how we are.

MONTEZUMA It is an interesting story. I am writing it for my paper. I think maybe these prophecies could be true in an unexpected way.

CARACOL Well, I can't read. Maybe you will tell me.

MONTEZUMA No one can make an army share victory. You can make a company share profits.

CARACOL Go on.

230

MONTEZUMA   This people sold oil rights leases to this company. A lawyer might be able to rewrite them more fairly. A share of the money they make can be used for schools—here, not far away—for medical care, for more seed, more food—more survival. That money would give you the freedom to preserve what you want. No more waiting for handouts. No more pleading for justice. No more having Indian children taken to schools to be whitewashed. The cacique of a Pueblo who led the people that way could well fill the role of a savior. I can get you a lawyer. He can help.

CARACOL (*to Hartman*)   Give me those papers.

HARTMAN   Warn him about carbon copies, Charlie. I don't want any grand gestures or—hey!

Caracol takes papers.

CARACOL   They threatened to grab our lands to get these.

MONTEZUMA   Oil companies can't just take land.

CARACOL   Indian agent, he threatened.

MONTEZUMA   Back in 1890?

CARACOL   "Your pueblos is not getting larger, it is getting smaller now; you don't need it"—that is what I heard he said. "If you don't lease to these good oil diggers, we will use that Dawes Act. We will get these lands declared public land, government land. You get allotments, instead."

MONTEZUMA   Communal land is exempt from the Dawes Act. Your land is held communally; even Spanish land grants acknowledged that.

CARACOL   I don't think we were told that.

231

MONTEZUMA Was any Indian bribed here? Favored?

CARACOL You see some rich man around? Tell him I'd like some.

MONTEZUMA What about the Indian Agent who threatened you?

CARACOL Some say he was paid by the company.

MONTEZUMA Is there proof the Agent was bribed?

CARACOL (*thinks*) Paying-off ceremony must be sacred to them. I don't think any Indian's seen it. (*smiles*) Maybe they got some big bribing dance.

MONTEZUMA If you were misled—if you were threatened—I can get the leases rubbed out.

CARACOL Good idea. We would like that.

MONTEZUMA You will need a lawyer.

CARACOL We have no money.

MONTEZUMA Let me worry about that. He will need proof the sale was wrong.

CARACOL These leases are proof.

HARTMAN Charlie, what's going on?

MONTEZUMA I mean proof of threat. Witnesses.

CARACOL They had no right to sell. They sold. These leases are proof. Witnesses. These lands. Sacred lands here.

HARTMAN When's the next iron horse leaving?

FLEMING Carter.

MONTEZUMA (*to Caracol*) In federal court it is no use to plead that land is sacred and that therefore its sale is proof of a crime. Do you understand? (*silence*) You know what they will call you.

CARACOL Why did you come here? To help your attack on the Bureau? We aren't Yavapai. Them you help about land.

MONTEZUMA You don't understand about the law, so you are disappointed.

CARACOL I am beginning to think you came here for your own glory. Make yourself so big, maybe white people say, if it's that big, maybe we should buy it for ourselves.

MONTEZUMA If you break the law, you lose. If you use it properly, possibly win.

CARACOL Best you take them off now.

MONTEZUMA Grandfather, I have seen over fifty reservations. They are plague spots on the map. Poverty, disease, and despair are the principal chiefs. It is essential to change that, get some Indian rights. And the only way I know is to know how to use the law properly.

CARACOL Stop talking their law in your language.

HARTMAN English again.

MONTEZUMA I prefer to continue. As we were.

CARACOL I guess not.

HARTMAN Problem here.

FLEMING Yeah.

CARACOL You are saying all the time: their law. What was I having before? Someone give me this suit, some church.

233

Say their kindness. What was I having before? They're
generous, been hearing. What was I having before? What
was mine I been having. My word for their law is hate.
Lawliss. You just want to be sharing it more.

MONTEZUMA No.

CARACOL Share their law—share their hate of red people.

FLEMING I don't hate anyone. I don't care, a man's green and
purple.

CARACOL I would like to see that man. He must be something.
You don't like black, don't like red. I would like to see that
green purple man you wait for to love like a brother.
(*silence*) Must be he has land you want, you don't care he's
green or purple. Must have something. (*to Montezuma*) No
right to sell. No right to lease. Not what they ain't owning;
and them no right to be buying. That's all.

MONTEZUMA I am afraid it is not.

CARACOL Sa-cred. There is one of your words.

MONTEZUMA Look, I know it was sold from despair—

CARACOL Well, see how I say it: This lands be sa-cred.

MONTEZUMA I understand—

CARACOL You are maybe ashamed to say that word: sa-cred.

MONTEZUMA I understand it is sacred.

CARACOL Part of the flesh of the people; them, part of it.

MONTEZUMA I said I understand.

CARACOL Shamed to say it; you make me shamed.

MONTEZUMA Now, hold on. I'm not ashamed.

CARACOL Then why is it you don't blame who kill your own parents? Because nothing is sacred to you. (*mocks*) "Don't blame no other Indians." Nothing sa-cred to you. Too shamed to hear their spirits calling: Remember us. Remember us. Revenge us.

MONTEZUMA You don't hear that.

CARACOL The dead have their rights. But not to you.

MONTEZUMA The welfare of the living is my concern.

CARACOL Words is your concern. Words won't fit in white man's court. Say sa-cred in some court, someone call you savage, primitive maybe. Throw you right out. That is what I think is scaring you, or maybe they take that suit. Take it away. Maybe jump some feathers up your nice hair there. I don't know. Could be you blush up so red you get took for some goddamned Indian finally.

MONTEZUMA I don't take that from anyone. (*rises*) Anyone!

CARACOL (*calm*) I am glad to see that.

Silence. Montezuma, angry, turns away suddenly.

CARACOL (*cont.*) Then I say to you: Your mother ain't dead.

Montezuma turns back, upset, stunned.

CARACOL (*cont.*) This is your mother. See how pretty. This being sold, being divide up for them. Is it time for that? For sharing money for that? This dividing her up. This stabbing into. This land Creator be making for all in one piece. This flesh, same as this flesh, and all the good life on it he put there?

FLEMING What do you think?

HARTMAN What do you think I think?

MONTEZUMA (*sits again*) Just like the summer. We're fighting now. This is not why I came to speak with you.

CARACOL I don't think that fighting is a mystery.

MONTEZUMA How do you mean?

CARACOL You been seeing divisions in people.

MONTEZUMA Religious factions.

CARACOL Is that some mystery? All this good being divide, being stab into.

MONTEZUMA Yes.

CARACOL Who can be peaceful, who can live right on it then?

MONTEZUMA I would like to speak privately again.

HARTMAN Christ on a crutch. He's back to Indian.

MONTEZUMA I heard about you. In Santo Domingo.

CARACOL I know some men there in Kiuwa.

MONTEZUMA One said I should meet you.

CARACOL I thought it was those two. You came to help them.

MONTEZUMA I would have anyway.

CARACOL That is interesting.

MONTEZUMA I was told at Santo Domingo you are not from this Pueblo. I don't know who you are, or your people, but I was told you were not born here.

CARACOL People will say anything. Especially near Santo Domingo.

MONTEZUMA Grandfather, one who knows told me.

CARACOL It is not for me to call someone I don't know a liar.

MONTEZUMA You know him.

CARACOL How can I tell without his name?

MONTEZUMA He is one of the clan who found you. A priest.

CARACOL Found me. Did he say I was lost?

MONTEZUMA They found you in the desert. That is where he said you appeared. Jornada del Muerto, south of here. Twelve years ago.

CARACOL He said that to you.

MONTEZUMA They were visiting with offerings at the old great serpent shrines; they came across you—

CARACOL What is his name?

MONTEZUMA I can't tell you.

CARACOL His name.

MONTEZUMA I don't want him punished.

CARACOL I would like to know it.

MONTEZUMA Grandfather, no.

CARACOL I have been trying to remember you to your own heart. His name I would like to know now.

MONTEZUMA People are struggling to survive. I would like to know, Why are they all being made responsible for a few old men's beliefs?

CARACOL   Did you prevent Tolson and the cannon from doing that already?

MONTEZUMA   Who hanged a man? As if any Indian needed others to punish him now.

CARACOL   He remembered who he was. He accepted.

MONTEZUMA   Well, I don't want another hanged for talking about—about who?

CARACOL   Maybe you are too baptized to remember. Maybe they held you underwater for too long. But though you live like them, they are not immortal; and they die. And when your time comes, then you will remember what you have not lived; you will beg friends to build you some lean-to on a mountainside near your people's home; for you will have seen these ways are worthless; they are lies. You will wish at least to die a Yavapai and not some white man mockery.

Silence.

MONTEZUMA   I've had this dream. I get tired fighting all this—Indian hate. Indian self-hate. That if I could just accomplish . . . some advance. Somehow. I could just go home to the mountains and at least die a Yavapai. (*silence*)   I don't know how you knew. Grandfather: I'll do my best. (*to geologists*)   Gentlemen: a talk.

HARTMAN   Is he going to listen to reason?

MONTEZUMA   Of course he will. It's not your reason, however.

FLEMING   Carlos, look, what's your opinion?

MONTEZUMA These leases aren't any good. At very least, they're flawed.

HARTMAN That isn't our problem.

MONTEZUMA Mr. Hartman, you and he are employees of Hopaho Oil. In 1890 these leases were obtained I believe by deception, which caused despair, which caused them to sell.

FLEMING Charlie, we're just geologists.

HARTMAN What about going ahead with the survey?

MONTEZUMA You said your arbitrator is coming.

HARTMAN Mike Stolsky? V.P. for Tribal Affairs?

MONTEZUMA I suggest you wait for Mr. Stolsky.

HARTMAN Not on his account, I'm not waiting.

MONTEZUMA I'd think in this case you'd like to keep your own word—

HARTMAN He had no right to kick us off.

MONTEZUMA Let's try again when Mr. Stolsky arrives.

HARTMAN I've had a neckful of this gabble. George, you coming?

MONTEZUMA Waiting for your arbitrator, which you promised, is Very Good Advice, my friend.

HARTMAN Whose friend?

MONTEZUMA He is their spokesman. I'm giving you my best advice.

HARTMAN Whose friend?

MONTEZUMA He's not nobody. He has rights.

HARTMAN (*seizing contracts*)   These are my rights, "friend."

Suddenly he slashes two melons off the vines.

HARTMAN (*cont.*)   This is my pleasure for being kept waiting.

He chops one melon in half, tosses half to Fleming.

HARTMAN (*cont.*)   Peace, Chief. Come on, George. Let's get the hell down to what we're paid for.

Geologists go.

MONTEZUMA   I saw aspens yellowing this week. I guess summer is really over. It was between Santa Fe and Los Alamos. It was beautiful there.

Fleming returns.

FLEMING   Say, let me pay for the melons, okay? Must have been hard getting them through the summer. I'm from farming people myself. How's a dime? I saw a dime for four in town. Dime'll be okay, won't it? Catch.

He flips dime; it drops.

FLEMING (*cont.*)   You keep it, okay?

Fleming goes.

MONTEZUMA   I'm sorry.

CARACOL   Be sorry for their children.

Caracol draws four circles in dust and divides and redivides them as he speaks.

CARACOL (*cont.*)   Who rises by greed—divide by greed. Who rises by injustice—divide by injustice. Who rises by hate— by hate. By murder—murder. By division—division. Divide them too. Then that divide too. Down to the littlest division; and divide that too. And angry earth howl up (*throws pinch of dust up*) and destroy them.

MONTEZUMA   They think it is you, don't they? The Anasazi come back. Old Kiva Man. (*silence*)   I know they'd been praying at the old shrines when they found you. There must be other reasons too. (*silence*)   You believe it, don't you? The prophecy; the change of the worlds. (*silence*)
Grandfather, it is important to know if you have accepted this if I am to help you.

CARACOL   Wassaja—come close.
Wassaja—hear me.
Wassaja—this is true.

Foreign dividers in lands they were born in—they destroyed each other; they drove each other away. Civil War was perpetual midnight; all sorts of terrible creatures were in it. Till they came here. Till they found us to destroy instead. Till they could do to others what they were doing to themselves. Do to others what you want done to you: That is the law their god gave them. When the worlds are changed, the prophecy is saying, destroyers go mad. Turn back on each other. Brother kill brother, and brother kill brother. Divide and destroy, destroy and divide. We will rise back to where we began, and in new and lawful unity, and at peace, and worshipful to the Creator. That is what I am telling you. The way they are, it is a sure thing.

MONTEZUMA   Is that what you think is promised?

CARACOL (*stung*)   I have no more to say to you.

MONTEZUMA   I am going to Santa Fe to see a lawyer. Consider what I said. I'll be back when this Michael Stolsky arrives.

241

CARACOL Nothing here concerns you now.

MONTEZUMA Pride without reason's the history of failure. They'll fail. I don't want you to fail, Grandfather. I know how to fight with their weapons. Be patient. (*silence*) Take care. (*silence*)

Montezuma goes.

CARACOL Oh, my child, oh, my boy. What a warrior I would have made of you.

Caracol lowers face to dirt and rubs it back and forth, then raises himself up.

CARACOL (*cont.*) Earth, hear me! Sky, hear me! You winds knowing me, hear me! Today I face what is to be done in this world and what was told in the prophecy!

Caracol returns to Stolsky. He sits.

CARACOL (*cont.*) That is a true account of what happen.

SCENE 2

MONTEZUMA Perhaps Stolsky's mind flashed; lands gone, I've seen them get old. Oklahoma is full of them. The crippled, the wrinkled, the half-blind brown old Indian generals: each who fought for some patch God gave the people and lost an entire continent; now themselves lost, in old pride and old dreams, in peyote religions or alcohol binges, watching the Southern Plains lightning-cracked skies, playing cards, telling fabulous lies, stupefied by the dumb cattle they raise—unhorsed, dislodged; unarmed—utterly.

★ ★ ★

Osage, Pawnee, Kansa, Oto. Muskogee, Cherokee,
Choctaw, Mesquaquie. Comanche, Ponca, Kiowa, Apache.

Some of them get just crazy as babies. He must fear it,
this man of progress—regression.

STOLSKY I thought you got me here on business. I mean, to
work out something. I mean, why are we here?

MONTEZUMA The old medicine man's ferocity, his acquired
contempt for whites—I know well enough. I wrestle with
this moment and decide this: Caracol must've seen. If Stolsky
only fears, if Stolsky cannot understand, he cannot play his
part. I must tell the truth I know and help—and perhaps, I do
not know, felt compassion just once for the enemy.

CARACOL I try to convert once, you know. On San Carlos.
This Dutch Reform mission. Good minister there. He gets
me not drinking. Tells Jesus forgive all. Well, he be kind, I
listen to him. Bible stories I really like. That Christian
ceremony stuff is hard, it is not made for Apaches, but I am
trying. I am taking my new wife to services. Mary Isabel
they call her. She is trying to find Jesus too.

Well, no one sit next to us at service. We sit down,
people jump, move over. No one share a prayer book with
us. Minister says, 'Cause we can't read; but I seen it ain't
that. I been Christian then. Some come up, say, How many
white women you kill, how many white children you kill,
how many white people you kill? I turn my cheek, I don't
say nothing. How many us Apache you kill I don't say. No
one come up, say, Okay Christian, welcome to us. Not to
Apache like us; maybe been different for others.

★ ★ ★

Stolsky, we lose a long war. Regret just useless, I guess.
Ain't no one listen to no loser complaining. But I seen my
babies' future then. Not Chiricahua. Not 'Merican either.
Christian coyotes they want 'em to be. Dogs more 'Merican
than my babies. Mice in the mission more. Lizards more.
Even snakes, rats, owls that evil trash, more.

So I dunno, I am not going to all the services. I am
getting drunk again sometimes too. Not much to do there,
you know. I got gambling some too, horse racing, you
know. So minister comes to complain. So I am saying to
him, You were fooling with me! I am drunk when I'm
saying this. These ain't no Christians loving their brothers,
and I ain't some goddamned dirty-leg coyote. I am still
Caracol! I been racing horses before you was born! (*silence*)

Church expel me. Say I don't love Jesus. Gambler trust
chance, not Providence. You are expel, you are damned. So
then I been knowing my whole sorrow, 'cause I try
everything to be Christian and good, but I am nothing
then. Not Apache, not a Jesus man. Nothing. So I tell my
babies I am nothing and they ain't nothing! This is no good,
I am telling them; and I raise my blade, and Mary Isabel
screaming—(beat)

How come I'm having children, I dunno. 'Cause I am so
stupid, I guess. I am stupid and dumb. To bring them into
this—world. This—'Merican light.

So I kill them. I chop them down. I don't know what
I'm doing. Just remember Mary Isabel scream. Arms and
legs hurt. Just cover in blood, I remember. Then Mary

Isabel stop scream. Then I hear it: One baby she's crying, *Mama mama*! Well, I look. Well, she doesn't be dead. Then the other too. Not touch at all. Not stab or nothing. Both of 'em fine. Well, my shaking get worse. Then I seen it. My own foot, bleeding. All these toes here; lying around just like dead soldiers. 'Cause something turn my blade aside. Something protect my babies. Drive that blade down on myself. Well, first I am amaze. Who done this? Who done this?

Then I hear him. He hollers from the west: Get back! They do not belong to you! And then am I scared. And his fist come from the east behind me, just slam my body to the earth.

I didn't ever hear of that one coming to no man before. We are saying our Creator, we call Yusen, he makes the tribes of the birds and the beasts, and a big fight between 'em which brings light to this world. Well. I ain't sure it been him. But, you see his face, you be pretty sure it ain't Jesus, maybe.

His fingers open there. On San Carlos his hand open and lift me up; this drunk Apache, he calm my heart, lift me up to put me on his lips, and he makes me to a word then, like a word come out his own throat. That word been, No.

That way he took my sorrow off; and he open my heart up and make me shout very loud out then, and mountains wake up, and look around, and shout back. I try looking for Mary Isabel and our babies, but he hide them in some cloud, and tell me go, and drive me away from my house. So before dawn I was gone from San Carlos.

STOLSKY You stole horses.

CARACOL Yes.

STOLSKY The army tracked you into the mountains. Then the blizzard.

CARACOL I guess.

STOLSKY Presume Old Terror dead. Yeah . . . I remember the telegram. December 30, 1894. (*silence*) Man in his sixties'd be sure to die there.

CARACOL Horse keep me going. He dies, finally.

STOLSKY How did you get here?

CARACOL Some of them Pueblos found me. They were gathering stuff for some ceremony.

STOLSKY Found you unconscious?

CARACOL Not in good mind.

STOLSKY Well, you told a good story. Or why'd they adopt you?

CARACOL I told my people and my name.

STOLSKY Caracol? They knew?

CARACOL My real name, that be just Mexican.

STOLSKY They think you're this messiah fella.

CARACOL Messiah is your word. We don't say that.

STOLSKY Come on. . . . How could you be?

CARACOL He is being reborn. Into some man.

STOLSKY The hell. You got crafty. You latched on to a good thing.

CARACOL When I been right again, and heal, they tell me they seen the mark of the prophecy, that is why.

STOLSKY What mark?

CARACOL That he come with so they know him.

STOLSKY What do you mean? How do they know?

CARACOL This.

STOLSKY Your foot?

CARACOL Prophecy say he's being reborn with this wound from before that is fresh now. He be lame.

STOLSKY For the love of—and you believe it?

CARACOL Same Indian heart in us, I guess.

STOLSKY How about pancreas. Same pancreas—? (*stops; suddenly*) My geologists . . . ! Where are they?

CARACOL That marshal will find them.

STOLSKY You sure? Why?

CARACOL They be where he's looking. (*pause*) I leave some things so they know who been doin' it.

STOLSKY Doing it, doing what?

CARACOL They were asleep—when I'm finding them. 'Neath some old willow tree. I knock their heads. I bind them up, hang 'em upside down. Put blue cornmeal down.

STOLSKY What are you saying?

CARACOL 'Neath them.

STOLSKY What are you saying, a ceremony?

CARACOL Just what has come to me best be done. Then I wash up in the stream some time; done some things need doing I know. Well, they wake groaning and cursing. Then the sun rise. Then I cut off their heads. Respect been paid to everything beneath 'em.

STOLSKY Jesus wept.

CARACOL Tolson be looking for me and the heads soon.

STOLSKY You kept the heads? Where?

CARACOL Safe.

STOLSKY Mangas Coloradas. What is it? Revenge for him, his head? What is it, that Smithsonian business? What? They were just—it was just—business. Why?

CARACOL See over there? Used to be peach trees. Bees humming round. Honey. I bet it sure been good honey.

STOLSKY How could you do it? (*silence*) The world isn't changed. You're going to hang.

CARACOL Maybe.

STOLSKY Not maybe. It was just business you—dumb Indian.

CARACOL Used to ride ten—twelve days, hear nothing but Apache. A lot of foreign noise this world's become.

Enter Edna Brightman, running.

EDNA *Chiesah, oh, Chiesah!*

CARACOL *Guwatzi.*

EDNA *Vengase. No esta bueno.*

She takes Caracol aside. She questions. He nods. Montezuma comes forward.

MONTEZUMA Observe the old couple's final talk. She speaks Keres, he Apache. She has about eighty words of Apache, picked up here and there. Also Tewa, fluently. He has Keres, but not as well, considerable Tewa, including crude jokes about Hopis and Zunis. But they both weave it together with Spanish, learned of necessity. Old empire governs the intimacies.

EDNA *Sí, sí. Es verdad, pero*—ah.

STOLSKY What's going on?

CARACOL I am trying to keep the peace here. She is angry.

EDNA *¡Caca cabron!*

STOLSKY Is she trying to punch me?

CARACOL Edna . . . *portate bien.* Edna. . . .

Note: Edna's anger may be surprising—but not comic. She is someone in extremity. If not dangerous, not comic.

CARACOL *(cont.; to Stolsky)* Tolson. He's back with the bodies.

STOLSKY Carter and George?

CARACOL They been dragging old people out of kivas and searching everywhere. This week the people are praying there. Pretty upset being dragged out, I guess.

STOLSKY They're looking for Old Kiva Man.

EDNA *Fuega d'aquí. Fuega.*

CARACOL Trueborn and Tolson, coming here. Pretty worry, I guess.

Edna pulls Caracol aside.

CARACOL *No importa ahora. ¿Quiere? Son tuyas.* I want the melons to be for her.

EDNA *¡No quiero, yo no quiero, ai Chiesah estupido, estupido, fuega!* (*stops*) *Adiós.*

CARACOL *Adiós.*

Edna goes.

STOLSKY You marry again?

CARACOL Widow I seen some.

STOLSKY Saying goodbye.

CARACOL I will surrender. To you now.

STOLSKY To me?

CARACOL I told her you take me to Santa Fe.

STOLSKY You can't just murder my employees and give up to me. What's the matter with you?

CARACOL Don't want a federal.

STOLSKY You planned this. You got me here to surrender to me.

CARACOL Surprise beat you here. You always was slow.

STOLSKY You're not telling me something! You knew I'd be here. Was it the boys stealing two melons? What was it? Showing off for Montezuma? Why did you do it? It makes no sense.

CARACOL (*silent, then*) Stolsky: Many times I have been wanting to die. Many times I wish I died in battle with Victorio. I am alive because it was promised: We would all go home again.

★ ★ ★

That was a promise when I surrender. Without that
promise, I never surrender. I miss my mountains in Arizona.
I miss my canyons. I miss my trees. I miss seeing my
creatures. Our Creator made us for each other. I miss seeing
my people getting piñon nuts in; I would like to be there
when they open that ground and bring up that nice fresh-
bake mescal. I would like to wake up mornings and smell
air I know and know everything is good. I would like to see
my daughters' womanhood ceremonies, and do right by
them. . . . I would like to be training young men like I was.
Now all that I been told I will not see. That is not our
Creator's plan. I have been told what I must do. That have I
done now. You be asking why, still. Well. We don't want
you around anymore.

STOLSKY   Well, I'm not taking any goddamned surrender!

CARACOL   Even surrender ain't good enough for you.

STOLSKY   People know I knew you; it'll all come out. I'll be
fired. Twenty-five years ago was different. It's my good
name now.

CARACOL   Been lucky then, maybe. Don't remember your
name was so good you couldn't take no surrender. Just
some soldier boy happy this Indian don't want to fight.
Maybe that surrender got you that good name, makes you
too good to take surrender. I don't remember you had it
before.

Silence.

STOLSKY   If surrender's all you want—okay.

CARACOL   See she gets those melons. Maybe another person
try to grab them.

251

STOLSKY   Get on with the surrender.

Caracol goes into melons. Brings out two sacks, opens them.

CARACOL   These are their clothes.

STOLSKY   They were just on a job, for Christ's sake.

CARACOL   Here is a pistol one wore. I found this machete near to the other. Here, some rock tools, I guess. Here, maps. For dividing into squares. Make into squares, see. Some writing they're doing.

STOLSKY (*reads*)   "No oil formations. Big—mistake. Substantial deposits yellow-cake pitchblende ore, worthless." The hell is pitchblende? Something "a good bet, abundant"—oh—"coal a good bet." For the love of— coal. . . . What's that?

CARACOL   Mask.

STOLSKY   The one from the old race? You wore that when you did it?

CARACOL   I will destroy this now.

STOLSKY   It's evidence. Leave it, I say.

CARACOL   No good to keep it around.

STOLSKY   Who made it? You had a helper?

CARACOL   Make it myself.

STOLSKY   The last face they saw? Christ.

CARACOL   And here are the heads of the foreign dividers.

STOLSKY   Aw, Aw, for the love of. Aw, aw put them back, put them down. What am I going to say back in Tulsa? They all know about you. I talk about those days all the time. What am I supposed to tell the families, what'm I supposed to do with these, you you—goddamned savage?

Caracol silent, then:

CARACOL   Send them to the Smithsonians.

STOLSKY   We have about an hour to sunset. (*silence*)   Last time to see—to see it as a free man. (*silence*)   Go on if you want to. (*silence*)
   We'll stop on the way back; tell her again. About the melons.

Caracol turns, goes. Stolsky picks up pistol, machete, mask. A chant is vaguely heard.

MONTEZUMA   Now he prays. He sings in the old tongue. These are the words he sends before him. (*Montezuma listens, and recites*)
   Oh ha le
   Oh ha le
   Through the air
   I fly, I fly
   Upon a cloud
   Far, far, far

Stolsky puts the mask down.

MONTEZUMA (*cont.*)   To the sky
   Oh ha le
   Oh ha le

Stolsky goes.

MONTEZUMA (*cont.*)   There I'll find the holy place
   Ah now the change comes over me
   Oh ha le
   Oh ha le

Through the air
I fly, I fly
Upon a cloud,
Far, far, far—

A shot. Silence. Stolsky returns. He holds up Caracol's head.

STOLSKY   They'll see I did it some ritual way. Ought to snuff the jabber you raised. Change the worlds, huh?

Stolsky puts on mask, holds head up high.

STOLSKY (*cont.*)   No way in the world we'll destroy ourselves for one old Indian in New Mexico who shouldn't have been there anyhow.

Enter Marshal and Trueborn suddenly, to one side.

TRUEBORN   Told you. Too late.

MARSHAL   Kill him.

Trueborn fires both barrels of shotgun. Stolsky is killed.

TRUEBORN   You were warned!

MARSHAL   Do him the favor.

Hands machete to Trueborn.

TRUEBORN   This head's Indian. Mr. Tolson?

Holds up Caracol's head. Marshal removes mask from Stolsky. His shotgunned face should be terrible, bloody, staring. Marshal turns away, covers his head with his arms.

TRUEBORN (*cont.*)   I don't understand Mr. Tolson. What was he doing? I mean, why the mask? Mr. Tolson? I don't understand.

Sunset light fades out. Rises again on the stage empty, except for the melons.

SCENE 3

Enter Carlos Montezuma.

MONTEZUMA   I am back from San Carlos Reservation. This is the woman who sent me there.

Enter Edna, with machete and basket. Her face is painted white. She begins to harvest the melons.

MONTEZUMA (*cont.*)   I told her I wished to piece this story together. She did not say so in so many words, but I gathered she believed it was myself I was trying to piece together. To heal. To find a truth perhaps I lost along with my parents. She herself lost twin sons. I checked for her. They'd been at Chilocco Indian School, Oklahoma, doing well, too. Meningitis epidemic. She was born around 1850. Baptized Edna Brightman, 1892.

EDNA   Charlie. *Guwatzi?*

MONTEZUMA   *Da'waa'eh. Está bien, gracias.*

EDNA   *Llega otra vez. Qué bueno.* (*returns to melons*)   *Qué bueno.*

MONTEZUMA   On Lakota reservations in the north many still say at ceremonies *Mitak' oyassin:* All are relatives. They also say the great earth family has been shattered. Everywhere I go I hear prophecies of danger due to the breakage.

EDNA   Charlie. *Ajuda me.*

They collect melons.

EDNA (*cont.*)   *Gracias. Yo creie que se me olvido.*

MONTEZUMA   I didn't forget you. I wish someone had been as eager to teach you English as to baptize you.

EDNA   *Ai, yo no quiero lo. . . . Yo no estoy completemente estupida porque yo no hablo ingles,* eh?

Edna completes filling the basket.

MONTEZUMA   The populace here was absorbed in time by other pueblos around. Hard-pressed, the pueblos endured nonetheless. As the population recovered, the land was hard put to support it. Some of the people found work around; it was easy to characterize: No one else would do it. A few got education. Many still pray in the old way. To put the great family back together again.

Since I was a doctor, disease of course got wind of me. I don't remember for sure how the course of it went. I think I was arranging a pan-Indian congress when it caught up with me. I died precisely as predicted: a lean-to. A mountainside. A Yavapai. Others, many others, continued my work. But that is not yet.

EDNA   *¿Está verdad; llego otra vez?*

MONTEZUMA   Back again. Yes.

Edna holds the last melon up to the sun. The light fades on the landscape, on the faces of the people, on the melon.

HANDS OF LIGHT

Gordium City, Phrygia, and environs.

CHARACTERS

ETEOCLES, a Greek traveler

CRACKY, King Midas' majordomo

TWO ADVISORS

MONEYLENDER

PARVUS, a farmer

GUARD (or policeman), Phrygian or Persian

MIDAS, King of Phrygia

MILA, his daughter

AN ACCOUNTANT

NUCIA, Queen of Phrygia

TWO ATTENDANTS

SOLDIER

HORSETAMER, an enlisted tribesman

GORDIAS, Midas' son

PERSIAN AMBASSADOR

CAPTAIN, former captain of the Palace Guard

OLD MAN, Horsetamer's father

OLD WOMAN, Horsetamer's mother

HOLY MAN

BAKER

FLUTE BOY

DOCTOR

Depending on the company, various guards, attendants, soldiers, and courtesans. Some doubling up is possible: Old Woman/Nucia, Old Man/Eteocles, Parvus/Horsetamer, Cracky/Captain, Two Advisors/Two Attendants, Holy Man/Baker, or even Cracky/Holy Man.

Some centuries before Christ, a series of kings in Anatolian Turkey, then called Phrygia, were named alternately Midas and Gordias. Most of what their reputations left behind can be summed up in two phrases: the Golden Touch and the Gordian Knot.

Although set in eighth-century-B.C. Phrygia, *Hands of Light* is obviously intended to be played in a modern mode, mostly in modern dress, and must have a pool table. Weapons should be pre-gun; that is, swords, lances, bows, clubs. If you want to do a play that is archaeologically authentic about the eighth century B.C. in Phrygia, this is one you will want to leave well alone.

I believe some wonderfully painted faces would help bridge the stylistic poles of a production: some kind of acknowledgment that the tribal reverence for earth and sun is not in the distant past—as, indeed, it never is.

Gordium City. ETEOCLES.

ETEOCLES   Gordium City, Phrygia. Midas, king. The brink of
West and East, and sun and earth, and war and peace.
   Troy was not far. Some ancestor of mine is buried with
its walls, his handbones gripped forever around unusable
stolen goods.
   The mind should scream. This one piece of earth. So
many hundred years, so many men, made so stupid, violent,
and debased. Strange. Instead, I feel at peace.

Enter CRACKY.

CRACKY   Greek.

ETEOCLES   Yes?

CRACKY   I knew it. Saw you get off the Smyrna shuttle, said:
Interesting. Dressed eastern, but not an Asian face. Bet he's
Greek.

ETEOCLES   I am Eteocles.

CRACKY   Hmm, employed in the Persian empire, maybe even
Cambyses' court? (*silence*)   Okay.
   Crackling; call me Cracky. I run the grain exchange,
supervise the gold markets for the palace, and do, say, odd
jobs for Midas. Traveler?

ETEOCLES   Something like.

CRACKY   Travelers have good stories, tell us some tonight, eat
with us. Midas loves a good story as much as he loves gold.
And the whole world knows, since his wife and daughter
went last year to Sicily to see her family, gold let's say is on

his mind. Here's a coin, it's a Midas. That's his portrait. We started minting gold this year.

Enter TWO ADVISORS.

Scene 2

1ST ADVISOR Cracky!

CRACKY The old guy's advisors.

2ND ADVISOR The captain's gone!

CRACKY Midas' old war chief, captain of the Palace Guard.

1ST ADVISOR The old dickhead actually deserted today. Took forty troops to Gordias.

CRACKY How's the market taking it?

1ST ADVISOR Going up like down had disappeared.

CRACKY That's the only sign you need to watch. (*to Eteocles*) You maybe heard? We have been establishing a kind of new order here, and it takes a—well—sorting out of people, kind of. Not everyone grasps the sacrifices that have to be made to get rich. The captain is the old type: horses, gore, war, and glory. But Gordias, Midas's own son—

1ST ADVISOR —He banished him six months ago—

CRACKY He's hardly full grown. You never know. You never know.

Enter MONEYLENDER, PARVUS, *and* GUARD.

LENDER Cracky, this farmer tried to stab me—me! Looka this suede, looka that hole! This is Bally, you cunt! Bally!

CRACKY Parvus?

1ST ADVISOR You know this hemorrhoid with legs?

LENDER I loaned Parvus gold to buy spring seed. He comes back, wants to pay a quarter of his crop. I say—

PARVUS I always paid back grain. Always.

LENDER —I don't wanna quarter of your goddamned crop, I want my gold and interest.

PARVUS Cracky, come on, I'm a two-legged ox. I can't get gold—

2ND ADVISOR It's gold to pay back gold. The law is—eight months old now.

CRACKY You sell wheat to the bakers, Parvus. Then you pay him back.

PARVUS The bakers want half my crop for enough to pay him back. I'm dead.

CRACKY I'm sorry.

2ND ADVISOR A bad example in a good time is a sorry sight.

LENDER Move him on; move, you ox. Oh! Cracky, the captain, the desertion; how's the market taking it?

CRACKY It's up.

LENDER I'll call on my broker later.

Lender, Parvus, and Guard go.

1ST ADVISOR We're headed for the palace. Midas' daughter is home from Sicily.

CRACKY Sorry, I'm due at the grain exchange.

1ST ADVISOR The boss said for you to come.

CRACKY   I'll be there for dinner. Oh. I've got him a Greek
storyteller, I think.

1ST ADVISOR   We like Greeks. They have unusual minds.

Advisors go.

CRACKY   You heard. And if you know any stories about gold?

ETEOCLES   There's only one story about gold.

CRACKY   Midas is gonna love you, pal. Remember: Cracky.
Dusk. The palace.

Cracky goes.

ETEOCLES   A Midas. So. You like to see yourself reduced to
this. Could be Eteocles has finally found a home.

He goes.

SCENE 3

Palace. A pool table. MILA, *Midas' daughter, Advisors, holding
cues, watch* MIDAS *shoot, Midas in front.*

MIDAS   We (*shoots*)   born of mud . . . have come so far by
knowing the sun itself is our sole progenitor and parent.
(*shoots*)   Born of mud. This old involvement . . . with the
irrational earth. Earth worships . . . the Goddess. Earth
mother (*shoots*)   stuff. I banned it years ago, when I
whipped the mountain tribes. Still, it comes back, the old
Earth thing. In new ways. Creeps back. Uses people. You
get to know . . . to sense it. Someone has a bright idea. In
your brother Gordias' case: Build dams. Irrigation. The old
earth—preoccupations. Creeping. Back. To send us
(*shoots*)   back from all this, to primitive times and fat-assed

goddesses with a sweet tooth for the unspeakable. But I knew. And I banished him. Your brother. He's gone, all right. 'Cross the Bosporus. He'll be safe there. (*shoots*)

MILA Father—safe from what?

MIDAS Temptation. Me. (*shoots*) Your grandparents? How are they?

MILA Well. But.

MIDAS I wrote you my dog died? Brutus?

MILA Yes.

MIDAS In these arms. I held him.

MILA You wrote, yes.

MIDAS Thought I had. (*shoots*) Why'd your mother stay so long?

MILA She will be back when she said.

MIDAS Didn't come with you, though. (*shoots*)

MILA I came early; you know I had a letter from Gordias—

MIDAS NO THAT IS NOT WHAT I ASKED! How is my dear wife, Nucia?

MILA She will—tell you.

MIDAS Wrote her about Brutus. Didn't get an answer. (*shoots*)

MILA It was me you wrote.

MIDAS Can't remember. You've been—how long?—a year? A year. . . . Didn't seem two days you'd left, poor old Brutus, old thing, just convulsed up like a fist, shat everywhere, whimpered four whole days, straightened his spine up while I held him, shivered, and just—anyway. . . .

See: damned green disease attacking those bronze reliefs I had made of you. Decay, I dunno. No, no problem—we'll cast them again in gold. Would you like that? Mimi?

MILA Father? What did Gordias do?

MIDAS (*turns away*) Banishment was mercy. (*shoots*)

1ST ADVISOR Dear Mila, he was not—*uhm*—sensitive.

2ND ADVISOR Lacking in sympathy—

1ST ADVISOR Your father was walking the shoreline alone one day—correct me if I'm wrong, boss—

MIDAS Sire. (*shoots*)

1ST ADVISOR Sire. Seeing the sands seduced away, is that right, Sire?

MIDAS Not wrong. (*shoots*)

1ST ADVISOR Had a vision. Our land shining in a golden light. So he determined—

MIDAS Gold, it's like—like jelled sunlight! Do you see? Permanent. Deathless.

2ND ADVISOR Unlike—*uhm*—the dog, you understand. . . .

MILA You mean because an old dog died, you banished your own son.

1ST ADVISOR No, no! Say rather loneliness—magnified certain perceptions—

2ND ADVISOR You and your mother being away, nothing soft was near to—

MIDAS Just say I established the greatest markets known to man! Gordias opposed me. In the markets, moneylenders. They draw on the treasury, pay us half the profits. Gordias—

MILA I don't understand.

MIDAS For gold to breed gold, Mimi.

MILA Gold doesn't breed.

MIDAS Like dragonflies in June, oh it breeds when you know how. (*shoots*)

1ST ADVISOR Gordias opposed him.

MIDAS Another Gordias, my father, he and I required the shock absorbency of women to live side by side. But I was loyal to him; not my son, not to me. I took our jerk-off scientists who love numbers, stargazing, all sorts of abstract guff; I set them to make gold from worthless metals. My advisors were unanimous it could be done.

1ST ADVISOR As it surely will be.

2ND ADVISOR As it must.

MIDAS Gordias buttonholed these bastards and said, "Build dams instead."

MILA Build dams.

MIDAS Do something useful for irrigation, he's cajoling 'em. We trade as, we are a farming people; you are *WASTING TIME ON MY FATHER'S FOLLY!* And then I knew him. My counselors pointed out: his plotting against my scientific effort, his Build Dams, it's why it's the same old thing, the banned Goddess thing, he meant to hurl us back to that. Well let him try his tricks *ACROSS THE*

BOSPORUS! or whatever, or whoever is using him mortal or otherwise, let him use him there, not here, *NOT AGAINST HIS OWN FATHER, NOT AGAINST THIS GRANDCHILD OF THE SUN.* (*turns away, shoots*)

1ST ADVISOR   Your father couldn't do otherwise.

MIDAS   Mimi, Mimi, Mimi. I really wanted to greet you with a gift, a great thing. Name it. (*silence*)
Oho. Is anyone else around here beginning to suspect it's some young man?

1ST ADVISOR   Of course. Genius!

MIDAS   Some good-looking kid she's been thinking of. Pining for.

2ND ADVISOR   Pining!

MIDAS   It's the year they turn their backs on old farts like us and look for younger farts.

1ST ADVISOR   Younger farts, wonderful!

MIDAS   Come on, Mimi. Who is it?

MILA   Mother will be home soon. For her sake, bring Gordias back. (*silence*)

MIDAS   I—this is, is—did she understand?

MILA   Think of her. A year away and coming back to this.

MIDAS   Fools are fooled, not me. Young and spends a year away—

MILA   Not what? Not fooled—about—?

MIDAS   Your mother.

Enter ACCOUNTANT.

MIDAS (*cont.*) Yes.

ACCOUNTANT The report you asked for. According to the tally sheets, the volume of loans is up nearly twenty percent this month. We're on the way.

2ND ADVISOR Raise 'em.

MIDAS Raise lending rates a point at—?

2ND ADVISOR Midnight.

1ST ADVISOR Double on the long-terms. Or we lose by being generous to the farmers.

MIDAS Double the raise on loans of six months or more.

ACCOUNTANT I can say with assurance we've got them all borrowing gold right now. I think we might top our last record day by a half today.

MIDAS Go make it breed; go.

Accountant goes.

MIDAS (*cont.*) There's a wonderful old fable; it somehow seems to persist. A magician on the Indian border could touch anything and make it turn to gold. Imagine. The sun, sunlight, jelled, on earth. Short of having that, what we have my friends is as good as it can get.

MILA (*to 1st Advisor*) What's happened to him?

MIDAS I told you that myself.

MILA You told me you hate your son, you hate your wife—

MIDAS I told you—

MILA   For reasons in your mind.

MIDAS   My—in my mind?

1ST ADVISOR   No, no, the world admits your father's a genius; we've gotten rich—

MIDAS   EXPLAIN THAT, GODDAMN YOU! In my mind?

MILA   You didn't want to give me a gift. You bribe people to believe you, that's all. (*silence*)

MIDAS   We want no one who is not happy here. You want your brother, join him; go on. But I warn you. His exile is a barren place. The tribes we hammered thirty years ago I deported there. They are poor as scorpions. And you will be.

MILA   And if bribes don't work, then threats.

MIDAS   You are banished. Deserters, both! Both!

MILA   Deserters jump. Banishment's pushing.

MIDAS   Be damned, damn you, go, get out. GET OUT, GET OUT!

Exit Mila.

MIDAS (*cont.*)   Foreign slut for a mother, what'd I expect? Fools are fooled, not me. (*to 2nd Advisor*)   Get her place at the table removed. Put friends around me, faithful friends. Tell the kitchen the Lion of Phrygia dines solely with his pride tonight.

2nd Advisor goes.

1ST ADVISOR   We'll celebrate the record day.

MIDAS   Yes. Yes, we will, by God, won't we?

1ST ADVISOR Yes.

MIDAS Let's shoot some pool.

Midas shoots.

(INTERLUDE)

ETEOCLES To recap a record day:
The captain of the Palace Guard deserted with some
soldiers at noon. Horsemen plunged out from Gordium
City; as the sun scrubbed the sky pure white, black dots
bounced on the glaring plain. It was a record business day.
No one saw them going away.

A peasant named Parvus tried paying back wheat. Kind for
kind, he'd always paid. No, Parvus; gold for gold now.
Phrygian prison's cool and quiet. Eight layers of palace shield
it from the blazing sun and the words of free men alike. In
prison, Parvus hears the king is good, his advisors, judges,
cops are bad; could the chief himself only hear our case, he'd
understand. But it is a record business day, and the chief
understands very well. In his way.

Mila, banished today, passes marketplaces in full cry,
investors plunging wildly with happy eyes. No one sees her
go away.

SCENE 4

Palace. Pool table. Everyone is in evening dress with brandy, cigars:
Midas, Cracky, Advisors, Eteocles, attendants, and courtesans.

MIDAS The upshot's, maybe, war with my own son, maybe not. The Persian king has sent cavalry and an ambassador to—my own son. Gordias. Forty years ago, Cambyses and myself sat on the ground together. We were young. The Persian had inherited a quarter of Asia. I'd just whipped the mountain tribes my father had begun to tame. I'd ended their degenerate Goddess worships, and pushed our borders out. The Persian and I battled. I killed two of his sons. Sitting on the ground, Cambyses agreed to end it there. Now he means to use my son to do to me the same thing I did to his. By God. We must be rich if he's gotten it up to meddle with me again. I'll squoosh them all like—this!

He holds up two squashed figs.

1ST ADVISOR (*to Cracky*) Here's how I read it:
Gordius plus Persian cavalry plus the captain to lead them plus the exiled tribes with a grudge equals an invasion. What do you think?

CRACKY I think: civil war. Buy iron; axles, too; the bronzeworks. And stockpile wheat. Buy up the farmer's debts, we'll take the wheat. Slip out now, go, go, go on.

1st Advisor goes.

MIDAS Storytime, Cracky!

Midas moves to the pool table, shoots intermittently.

CRACKY This is the Greek—

MIDAS I'm drunk as a donkey and all ears, let's get to it. (*shoots*)

CRACKY Eteocles.

272

ETEOCLES The story is strange.

MIDAS It's supposed to be, you ninny! (*shoots*) Just not too strange.

CRACKY A word of warning about—uh—the Greek weakness for the gods. How many times we hear this god or that intervenes just in time—

MIDAS Unlike our own. (*shoots*)

CRACKY —to save the hero. But: If your story is about real life, and it's soundly based and has a beginning, middle, and end, then it's okay to spice it with a little shake of the unnatural.

MIDAS Haw. A subject you'd know about. (*shoots*) Greek, the theme.

Silence.

ETEOCLES It concerns a mistake a mad king made.

CRACKY Uhm, that's not so terrific. If I can advise you—

MIDAS Whaddya mean? Love mad-king stories! Music! (*shoots*)

ETEOCLES It concerns a mistake of King Cambyses of Persia.

MIDAS Delightful. (*shoots*) Let's hear it, old fella.

Flute music.

ETEOCLES It begins in Cappadocia, a Persian province. There a wealthy Greek merchant lived. His business thrived. In his free time he studied nature, and when he traveled he sought out wise men who had secrets, medicines, knowledge. It was rumored he had acquired some himself. His business grew more successful. He married a beautiful girl. She read, she wrote, and was known for her gentle wit. If you ever

273

watched a person writing, you will know why he loved to watch her at this absorption.

Now you know how wealth breeds envy. And envy breeds rumors and gossip. Word came to Cambyses that this Greek's wealth had been acquired by witchcraft and that, further, he was not paying proper taxes. Tax collectors came. They examined, and they confiscated everything. Then royal investigators came. They questioned him; took his wife away; put him on house arrest. He wondered what he could do; he worried. Alas, news came: His wife had died in custody. Our hero, knowing what came next, fled. In no time Cambyses' cavalry was on his trail. He suffered all the shame and indignities that cities and cruel weather have to rain on the unlucky. And so he came to the city of Cyme.

LISTENERS   Cyme.

MIDAS (*simultaneously*)   Hold on. Cambyses leveled Cyme— why, just last year. He slaughtered thousands.

ETEOCLES   As you will hear.

MIDAS   Go on.

ETEOCLES   Cambyses himself joined the chase. He believed the Greek had fled with something very valuable. At the gates of Cyme, Cambyses howled demands that the city give up our hero. So the city sent a messenger to the Oracle of Apollo and said, "Lord Apollo, help us. If we don't give up this man, Cambyses will destroy us. What to do?" The Oracle said, "Let the Persian have him." The city was relieved.

MIDAS That's not right. Sanctuary is sanctuary. Go on.

ETEOCLES Our hero begged one thing. He said, "Go back to the Temple of Apollo. Walk around, remove, and bring me all the birds that have nested there. I wish them for a final meal." So a priest from Cyme went to the temple and removed all the birds from their nests for the final meal and placed them in a dark sack. There they banged and flapped against each other, and their terror and their squeaks multiplied until a terrifying howl rang out all the long way down the sky: "Impious wretch, wicked man, how dare you. Those who come to my temple for protection no man dare remove!" And the priest of Cyme understood and said, "Mercy, Lord Apollo"—releasing the glad birds hastily— "But how is it you protect your suppliants and yet tell the people of Cyme to abandon the Greek to Cambyses?" And the voice answered, "So that you suffer and never dare to come consult my oracle again about handing the helpless to their enemies. For this crime I turn my back on you forever—thus." The sky darkened. Then, as if a quiver had been upended and out all the arrows fell, lightning forked down everywhere and shook the earth. The priest of Cyme ran back. But no one would listen to him. Wild-haired, Cambyses' armies pawed the earth before their gates. A herald brought word: Send out the Greek! Debate began; fear killed it.

In his cell our hero became resigned. To his jailor, a fellow Greek, he said, "They are bound to hand me over." "Yes," the jailor said, "Cambyses is too powerful." Our hero said, "I am tired. You alone have been kind to me, of all the people here." And at this point he brought out from

275

under his shirt a stone vial of lapis lazuli, and said, "This is what Cambyses wants."

MIDAS   Why are you stopping? Go on. What was in it?

ETEOCLES   The prisoner suddenly burst into sobs and tears of grief. He said, "I wish I'd never seen this! My wife never knew; she couldn't tell them what they wanted to know, and they killed her. I brought it with me only to start a new life again; now I see I wasn't destined to live. I got it in the East in a land beyond the Tigris, on the Indian border, from a magician there. Two sips are left. Just one will be enough to make you the envy of all Babylon or Nineveh—

MIDAS   It exists. . . .

ETEOCLES   —all places where men live, from Sardis where the Pactolus flows to all the might of Persepolis. For one sip— of the two left—and everything your fingers touch will turn to solid, gleaming, yellow, perfect—"

MIDAS   GOLD? GOLD? IS IT TRUE? IT EXISTS?

ETEOCLES   Gold.

Music stops.

MIDAS   Is it true?

ETEOCLES   As you will hear.

CRACKY   Quick, man.

ETEOCLES   He gave the jailor the vial. The citizenry of Cyme came in their panic and turned our hero out the gates into the arms of wild-eyed Cambyses. By this time the Persian had so sunk into a rage, he sent him back again, dismembered, then laid siege to the city and slew them all.

276

MIDAS No! All?

ETEOCLES One lived.

MIDAS The jailor.

ETEOCLES He bribed his way to freedom, yes. Drank one sip—

MIDAS One's left, then. Where is he?

ETEOCLES I can tell everyone, or one alone.

CRACKY Out with it. Where?

MIDAS Silence! The evening's over. You are all excused. Guards, escort my guests.

CRACKY Midas, please—

MIDAS Get him out of here, will ya, go, go!

They go.

MIDAS (*cont.*) You are welcome here. Your name again?

ETEOCLES Eteocles.

MIDAS Eteocles. To the point. Where's this jailor?

ETEOCLES Dead. The Cappadocian Greek's alive. He overpowered him and sent him out unconscious.

MIDAS The one who had been kind to him.

ETEOCLES The only one.

MIDAS Necessity is harsh. Survival counts.

ETEOCLES So they say.

MIDAS You know where he is. (*silence*) Greek!

ETEOCLES   He has no more dreams, except of peace: to be rooted in one place. Feel rain and sun on his face, the wind on his scalp.

MIDAS   I would give him sanctuary here. He would be inviolable. Residence. Special worship after death. (*silence*)   Greek!

Eteocles withdraws from his shirt a lapis lazuli vial.

ETEOCLES   Sanctuary, residence sounds good. The rest impious. I will accept.

MIDAS   I knew it! I knew it was you! Take the palace. It's yours.

ETEOCLES   I prefer a quiet house, away in some natural place.

MIDAS   I know the one. In the hills—cypresses, cedars, pines in groves east and west, a blue stream nearby running southwest, over speckled round smooth rock, excellent hunting and, and an old lodge of mine, why—why, it's a wonderful place. I had it converted from an ancient Earth Goddess shrine, and you know how they built those. I shot an albino wild boar not half a day from the place; it is beautiful there, beautiful—

ETEOCLES   A woman for the house.

MIDAS   Choose one. It'll be arranged.

ETEOCLES   That portrait. Who is she?

MIDAS   She? Why, she—that—that is my wife who's been away. Nucia.

ETEOCLES   Nucia.

MIDAS Hold on. Remember who I am.

ETEOCLES Do you know what you want, Midas?

MIDAS Is it that—that it? The lapis thing?

ETEOCLES Do you know what you want?

MIDAS If you lie—

ETEOCLES I know.

MIDAS It's the stuff for gold?

ETEOCLES The last sip.

MIDAS Man. Take anyone else.

ETEOCLES I want her. And you?

MIDAS I–I'll–I'll—I'll do it for the national good. I'll do it, yes. Yes. I've lost the taste for her anyway. I'll whisk her to your house when she arrives. The Italian's yours.

ETEOCLES The house?

MIDAS The guards outside, they'll take you.

ETEOCLES This is it.

He hands the vial to Midas.

MIDAS The portrait—take it! You leave it and take her; it'll just be a temptation. I may—

ETEOCLES Break your word to me? I don't think so. Send her when she gets here. Midas: If you need me, come yourself. Otherwise, leave me be.

Eteocles goes.

MIDAS Need you for what, dummy? The portrait's twenty years old; *ciao,* Nucia! (*throws picture away*) Now . . . let's

279

just see if I'm rid of what good riddance to, and got what I need . . . in one stroke. (*drinks*)   Aw. Aw, shit, aw, AHHHHH! Ahhh! POISON, POISON!

Midas begins to shake, staggers to pool table for support, grasps billiard balls.

MIDAS (*cont.*)   Help! Ah, help help help me! Ah—

Lifts billiard ball up. Becomes still. It is gold. Lifts other up. It is gold.

MIDAS (*cont.*)   Ye gods . . .

Enter Cracky.

CRACKY   What's happened, are you all—oh? Is it—

MIDAS   Gold. . . . (*gives one to Cracky*)

CRACKY   Gold.

MIDAS (*holds up other ball*)   The sun on earth. Jelled. The sun on earth! Ah. Ah, run. Run old buddy. Alert the world. Your master is—like—a god. . . .

CRACKY   Gold. (*runs out*)   Gold! Gold!

SCENE 5

A forest road. Enter NUCIA *in a cart, pulled by* TWO ATTENDANTS.

NUCIA   Why are we stopping? Is Midas meeting us here?

IST ATTENDANT   No, ma'am.

NUCIA   Is something wrong? You know, I got off the boat, I thought how good it is to be home. (*stops*)   I was— surprised—Midas wasn't there. Is he angry?

IST ATTENDANT   No, ma'am.

NUCIA My son, I was sure he'd—is he in the city?

1ST ATTENDANT No, ma'am.

NUCIA I wrote him I'd been sick. . . . This is the road to the hunting lodge. We're not going to the palace?

1ST ATTENDANT No, ma'am.

NUCIA Poor Midas. Has he arranged a little love nest for his returning wife? To reclaim her from Distance, the great rival.

1ST ATTENDANT No, ma'am.

NUCIA I don't understand. Is something wrong?

1ST ATTENDANT I don't know, ma'am.

NUCIA Then why so . . . tight-lipped? Is Midas—something's happened to him? Please. Say something.

1ST ATTENDANT Your jewels, ma'am. Please.

NUCIA My what?

1ST ATTENDANT Please.

NUCIA A bandit's life here is shorter than a mayfly's. Please don't.

1ST ATTENDANT No, ma'am. The jewels, please.

NUCIA (*gives jewels*) All young people are immune, you don't believe me—

1ST ATTENDANT No, ma'am. The rings, too.

NUCIA You are not from Midas.

1ST ATTENDANT We are, ma'am. The shoes, too. Please.

NUCIA Are you going to—what are you going to . . . do? I have—I have been ill. I *am* ill. I have very little time left. I

281

just want peace. No one knows yet; give me what's mine back, I will forget this. Take me home.

1ST ATTENDANT Ma'am.

NUCIA Yes?

1ST ATTENDANT Your shoes please, ma'am.

NUCIA You will die for this!

1ST ATTENDANT No, ma'am.

NUCIA Have I ever hurt you?

1ST ATTENDANT No, ma'am.

NUCIA Or anyone.

1ST ATTENDANT I don't know, ma'am.

NUCIA Where's the captain? You're under his command.

1ST ATTENDANT You won't be seeing him, ma'am. Ma'am— the shoes?

NUCIA (*throws shoes*) Chase them, run scum run if you want them.

Enter Eteocles, carrying her shoes.

NUCIA (*cont.*) For heaven's sake, help me. These men are traitors. I am Nucia.

ETEOCLES I know.

NUCIA Help me, you'll be rewarded. The king—the whole nation—kill them.

1ST ATTENDANT You are Eteocles?

ETEOCLES I am.

1ST ATTENDANT   King Midas, Lion of Phrygia, great-great-great-great-great-grandchild of our Father Sun, says he does forthwith divorce this woman and give her to you to be your wife and do with as you will.

NUCIA   No.

ETEOCLES   Come, Nucia.

NUCIA   First . . . tell me—what? . . .

ETEOCLES   Suffice to say for now that you have been traded. The rest, for what, I'll fill you in at home. (*stops*)   Do you read, Nucia? Do you write?

NUCIA   Read? Write? What for? You looked insane when you asked that.

ETEOCLES   I am sorry. I will teach you.

NUCIA   Traded? By Midas? . . . To you?

ETEOCLES   From varnished to unvarnished. I know.

NUCIA   Varnished to unvarnished?

ETEOCLES   Varnish strips. Your real grain will be beautiful. It's in your eyes.

NUCIA   Stripped? Like an old chair? (*laughs*)

ETEOCLES   Why are you laughing?

NUCIA   Oh . . . suffice to say for now you won't soon forget this—this—grain. "I'll fill you in at home." This—grain. What a good bargain you have made.

ETEOCLES   You'll need the shoes.

NUCIA   They were no good for walking anyhow.

They go. 1st Attendant retrieves shoes.

2ND ATTENDANT We couldn't have got her to Gordias.

1ST ATTENDANT We should've tried.

2ND ATTENDANT And if she croaked on the way? She wanted to kill us.

1ST ATTENDANT Should've deserted with the captain.

2ND ATTENDANT We'll go now. Bring her stuff.

1ST ATTENDANT For proof?

2ND ATTENDANT No one's going to believe us without it. Hey—you get that reading and writing bit?

1ST ATTENDANT Yeah?

2ND ATTENDANT Wait till he finds out she don't do windows either.

They go.

SCENE 6

Palace. Enter Midas in gold robes, sits on gold chair, picks up gold fork, tastes food laid on table. Enter Guard.

GUARD The felons and prostitutes have been bathed. They're dressing.

MIDAS Am I a god or not?

GUARD Lord Midas! It is a good thing that you are.

MIDAS The good thing is that I am. The bad thing is that I'll never know if I am or not. Send me one in. It's Judgment Day.

Guard goes, returns with Parvus.

GUARD Parvus. Farmer. Attempted murder of a moneylender.

MIDAS Prepare the rest.

Guard goes.

MIDAS *(cont.)* Attempted murder. Why? Come closer. I will understand if you explain.

PARVUS I didn't stab him. I just—it was the sun, I lost my head. I'm—they're doing things.

MIDAS Doing things.

PARVUS In your name. I'm losing everything. I dunno how to make the bad luck stop. They got drought. I—I'm just an animal, just send me back to the fields. It's all I know. The land. I don't know gold. Stuff like that.

MIDAS Parvus, approach. The law requires death. I will be merciful—thus, my son.

Touches Parvus, who turns to gold.

MIDAS *(cont.)* More valuable to me than any farmer dreamed. . . . Guard!

Enter Guard.

MIDAS *(cont.)* Pour 'em in. Let's have 'em.

Exit Guard.

MIDAS *(cont.)* Heavens, you above-people who watch over my worthless so worthlessly, watch. Be shamed by Midas. He turns this felonious mud into a pillar of the treasury.

Enter Guard with prisoners.

MIDAS (*cont.*) Draw that screen and leave.

Guard draws screen across the prisoners, goes.

MIDAS (*cont.*) Welcome. Oh, don't pull away, come close, come. You are the guests of Midas now. Behold: the hands of light.

Enter Cracky.

CRACKY I thought I heard a scream. Oh.

MIDAS Like it? What do you think?

CRACKY Uhm . . . amazing. Yes, statues. . . . Marvelous.

MIDAS I executed them myself.

CRACKY Pornographic statues. Well, well.

MIDAS What statues?

CRACKY Well, suggestive statues. And worth their weight, of course, in—

MIDAS Clam up, you. Just shut it!

CRACKY Did I say something wrong?

MIDAS Pornographic?

CRACKY But, I mean, look at them.

MIDAS They clung together as I got near.

CRACKY But it's exciting.

MIDAS It was with fear!

CRACKY Fear. Oh.

MIDAS Of justice.

CRACKY Justice. Oh. Well. If you say so. Justice seems to have got his little paw on a tit here, ha-ha.

MIDAS What shall a man, much less the great-great-great-great-great-grandchild of the Sun above, say when he's executed the justice of the realm and his best companion calls it pornography?

CRACKY Oh that mood. Well I apologize. Musta been fearsome.

MIDAS Get away from me. Stay away.

CRACKY Hey. Who runs the markets for you? You count on me.

MIDAS If you see me coming, by God you squeeze back into the shadows, you rotten little tub of slander, or I'll turn ya into the ugliest nugget seen on earth.

Midas goes.

CRACKY Midas! What did I do? Wait—well. Gordias, Mila, now me. But me—at least I was useful. Be damned then, old man!

Enter 1st Advisor.

1ST ADVISOR Invasion for sure, Cracky. The border tribes, they've gone over to Gordias' forces.

CRACKY He's draining the prisons to fill the treasury. Look.

1ST ADVISOR Scary. No more prisoners, old Hands of Light will turn elsewhere.

CRACKY He's already gilded too much mud; gold's losing value daily.

1ST ADVISOR Tell me what to do.

CRACKY Buy what people need: grain, cotton, beans. Unless you mean to flee. Then something portable—jewels.

1ST ADVISOR You, what are you doing?

CRACKY Been buying grain, I've got to stay. Just get out of gold, that's my advice.

1ST ADVISOR Jewels.

CRACKY Pay anything but do it now. You're going?

1ST ADVISOR It's gambling too much, staying.

CRACKY Gordias doesn't frighten me.

1ST ADVISOR Cracky, I fought the old campaigns, I know those border tribes. If they're let loose on this city—

CRACKY Gambling is the life, my friend. Remember me to— wherever.

Cracky goes.

1ST ADVISOR Not my life.

1st Advisor goes.

SCENE 7

The Bosporus. Enter HORSETAMER, SOLDIER. *Opposite, enter* OLD MAN *and* OLD WOMAN. *Old Man carries a lance.*

OLD MAN Horsetamer.

SOLDIER Look at that geezer. And look at her. They don't make them like that anymore. Real tribesmen, huh?

HORSETAMER Boy, that's my parents. (*to Old Man*) This is my friend. He deserted Midas with the captain. I'll be breaking a few ponies for the cavalry.

SOLDIER You people Midas exiled here, it's good to see you come out of the hills for Gordias.

OLD MAN (*ignoring him*) Not for Gordias. It's to go home. Boy: They are all saying it's going-home time for us.

HORSETAMER Yes, sir.

OLD MAN I brought this. Take it.

Hands spear to Horsetamer.

HORSETAMER See this? My father fought Midas' father, then Midas. He even wiped out the captain's cavalry once.

OLD MAN He wiped me out twice. That's why we're here.

HORSETAMER He was also a Spirit Man, you people call it a Holy Man maybe. Spirits kind of used him as a mouth to speak to us. Even Earth Mother, people say, used him as Her voice.

OLD MAN You are my son's friend. I do not want to embarrass him. But my son is a fool. He was born after Midas and his crazy father tried wiping out the old ways. But we held him up to sky anyhow. We rolled him in earth. We dedicated him to Earth Mother. I taught him what I know. I promised Her he would take my place if the people could go home again. Now we will go home; he still refuses to take my place.

HORSETAMER Things don't change for my father.

OLD MAN Horsetamer, he's a big man. Regular grizzled veteran. Border guard. Breaks horses 'cause he's got the good hands. Thinks he bought those good hands at Woolworth's, maybe, or a 7–ELEVEN, those good hands the horses know right off where they come from. You see 'em get calm like that. She gave him these, She who is Earth. Not for breaking cavalry ponies but for helping the people live. I wanted to hear him say he accepts to take my place as a Spirit Man. I know I never will hear that now. But I also know he will not escape what he is. She who is Earth will lead him by the hands.

HORSETAMER I can't make a living in that old-time stuff; he can't either. That's what being banned means. It's over.

OLD WOMAN Earth and Sun are in a balance; no man can ban that. Not Midas. No man. I guess Earth Mother is lonely now. No one bringing Her gifts anymore, shrines killed, no one to talk to. Bring Her this from me. Speak to Her when you get back home.

HORSETAMER I don't get it. After thirty years here, you mean you're not coming? (*silence*)

OLD MAN Got other things to think about. I am going to the mountain soon.

SOLDIER Mountain, what mou—? Oh.

HORSETAMER I better stay here.

OLD MAN You have never seen your own land. There is nothing to see here.

HORSETAMER Father.

OLD MAN Say what the people said before battle. That is all I would like to hear from you.

HORSETAMER You sun, you live forever. But we are born and must die. You mountain, you live forever. But we are born and must die.

OLD MAN Safe journey.

HORSETAMER Wait.

OLD MAN Come a few yards with me if you like. It will be good for your mother. But then I got to go alone.

They go. Enter PERSIAN AMBASSADOR, CAPTAIN.

AMBASSADOR I am the ambassador from Persia, Captain. You are Midas' old hunting hawk.

CAPTAIN I've sent for Gordias.

AMBASSADOR It is an irony of history that we stand here together as allies.

CAPTAIN I don't know history, I don't know irony. I know I whipped your regiments forty years ago, then again two years later.

AMBASSADOR You made Midas Midas; his military arm. Now you are making Gordias. But he's what, eighteen? Commands no loyalty, commands (*mocks a stutter*) n-n-n-nothing, if you follow me. The tribes you subdued: for Midas. They'll follow you. Not Gordias. He's a flapping glove; it's you who are the fist. Lose Gordias. Wipe Midas out. Be king. You.

CAPTAIN (*silence*) Prefer the company of my ponies.

AMBASSADOR You'd be very rich, Old Hawk.

CAPTAIN Maybe not rich enough to protect myself from the likes of you?

AMBASSADOR Cambyses, and all Persia, thought when you deserted, you'd decided.

CAPTAIN He misunderstood my desertion. You've insulted my patriotism, my integrity, and my intelligence. That's enough for one day, even for you bunch.

AMBASSADOR Cambyses believes the stories coming out of Gordium City are true. It's obvious you don't.

CAPTAIN The golden touch? Save that garbage for the stupid. . . . Gordias.

Enter GORDIAS and Two Attendants.

GORDIAS These t-two men have ju-ju-ju—

CAPTAIN Just.

GORDIAS Just arrived. I don't know wh-wh-what to say. It's all true. Amba-amba-ambassador, it's true, I-I-I—

CAPTAIN Slow down, boy.

GORDIAS True! They brought her shoes, her jewels for proof!

CAPTAIN (*to Gordias*) Privately. Not here. You two. Ambassador.

Gordias, Ambassador, Attendants go. Captain goes. Enter Mila.

MILA The world's reversing. Turning back. Going back . . . somehow. I couldn't breathe last night. I couldn't sleep. I walked down to the beach. Up and down the sands, torches burned. Boatmakers boiled pitch in tubs. Carpenters with adzes joining keels and ribs, invasion craft being prepared. Exiled tribesmen stood and watched. Often leaned on spears, one leg slightly bent. As if to take that first step home. As if. I watched them watching. I have always been told they are ferocious and terrible people. In fact they seem—well, gentle. I was scared to speak to any of them until one turned and saw me and smiled. He said, "We are going home." Them. With every cause to hate Midas—don't even think of Midas. Just remember love of home. And I do, too.

Enter Horsetamer.

MILA (*cont.*) You. Please take a message to my brother. I am going on ahead. Home. With Mother there I think there's hope. I can't not try. Are you all right?

HORSETAMER I'll tell him.

MILA Thank you. For everything.

HORSETAMER Like what?

MILA Don't hate me.

HORSETAMER Lady, I hate being poor, that's all. I'll tell him.

Turns away.

MILA I am not my father.

HORSETAMER Me neither.

Mila goes. Enter, opposite, Captain.

CAPTAIN Horsetamer!

HORSETAMER Cap'n?

CAPTAIN You promised me twelve ponies by this week. I need 'em and you're late.

HORSETAMER I got just one ass, Cap'n. Breaking horses right takes time.

HOLY MAN *enters, pushing enormous ball of rope.*

HORSETAMER (*cont.*)   Watch it, Cap'n!

CAPTAIN   You know Gordias' holy man; you're fellow tribesmen, aren't you?

HORSETAMER   I know him.

CAPTAIN   He's a spirit man, like your father.

HORSETAMER   Not like my father, no, sir.

CAPTAIN   Well . . . in this part of the world, this old fraud's what brings social order. (*to Holy Man*)   Is that it? Gordias' knot?

HOLY MAN   The horsetamer's father was a rival. I hope he has not been slandering me.

CAPTAIN   Get on with it. What's this ball of filthy rope supposed to do for us?

HOLY MAN   Oh. Dream commanded it. Divinity guided my hands.

Horsetamer goes.

HOLY MAN (*cont.*)   Good riddance. In the dream I saw the umbilical cord of all things, entangled, knotted, and entwined from the navel of the world to the navels of all things, and in the center, Gordias' own, signifying his power over all to come. By him all is related; all is one, or it is nothing.

CAPTAIN   Right—before we leave, roll it through the camp and make sure the fucking Persians see it. Say, Until a man can unravel it, Gordias and Cambyses will hold the whole throw of the world between 'em, and tell 'em they're all included here. (*pays him*)   Got that?

HOLY MAN   All is related, all is one, they are, my captain.

Enter Gordias.

HOLY MAN (*cont.*)   Ah, Lord Gordias. I have a nice surprise for you.

GORDIAS (*ignoring him*)   Captain.

Gordias and the Captain confer on one side. Enter opposite, Ambassador and Guard.

AMBASSADOR   Say, Eteocles. Say, Gold. Say the price was Nucia. Cambyses will understand. Find out what he wants me to do. And hurry. Gordias doesn't want rumors spreading; go now. Eteocles, Gold, Nucia, remember.

Guard goes. Holy Man starts pushing knot, bumps Ambassador.

AMBASSADOR   Watch out with that thing!

HOLY MAN   Oh, it is the mystery of all things, all that is related, all that is one.

AMBASSADOR   I am sure it is in good hands. Excuse me.

HOLY MAN   We are related, even you and I. Buy me a beer, I will tell you how.

AMBASSADOR   Related, related? I am the Persian ambassador! You—you are crud. Absolute crud.

Ambassador goes.

HOLY MAN   Yes, that too is a mystery.

Enter Horsetamer.

HOLY MAN (*cont.*)   Don't try to make trouble for me! There's enough for all. You understand. Just business.

HORSETAMER Message for Gordias, that's all.

HOLY MAN Oh. Good. Well, off I go.

Holy Man pushes knot out.

CAPTAIN You think it's true?

GORDIAS They had the sh-sh-shoes; the jewels.

CAPTAIN We'll start preparations now; we can go in three days. Tell your sister—

HORSETAMER Cap'n?

CAPTAIN Yes?

HORSETAMER Man's sister's headed back for Gordium City. Said to say it to him.

GORDIAS How long ago?

HORSETAMER Not long.

GORDIAS Well, go after her! How, c-c-could you let her?

HORSETAMER Sir?

CAPTAIN (*to Gordias*) Let me. (*to Horsetamer*) Go after her. Don't bring her back, we're moving out. I make you responsible.

GORDIAS I'll see he, g-gets help. Come on.

Gordias and Horsetamer go. Enter Old Woman, opposite. She watches.

CAPTAIN I know you. How?

OLD WOMAN You sent us here. Long time now.

CAPTAIN Oh, yes. Spirit Man's number one. How is the old brute? (*silence*) I'll bet he never thought he'd get home

296

again. I didn't. (*silence*)   Old Woman: Midas ended up doing to us all what he did to you bunch first. Tell the old savage that. It'll make him laugh. (*silence*)   Tell him I said hello.

Captain goes.

OLD WOMAN   Earth Mother: Old Man is gone to the mountain. Earth Mother: He is going to you. Now my child is going; my son too is going. May you help him bring good back again. May he get home safe again, thanks to you and Father Sun. May he bring balance and good back again, thanks to you and Father Sun. I am praying, May good come back to that land again. May balance come back to that land again, thanks to you and Father Sun. May good and balance come back again, that is all I am praying now.

Old Woman takes out flints. Tears cheeks, tears arms.

OLD WOMAN (*cont.*)   Good, come back! Good, come back! Toss evil men to hell.

SCENE 8

Forest. Two Advisors enter, breathless.

1ST ADVISOR   We'll keep on south. Phoenician ports. Whatever sails first, to Tunis, Egypt—

2ND ADVISOR   Rest a sec. (*sits and opens bag*)   Jewels. New lives. Alabaster head of a girl. It's got to be a collector's piece.

1ST ADVISOR   That's Midas'.

2ND ADVISOR   Was.

Enter Mila.

297

MILA You. And you.

1ST ADVISOR You're supposed to be with your brother.

MILA You stole that. That head. You're running away aren't you?

1ST ADVISOR Mimi. See the moon? See the city beneath it? It's crumbling like a clod of mud. Your father's why. Don't go. The world is ending; no one cares. Midas makes them rich.

2ND ADVISOR He is also magical. Everything he touches turns to gold.

MILA That is ridiculous.

1ST ADVISOR (*hesitates*) Yes . . . yes, indeed it is. Would you like these pearls?

MILA What for?

1ST ADVISOR They would suit you.

MILA Excuse me, let me pass.

1ST ADVISOR Mimi. I would love to see them on you, on your bare neck. We could make them bounce. See?

MILA Don't. Please. I have an armed escort, I warn you.

2ND ADVISOR Must've left 'em in your other pants.

MILA I got ahead. Please; I said, please don't. Don't, please—

1ST ADVISOR (*pulls her to the ground*) Oh, we'll just roll on the ground together, come on, just roll, come roll, come roll.

Enter Horsetamer, Soldier.

1ST ADVISOR (*cont.*) Oh, hell.

298

HORSETAMER Don't get so far ahead, it's not a good idea.

MILA Roll on the ground with them, you bastard, roll with them!

1ST ADVISOR No need for that point in my neck. We'll go our way, you go yours.

MILA The alabaster head's of me.

She takes it.

1ST ADVISOR Your friend's blade's hurting my neck, Mimi.

HORSETAMER I can't take 'em prisoner and keep watch on you.

MILA Do what you want. I'm going on.

Mila goes.

SOLDIER Aw, she's off again. We better do them and catch up. Kneel.

1ST ADVISOR Have pity.

2ND ADVISOR Midas liked to hear yes. That's all we really did, say yes.

SOLDIER Got no time for you. If you want to pray, pray; but do it now.

2ND ADVISOR Please don't.

1ST ADVISOR I have a prayer.

SOLDIER Get on with it.

1ST ADVISOR You gods, hear me. I give thanks. I give thanks I did say *yes*. I kissed the rear end of my king and it was sweet. I give thanks it saved me from slavery, hillsides, and

299

the soul of a sheep. That's all I, born a shepherd, might have been. But I slept between silk sheets from China. I ate at a great king's table. I woke with my nose between adulterous perfumed breasts. For all that, I give thanks. For now I'm dying not smelling of mud or sheep or with my nails black or without a name; but I have had a name; and it has passed from mighty lips to mightier ears, and I was not nobody, and I die smelling of perfumes, oils, spice. I give thanks I shared in what little light shines on this unfair earth. I give thanks I never cared therefore if our leader dabbled in evil and lies or the nation fell apart.

2ND ADVISOR   I give thanks, too.

SOLDIER   Shut your eyes.

He raises his sword.

HORSETAMER (*pushes blade down*)   No killing here.

Horsetamer picks up earth, holds it to 1st Advisor's mouth.

HORSETAMER (*cont.*)   What's this?

1ST ADVISOR   Agh, stop. Dirt.

HORSETAMER   In the old way here they'd say it was your Mother. Maybe you heard that.

1ST ADVISOR   Yes.

HORSETAMER   All that thanks for what gave you sin, none for what gave you life. It's no way to die. Or live.

1ST ADVISOR   No. I'm sorry. I give thanks.

2ND ADVISOR   I give thanks, too. Goodbye, my friend.

1ST ADVISOR   Goodbye.

SOLDIER Now?

HORSETAMER Not here. Turn your back, turn.

SOLDIER They were raping her.

HORSETAMER We stopped 'em. They scared her; we scared 'em too.

2ND ADVISOR He's letting us run. Come on!

Advisors go out. Horsetamer begins to undress.

SOLDIER Why? What's with you?

HORSETAMER See this circle? Of white stones. Here.

SOLDIER It's almost buried. So what?

HORSETAMER It's an old place people left prayer offerings. It's sacred to us. They'd stop here, then bathe, then go on to the shrine. *(laughs)* Hey. I guess those two are my offering, huh?

SOLDIER You're going to bathe.

HORSETAMER Well . . . just get this exile dust off. There's a stream back there.

SOLDIER You're what? Going to look for the shrine? You are, aren't you? But you said all that stuff's crap. We're responsible for the girl, and she's half a mile ahead already.

HORSETAMER Well. See—I promised him. Them. He—he was a real spirit man, you understand? No. Well. *(silence)* Oh, hell. I'm just a naked man who can't explain himself. Do what you like.

Horsetamer goes.

301

SOLDIER Hey. Hey, wait, don't leave me out here alone. Hey, wait.

Soldier follows.

SCENE 9

The city. Night. Enter Cracky. Behind him, BAKER.

CRACKY You are following me.

BAKER Yes. From the grain exchange.

CRACKY What do you want?

BAKER I'm going broke. I bake bread.

CRACKY What do you want?

BAKER You're selling grain to speculators; they hoard it.

CRACKY So?

BAKER What am I supposed to bake with?

CRACKY What do you want?

BAKER Sell to us direct.

CRACKY Tell your friends if the baker's art dies in Phrygia, don't look for me at the funeral.

BAKER Give us a break. If we can't afford the flour, no one's going to have bread.

CRACKY Can't help you. Good night.

BAKER You have to! It's you in charge, you!

CRACKY You wanted gold. You got it. I bought wheat. I sell it. To the highest bidder. What's your complaint? That I was smart? You weren't. You're like the farmers. Stop the pampering, they squeal like piglets. You've had it good. Now use your wits.

BAKER For the love of heaven, we're bleeding to death.

CRACKY Make you competitive again, inventive—look at it that way. Good night.

BAKER You can bleed too!

CRACKY Ah. The killer croissant's loose. And my mother warned me, too. Good night.

As Cracky goes, Baker suddenly stabs him.

CRACKY (*cont.*) What—?

BAKER How's this, inventive? How's this?

Cracky stumbles out, followed by Baker.

SCENE 10

Palace. Midas, FLUTE BOY, *Guard.*

MIDAS My daughter? Here? Where? Why'd you let her see the statues? Tell her I'm gone, get rid of her. She mustn't see me.

Guard goes.

MIDAS (*cont.*) What do you want?

BOY The song's ready.

MIDAS Song?

BOY You asked for. (*Midas laughs*) You remember—

303

MIDAS Battalions have deserted, grain is unavailable, boys hunt in packs with firewood clubs for someone to beat up; the rich scuttle to their armorers and double bolt their gates, the poor stomp rats to eat, the rats snaffle their own babies up when they can't get someone else's, and you want to sing your little song? Haw-haw! Well! Someone still prefers court to the hillsides—haw—must be—haw—the better view haw-haw of our slide back to the prehistoric slime! Haw! Your little song! Haw-haw-haw-haw-haw!

BOY We weren't shepherds. Farming people.

MIDAS Oh! Haw, farming people! Haw! I don't remember; you tell me that?

BOY You didn't ask.

MIDAS No . . . no fear in your eyes. So I don't know you; 'cause I only want to know 'em when they fear me so much I'm scared why. . . . Farming people.

BOY My mother died two—no, three years ago.

MIDAS Father?

BOY He sold me to Cracky to pay some debt.

MIDAS Hate his every breath?

BOY Old Parvus thought it'd make me safe.

MIDAS Parvus.

BOY My father's name. I wonder if he's safe.

MIDAS He's safe.

BOY You know him?

MIDAS He's safe. If I say it, it should be good enough. . . . Now, about that little ditty you were doing. I remember; lyrics were the damnedest things I ever heard. "Midas was old, Midas was frightened." What kind of stuff is that?

BOY I was putting down what I saw.

MIDAS You're supposed to cheer me up.

BOY I'll work on the words some more.

MIDAS Do that. I don't want to get eardrum cancer or something.

Enter Mila.

MIDAS (*cont.*) You best go.

Boy goes.

MILA You—monster.

MIDAS I can see that being an old charmer won't get me diddly with you this time. You saw?

MILA I saw. I heard.

MIDAS About your mother.

MILA I heard.

MIDAS You heard.

MILA How could you?

MIDAS Sell my wife?

MILA How?

MIDAS I bought her in the first place. No . . . no answer. Can't think about it anymore. Why'd you come back?

MILA I thought you needed me. That you were helpless.

MIDAS No.

MILA What happened?

MIDAS Dunno. Sometimes you think you're up to one thing. But you're up to another really. Perfecting solitude. Kind of. I dunno, really. When you get it right, you have got a bubble around your body, kind of. No one can reach in. You can touch nothing. Things—got out of hand. Totally.

MILA I thought you were sick.

MIDAS No.

MILA Gordias is coming.

MIDAS With Persians?

MILA And the tribes.

MIDAS The tribes!

MILA What do you think you can do?

MIDAS It doesn't matter.

MILA Give in. Now.

MIDAS Give in?

MILA Now. Before he comes.

MIDAS Look: Here's a riddle. Life comes from this beneath your feet. It goes back, feeds more life. I can hold it here. You saw. In gold. I hold it here. I rob death. Earth. Nature. Hell. The cycle of things that comes and goes and gives all kinds of beauty. It stops here—in this monotony. But: It stops. Then who do I give in to? To what? My traitor son? Enemy nations?

MILA Your—own goodness.

MIDAS What goddamned goodness? Use your eyes, you ninny!

MILA If there's no cure for you, it doesn't matter.

MIDAS A cure, sure there's a—

MILA Is?

MIDAS The Greek had the power; he doesn't now. I tell you for a fact it doesn't wear off like finger paint. All I have to do is go beg the Greek. And your mother, probably. Beg.

MILA Then do it.

MIDAS Who is like this? No one and nothing. Look what I am.

MILA Who—what are you? You know you can undo this, how can you refuse?

MIDAS That's what I am saying. Look!

MILA Saying what?

MIDAS Knowing you can when you—can't—it's all part of it. Look what I am. . . .

MILA Part of what?

MIDAS *(thinks)* Evil. I guess . . . you can. But you can't. No way back. You go on. It goes on. To the natural end. See, I'm a damned man, Mimi, and I know it. Damned, and I know it.

MILA No.

MIDAS Why dwell on it, it's no fun. Let's, oh, let's just—let's get some entertainment, get my mind off this. (*calls*) Boy! Come back here! Want my daughter to hear your song!

MILA Go to the Greek. Please. I will go with you.

MIDAS You wait till you hear what this scurrilous little skunk's made up about me. You'll like it.

MILA You can cure yourself. I'll go with you.

MIDAS I said no. Cut it out. No means no.

Enter Boy.

MILA Why? When you can, why won't you?

MIDAS Sing it, you little stinker.

BOY Should I?

MIDAS Your little ditty, sure. Mila?

MILA I'll show you *no*.

She grasps his hand. Turns to gold.

MIDAS Oh. Aw. Aw, now. No.

Midas walks around her, examines her. Boy sings.

BOY Midas was a frightened old man
Afraid of death was he
He lost his force and wanted more
So by gold he set his store
Now gold's not life but an open sore
He wishes things like they were before.
Oh Midas he is a mad old man
Afraid of gold is he
He's wandered into the golden night

Shadows shiver and starve
Shadows take flight
Midas borrowed so much, credit got tight—
Poor old man with hands of light.

MIDAS Aw, aw, no. Aw, no, no, no, no.

Midas flees.

(INTERLUDE)

ETEOCLES When Midas was a youthful buck, he hunted wild
boar alone and made sure at the kill while lifeblood jetted
out the wound to stare the amazed and dying beast right in
its fading eye, and say:

When you fled, churning underbrush in terror, it was I
behind you—Midas—like a dream. The unexpected has a
name. Shout beast if you like, you will not be shamed. All
the force earth piled in you is nothing as to Man's, and of
men, Midas number one, direct descendant of the sun.

And yanked the leaf—shaped bronze from the glistening
red—soaked flank. Silence, Midas, and flies hover. But: The
shivering creature just shifts one eye to the side, stares back
awhile and dies.

Now an older Midas, hands buried in gold robes to
protect what he might touch, himself hurtles through the
pathless thorns crashes through the underbrush leading to
Eteocles' house and recalls the dying boar's look, decades in
translation from beast-eye to man-mind, but arriving finally,
and saying: "Boast, Midas. The unexpected has its ways.
Someday you'll get yours."

SCENE 11

Forest. Nucia is digging a hole. Enter Midas.

MIDAS   Nucia.

NUCIA   Apparition. Hm.

MIDAS   It's me.

NUCIA   You remind me of him.

MIDAS   I am.

NUCIA   (*peers at him*)   No. I'd have died for Midas. I wouldn't catch a cold for you. (*digs*)

MIDAS   You don't want to see me.

NUCIA   Oh, well. I did. Getting off the Sicilian boat, I looked for your face. That's not all, to be truthful. Ever since, I begged to see you. Since I was shuttled to Eteocles, like some squawking hen one farmer owed another, I begged to see you. To see what I'd been traded for. It was hard to believe. Eteocles wouldn't let me. He said you'd come. He didn't lie. He never does.

MIDAS   I came because.

NUCIA   You want a cure. Eteocles said you would, one day.

MIDAS   Help me. If you have even an atom of old love.

NUCIA   Love. Ah, love. Easy to hurt; hard, hard to kill. When you kill it, it makes you wonder.

MIDAS   Wonder?

NUCIA   If you ever had it. You see—Eteocles—wanted me, oh—oh, in that way men want women when they have lost

310

another they cannot replace. Angry. Hard. Desperate. It was repulsive. When I'd have to give in inch by inch—I kept, I couldn't help—thinking: Midas made me do this. Once I refused a favor. He bolted me in a storeroom for three days. It was dark. Damp. Turnips don't say much . . . I may have killed it there—the love, I mean. You mentioned love?

MIDAS Stop.

NUCIA Why? You always loved a story. Here is a surprise. Greeks call it a reversal. They have words for everything. It surprised me. It will surprise you too. When he opened the cellar, I was so furious I fell on him. I was a very crazy angry woman, and I hit him. And I sobbed. Because I felt this thing. Impulse. A passion so full of hate and full of love . . . it made me wonder. Afterward, that is. When nothing was left undone, just us panting like shot birds on the ground. . . . Nucia! I said. What have you been telling yourself all these years? What? Ah. I am possessed, Midas. I possess him too. A different thing, no? It is what you wished on me. What dirt you wished, I have embraced. Are you glad? If you are not, you are a fool to come here.

MIDAS I had to. What will I do?

NUCIA I don't know. Perhaps . . . can you, well, can you stick a finger in and end it?

MIDAS Gordias is marching against me.

NUCIA The usual boy's stuff.

MIDAS I—she grabbed my hand. I touched her: Mila. Mimi.

NUCIA You haven't. . . .

MIDAS Yes.

NUCIA Fry in hell . . .

MIDAS Nucia—

NUCIA But first learn what I had to: that you are nothing, really. That when it comes to it, you will praise darkness if you are asked to, or mud, betrayal, unnaturalness, anything, with your whole heart, because that is what you really are: nothing.

MIDAS Intercede for me.

NUCIA Here? Remember where you are: It's the old Earth Mother shrine you made a hunting lodge; and now you— you, begging on your knees in this of all places, for intercession—

MIDAS I need Eteocles.

NUCIA You need. You need. Always you need. You destroy and—then you need.

MIDAS Please.

NUCIA Get your hands away from me. I have been turned to gold once. I am not your wife. I am not a queen. I am not a mother. All I am is flesh. That is all. No wish to be made gold again.

Enter Eteocles.

ETEOCLES A lot of noise for midnight, Nucia. I figured we had an important visitor.

MIDAS Eteocles: How'd you cure yourself?

NUCIA Remember what you promised me; your vow; remember.

ETEOCLES Nucia. He's guessed a cure exists. That's why he is here.

NUCIA Your vow.

ETEOCLES My word's good. Midas, there are resins. There is a compound substance. When it is taken, you can undo the gold. Normal motions, normal powers will return.

NUCIA That's enough.

ETEOCLES I promised not to tell; until an event in the future.

MIDAS Will it be soon?

NUCIA Get rid of him.

MIDAS Nucia, not even for—?

NUCIA I have no daughter. I have nothing. I have this.

MIDAS Gods in heaven, I repent. Forgive me.

NUCIA Get—rid of him.

MIDAS I beg you, I repent.

NUCIA You do not beg here or repent. You learn. What I had to. That you are nothing, really, nothing at all. That you will praise darkness, mud, fear, betrayal, and pain *with your whole heart because it is all, all, all that you are!*

ETEOCLES Nucia.

NUCIA Get rid of—him . . .

MIDAS I am going.

ETEOCLES Until I can, I can't.

MIDAS I am going. I am going.

Midas goes.

NUCIA I made you admit there's a cure. I made you promise you won't reveal it while I live. Promise again.

ETEOCLES What do you really want? Say it.

NUCIA Really want? Die instead of me. . . . No?

ETEOCLES Come to the house. I have been mixing medicines. They will ease the pain.

NUCIA My dear, it is too late. Look at me. You can tell. Oh . . . Eteocles? You used to frighten me—can it be you are afraid to, now?

ETEOCLES You are a monster, Nucia. Monsters can't be frightened.

NUCIA Lucky monsters. (*digs*)

ETEOCLES Come have the medicine.

NUCIA I had a thought. Digging this, my own grave. That it's the only honest labor in my whole life. So. I'd better finish it. I'd like to leave one honest thing I did. It helps. . . . I have actually envisioned it: my death. It is a kind of wide and bright forcelessness; and sweet. All the murk and terrors, gone. Oh. I feel like a cinder burning. Oh!

ETEOCLES Come in the house. The medicine.

NUCIA Must finish it.

ETEOCLES Stop that. Come.

NUCIA If we'd had more time. I knew nothing, really. Do you understand?

ETEOCLES I do. Nucia. (*climbs down into hole*)   Come.

NUCIA Can't. Finish. Oh! Oh, help me. I am so frightened. Oh, help me . . . *Greek!*

She dies.

SCENE 12

Same. Eteocles buries Nucia. Enter Soldier and Horsetamer.

SOLDIER That dust cloud on the plain. It's the invasion, it's got to be; they've crossed the straits. We've lost the girl and we're going to miss the battle.

HORSETAMER Someone being buried.

ETEOCLES Are you from Gordias?

HORSETAMER Yes.

ETEOCLES Saw the dust cloud. Guessed he'd send someone on ahead. This is his mother. I am the one you want.

HORSETAMER The one I want?

ETEOCLES She wanted to be buried here. Let me finish. Then you can take me.

HORSETAMER Take you.

ETEOCLES To Gordias. I'm the Greek—ah. I see. He didn't tell you. He wouldn't, no. I gave Midas the power to change things to gold.

SOLDIER Change things? To gold?

ETEOCLES With a touch. Like that. It's really something to see.

HORSETAMER Bury her. We'll wait.

315

SOLDIER With his hands?!

HORSETAMER Greek. Is there a goddess shrine near?

ETEOCLES The whole ridge. The building is in the grove. Why?

HORSETAMER It's a powerful place.

ETEOCLES Is it?

SOLDIER But, but . . . if anything . . . if Midas . . . if he touches—I mean, what'll Gordias do with him?

HORSETAMER Friend. I'm just going to see for myself. I won't be far.

Horsetamer goes.

SOLDIER Greek: What'll they do with Midas?

ETEOCLES What would you do?

SOLDIER If everything he touches turns to—I got it. Take him with a net! Hoist it on a pole, take him to the cellars!

ETEOCLES The inventiveness of man.

SOLDIER I got a better one! Tie his arms around a frame or pole, leave space around his hands—then take him to the cellars!

ETEOCLES It always ends belowground.

Eteocles sprinkles powder on grave.

SOLDIER What's that? To feed the spirit?

ETEOCLES It's not what you Orientals do. But, she was not one of you. I think we can go. I have something Midas will need.

Enter Persian Ambassador and Guard.

SOLDIER Who are you?

AMBASSADOR You are Eteocles? *The* Eteocles? I have come from Persia; I have found you, it seems.

SOLDIER What's going on?

AMBASSADOR You have caused Cambyses frustration. He has no tolerance for frustration. He'd like to see your face. Be joyful, Greek, a great, great king has sent for you.

ETEOCLES It is not a new experience.

AMBASSADOR Give him a new experience.

Guard clubs Eteocles unconscious. Enter slowly behind them, changed somehow, Horsetamer.

SOLDIER Hey. That's our prisoner.

AMBASSADOR We're your allies. Who's he?

SOLDIER (*to Horsetamer*) We've got a problem.

Horsetamer, oblivious, goes to grave, squats, sprinkles pine needles on it.

AMBASSADOR What's he doing?

SOLDIER Come on, will you? They're taking our prisoner.

AMBASSADOR Your pal is in a trance, I'd say. (*to Guard*) The Greek's head. We'll send the face as requested.

SOLDIER Hey, stop that. (*to Horsetamer*) What's with you? Come on—

Guard raises sword.

HORSETAMER (*not looking up, quiet, in a soft, woman's voice*)   This is my shrine. This man is protected here.

GUARD   What should I do?

AMBASSADOR   Take it.

Guard raises sword again.

HORSETAMER (*same voice*)   Do you know who I am? This is my shrine. By him will what is mine be restored. This man is protected here.

GUARD   *Was,* cunt.

Horsetamer leaps onto Guard's back and breaks his neck.

HORSETAMER   THIS! is my shrine you violate. THIS! man is protected here. BACK OFF OR BE LOST!

He tosses the Guard's body down, looks around, falls over unconscious.

AMBASSADOR   I'm the Persian Ambassador, I'm the Persian Ambassador! What's this man, who is he?

SOLDIER   Pick up the Greek.

AMBASSADOR   We're allies, dimwit, allies!

SOLDIER   You get to carry him, ally. Horsetamer? . . .

HORSETAMER (*recovering*)   I saw her. I followed her back. She was tall and dark and like a tree but like a smiling woman too. I told her they are our allies, but I could not stop her. Are you all right? She is angry. We better get out of here. . . .

SOLDIER   Keep your distance! It was you.

Horsetamer is silent.

SOLDIER (*cont.*)   You spoke in a woman's voice. You broke his neck like a twig. (*silence*)   "She will lead him by the hands." Is that what he meant, your father?

HORSETAMER (*really scared*)   I got to get out of here . . . !

SOLDIER   Oh, no. I'm not taking the blame. Help him carry the Greek. We're going to the city, where we should've been in the first place—Spirit Man.

HORSETAMER   My friend—please—

SOLDIER   Keep your distance! Move.

They go.

SCENE 13

Palace cellar. Darkness. Midas is bound. A Guard tows a Moneylender through.

LENDER   Where now?

GUARD   Day of Judgment. They're waiting.

LENDER   Midas! Witness for me! I was doing what you told me! Why doesn't he answer? Midas! Save me!

They go. A soldier brings Eteocles in.

SOLDIER   Wait here.

Soldier goes.

MIDAS   Greek?

ETEOCLES   Midas?

MIDAS   It is hard to see at first.

319

ETEOCLES Is that you?

MIDAS Not sure. Not like me at all.

ETEOCLES A normal prison feeling.

MIDAS Will we be executed?

ETEOCLES I doubt a son can start a fresh regime with the execution of his father.

MIDAS Nucia will save you.

ETEOCLES She died, two days ago.

MIDAS Ah.

ETEOCLES She came home sick. With—whatever was inside. It took its time. It doubled back once and then returned and devoured her, that's all.

MIDAS There was pain?

ETEOCLES Yes.

MIDAS You . . . at least . . . saw that she died peacefully? I hope.

ETEOCLES I—(*silence*)

MIDAS I only—I mean—not more than she could bear. (*silence*) Oh . . .

ETEOCLES Midas. The event she mentioned. Or did I? It was her death.

MIDAS I don't care. . . . I praise this dark, this mud, and rats and betrayal and unnatural place, for that is all I am. She was right.

ETEOCLES I am released from my vow.

MIDAS Your—? I wish I was dead, I don't care.

ETEOCLES You didn't value her.

MIDAS No.

ETEOCLES But you did not kill her. (*silence*)   I can cure you now.

MIDAS What cure?

ETEOCLES The dead don't want remorse; and can't give forgiveness. What is still living is what needs you. To give back what you took.

MIDAS The gold?

ETEOCLES The gold.

MIDAS Tell me. Was the fighting in the city bad?

ETEOCLES Surrendered easily, I'm told.

MIDAS Nothing worth defending.

ETEOCLES Don't turn away from it, Midas. The gold.

MIDAS Give it up?

ETEOCLES Undo it. You can now if you will.

MIDAS There is . . . this fist in me. Just—whamming this greed on. No control. Scroonching me up into this—hate. Hate. Of everything that is not what I am. I am nothing. Got to grasp at—everything. Can't reach it; must smash and hate. . . . When you undo the gold, Greek, will your stuff undo that too?

ETEOCLES (*pause*)   Something will. Stay where you are. I took care to keep this with me. Don't move—let me. This is it. Take it on the tongue like a baby. Careful. Swallow.

MIDAS   Is it . . . will it work?

ETEOCLES   In minutes the power will be gone. Then you can restore whatever you turned to gold. Midas?

MIDAS   Yes?

ETEOCLES   It's over.

MIDAS   Perhaps. . . .

ETEOCLES   I'll begin to untie your hands. That's already safe.

MIDAS   Eteocles. In olden times here, Phrygians held sacred both Father Sun and Mother Earth. Or so I was told by my nurse. She had been a priestess once, had the tattoos, everything. She told me, as my grandfathers and my father built the city, and more turned to trade and fewer farmed, the great Goddess was being forgotten. Nurse told me we would pay one day.

ETEOCLES   You said?

MIDAS   I was a child.

ETEOCLES   You said?

MIDAS   Someone else will, maybe. I am Midas, Lion of Phrygia, directly descended from the Great Sun above. The Goddess, I have been told, is a weak and cruel and dirty thing. I am a child only of the light. My hands, hands born of sunrise. Before me, my father thought the same. Before him, his.

ETEOCLES   (*finishes untying hands*)   Free. Touch something.

MIDAS   I better not. I can't.

ETEOCLES   Take my hand.

322

MIDAS I just can't.

Enter Guard.

GUARD Gordias sends for you both. It is the Day of Ju—aw, fuck! He's free!

ETEOCLES It's safe. Midas. (*takes Midas' hand*) You see? Nothing to fear. Look.

MIDAS Human flesh. Things as they are. How good. How good.

GUARD You two come with me.

They go.

SCENE 14

Palace. Screen with gold figures behind it. Gordias, Captain, and Horsetamer are in front.

GORDIAS (*to Horsetamer*) Go on. Tell me wh-wh-wh—who it is.

Horsetamer goes behind screen.

GORDIAS (*cont.*) As for Midas, only r-reason can undo unreason. Th-th-that is what we must restore. Reason. With it will come politics, agriculture, trade, and s-s-some sort of workable national life.

You think I'm weak.

CAPTAIN Young.

GORDIAS Will you help me? What would you do in my place?

CAPTAIN I'll help you when I can.

GORDIAS My s–sp–sp–sp—

CAPTAIN Speech.

GORDIAS That is not what I meant by help. I do not know what I meant. But I say it again: Reason must undo unreason. R–reason is my authority, not speech. If not reason, what?

Enter Horsetamer.

GORDIAS (*cont.*) Well?

HORSETAMER Yes. It is your sister.

GORDIAS I sent you to protect her.

HORSETAMER Yes.

CAPTAIN Yes, what? Yes, sir! (*silence*) Hopeless.

GORDIAS You f–failed to protect her.

HORSETAMER Yes.

GORDIAS You murdered a Persian ca–ca–cav—horseman.

HORSETAMER I saw a woman doing it.

GORDIAS Others saw you.

HORSETAMER I know.

GORDIAS Protecting the G–greek.

HORSETAMER Yes.

GORDIAS But not my sister.

HORSETAMER That is what she did, yes.

CAPTAIN That is what you did!

HORSETAMER Cap'n.

GORDIAS Speak.

HORSETAMER I want to go back to that place.

GORDIAS My mother's grave.

HORSETAMER The old shrine, I mean, yes.

GORDIAS You neglected your duty. You (*stops*) killed an ally of ours. Why do you think you should go back?

HORSETAMER I want to restore the shrine.

GORDIAS What is he saying?

CAPTAIN You want to do what?

HORSETAMER Make it as it was.

GORDIAS What makes you think you can do that?

HORSETAMER Well—I can work wood. I know from my father and mother what paintings used to be on the walls.

GORDIAS Does this man understand what he faces?

HORSETAMER I was brought up in the old ways. If you want to prosper, you will need someone to restore it.

CAPTAIN Are you pretending to be a Holy Man?

HORSETAMER No, sir.

CAPTAIN Take tribesmen in the army, you always end up with this. Don't linger on it, it's petty. Assert authority. Restore order.

GORDIAS H-h-horsetamer: I d-don't believe you know what you did. But you did it. Worst you ne-ne-neglected to protect my sister. You will be be-be-beheaded at sunrise.

CAPTAIN Earth gonna protect you now, Horsetamer? Spirit Man promise you that?

HORSETAMER She is back. That is all I know.

CAPTAIN Don't count on it, son.

Enter Soldier.

CAPTAIN (*cont.*) Stand over there. (*to Soldier*) Midas?

SOLDIER Outside, Captain. Captain, his—magic—it's gone.

CAPTAIN Bring him. And Eteocles.

Soldier goes.

CAPTAIN (*cont.*) I'll help you when I can. But watch him.

GORDIAS You are frightened.

CAPTAIN I know Midas.

GORDIAS I am not frightened. Reason must undo unreason. If not reason, what?

Midas and Eteocles are brought in. Silence.

GORDIAS (*cont.*) If—(*stops*) if ruin had another name it would be yours. You. Made everyone angry. Now you are pitiable. But th-at will not put you beyond judgment. Is there anything you wish to deny?

MIDAS Nothing.

GORDIAS I wi. I will weigh other matters first, then. You are Eteocles. You buried my mother.

ETEOCLES Yes.

GORDIAS Gave her final rites.

ETEOCLES In a fashion.

GORDIAS Thank you. I know she was sick. I had a letter. Is she buried where she wished to be?

ETEOCLES Yes.

GORDIAS Th-thank you. I will visit soon. Now: the power you gave Midas.

ETEOCLES It is gone now.

GORDIAS I d-d-don't wa-wa-want it! That is not what I meant. But you knew what it was.

ETEOCLES Yes.

GORDIAS You must bear responsibility for all this.

ETEOCLES Yes.

GORDIAS No excuses?

ETEOCLES What would be the point?

GORDIAS None.

ETEOCLES I wanted safety from the Persians.

GORDIAS To be consistent and rational, your sentence must be harsh. G-given other things, it would be repugnant to carry it out here. At the request of Cambyses, I will extradite you to the Persians.

MIDAS I gave him refuge here.

GORDIAS And?

MIDAS You can't give him to Cambyses.

CAPTAIN He has said he will, he will!

MIDAS Old Hawk who flew the coop got himself another handler, eh?

CAPTAIN I could see you pawing earth. I only wondered when, not if.

MIDAS Who's in charge, you or him?

CAPTAIN You only need to know it isn't you. It's him.

MIDAS I want to make an appeal.

CAPTAIN Make it to him. Your king.

MIDAS I'll make it to the real power here.

CAPTAIN If I was, I'd have you muzzled.

MIDAS To prevent me making an appeal?

CAPTAIN For the center of attention. Muzzle him.

GORDIAS I w-will not need that. Appeal for what?

MIDAS We have a law of sanctuary. I granted him sanctuary. I do not know of a way you can ungrant it.

GORDIAS He bought it.

MIDAS That's not a crime.

GORDIAS The result is around you.

MIDAS Oh. He single-handedly ruined the country.

GORDIAS He wasn't accused of that.

MIDAS Bears responsibility. Your words.

GORDIAS Not for that.

MIDAS Oh. Not for that.

GORDIAS That began before.

MIDAS Say what you mean, son. Is it easier if I turn my back? You always liked to talk behind my back.

GORDIAS It be-be-began with you.

MIDAS So did a lot. What's his crime?

GORDIAS Look around y-you.

MIDAS In the room, you mean?

GORDIAS Your . . . daughter. My s-sister.

MIDAS What family feeling this boy has. Except for his father—

CAPTAIN For God's sake, muzzle him.

GORDIAS N–no.

CAPTAIN He's making you a spectacle.

MIDAS Oh, Old Hawk. Oh, my friends. When a son tries his father, it's bound to be a spectacle, muzzle or no muzzle. Heaven itself sees how wrong it is. Bringing Persian horse into my country and my city only makes it worse. Now, this bend-over-spread-your-cheeks gift of the Greek to Cambyses, my old enemy—I'd say my son appears to be Cambyses' man, less king than foreign agent and less man than king.

GORDIAS Y-your country?

MIDAS My city. My law. And my appeal. Eteocles' only crime is for what is in this room?

GORDIAS His complicity is enough.

MIDAS Nothing more.

GORDIAS Enough.

ETEOCLES Midas, in the cellars you said some things I think you are forgetting—

MIDAS I am nothing. I know. In my own land. He's stolen my country and my captain, rubbed a butt itchy for his father's throne up against my enemies; no, I didn't forget that. But you forget: That of this matter in this room, your crime so-called, from these folk down to these objects down to this invaluable piece of cheese—which constitute your so-called crime—I alone have sole authority. Thanks to Eteocles, I can, I do, I pray I will restore them thus to life. Thus. Thus. Thus. Thus. Thus. Thus. Thus. Trooper, are they stirring or not?

SOLDIER (*suddenly kneels*) Lord Midas!

MIDAS No victims, no crime. No crime, no sentence. No sentence, nothing. Set Eteocles free.

GORDIAS What's happening?

SOLDIER The gold, it's kind of—it's bleeding out! They're stirring!

MIDAS I have done this, I, Midas, Lion of Phrygia. Behold: hands of light.

GORDIAS (*to Eteocles*) Ha-have they been dead?

ETEOCLES I don't know what, some other state.

GORDIAS H-how long? How long for th-them to r-r-return to life?

ETEOCLES About a day. They won't have much power to move or talk at first. Then yes.

GORDIAS We'll wait. If what you s–say is true, I w–w–will commute to banishment.

MIDAS There's a man named Parvus. Cracky bought his kid when he couldn't pay his way. If I were still king, I'd see them brought together for a nice little family reunion. Restore some family values here. The kid's a musician somewhere around. It's hard to know what Gordias will do. In fact, if I hadn't pulled this thing off, I have no doubt my poor boy would've sentenced me to death, maybe sent me to Cambyses even.

GORDIAS I?

MIDAS (*to Captain*) How'm I doing?

Captain turns away.

GORDIAS B–b–b–bring in the Persian!

Soldier goes.

GORDIAS (*cont.*) Y–you m–m–must think I am like you!

MIDAS Not much.

GORDIAS No. Nnn–not much! You sentenced f–farming to death. Trade, to death. Th–the faith, the tribes who accepted your sovereignty, to d–d–deh–deh–death! By abusing that faith. The p–poor to death by aban–aban–abandoning the tradition th–that no ma–matter how li–little, n–no subject of yours w–would g–go without wh–while you we–we–we–were with! For gold.

MIDAS That answer's clear enough.

GORDIAS T–to sentence y–you, clear enough!

331

MIDAS Excuses to sentence anyone.

Enter Persian Ambassador, followed by Holy Man, pushing knot.

GORDIAS This is Midas. Re-repeat your offer in front of him.

AMBASSADOR Cambyses will take him from you if you wish, for obvious reasons.

MIDAS What's he want, to fry my nose? I'm not afraid.

AMBASSADOR When he let up you were to take it as a signal to make gold for him.

MIDAS Good luck, pal.

AMBASSADOR And of course to execute him, which you cannot do.

GORDIAS P-pay attention. Midas c-can't make gold now. Can you?

MIDAS Well, not now, no, not anymore.

GORDIAS He can do nothing here. We want g-g-good relations with allies.

MIDAS No, no, no, that's not the way to go about it.

GORDIAS But if your l-l-l-lord wants v-vengeance, he w-will not find it here. I will b-banish him. This old stimulus. For hate. Midas will be gone.

CAPTAIN Good. Good.

MIDAS Banish?

AMBASSADOR Cambyses will expect thanks for his help.

GORDIAS He'll get what's reasonable.

CAPTAIN Good.

MIDAS Banish, banish me?

GORDIAS With the Greek.

ETEOCLES Midas. You can't stay.

MIDAS He can't banish me!

ETEOCLES He has.

MIDAS He can't, he can't, he can't, he can't! No son may judge, may send away, his father; he can't. If the father is a killer—it's his father! If he is a thief, his father; if, if, if he does the damnest to the most helpless and rubs it in with dirt, it's still his goddamned father. I AM YOUR FATHER! I am all of yours . . . Midas, Lion of Phrygia! I!

GORDIAS I have t-t-tried to be reasonable.

MIDAS I AM SPEAKING, SHUT YOUR MOUTH!

Midas whirls, strikes down Gordias.

CAPTAIN Get up. You've got to.

Gordias struggles up.

MIDAS O Great Sun, ancestor of us all! Look down on this, my child, who I did my best to make right, O you source, remember me, me, me, hear my hate, and strike him down to dust before he banishes me!

Midas strikes Gordias down with both fists.

MIDAS *(cont.)* To dust!

CAPTAIN Get up. Get up, I say, he'll kill ya, you've got to get up.

MIDAS Feel 'em, the hands! To dust, to dust, to dust, to dust, to dust!

HORSETAMER Midas!

MIDAS (*stops*) Who is this?

HORSETAMER Midas! (*spreads hands out*) Look: I want to show you something.

CAPTAIN Keep that man back!

MIDAS Leave him—who's interrupting, who is he?

HORSETAMER I want to show you something.

MIDAS Who are you?

HORSETAMER Horsetamer.

MIDAS From mountain people?

HORSETAMER Yes. Spirit Man was my father.

MIDAS I knew him. Hands mean something?

HORSETAMER Maybe so.

MIDAS Something you learned from Spirit Man.

HORSETAMER Just something I want to show you.

MIDAS They been hiding something from me. What? Let him loose!

GORDIAS Release him.

Horsetamer is released.

MIDAS It's something they kept back from me? Whaddaya got?

HORSETAMER Your own hands: Look.

MIDAS My own hands?

HORSETAMER Put them in front of your eyes. Don't be afraid. They are still powerful.

MIDAS Afraid! I whipped your father's butt, and the son says, Don't be afraid. Watch this, all of you! I am afraid of—nothing.

Midas puts hands over his own eyes.

HORSETAMER I am going behind you now.

MIDAS Your voice—it's like his, isn't it?

HORSETAMER Putting my hands over yours.

MIDAS Like Spirit Man's. . . . What's going on?

HORSETAMER Don't be afraid.

MIDAS Show me what you promised; I'll show them all who I still am.

HORSETAMER What do you see?

Horsetamer is behind Midas, his hands over Midas' hands.

MIDAS Dark. What'm I supposed to?

HORSETAMER Press softly. What do you?

MIDAS Yellow spots. What'm I supposed to—?

HORSETAMER I want to show you something.

MIDAS What'm I—?

HORSETAMER Press harder.

MIDAS Ah.

HORSETAMER What do you see?

MIDAS I-I dunno, yellow spots, things spreading—wings!

HORSETAMER Wings.

MIDAS Spreading wider.

HORSETAMER A female eagle?

MIDAS Yes. That's what it is—oh! It's fading.

HORSETAMER Press harder.

MIDAS Ah? Harder!

HORSETAMER Beautifully she comes, you see?

MIDAS Yes.

HORSETAMER Beautifully she comes, you see.

MIDAS Harder. Press harder!

HORSETAMER Beautifully she comes, you see.

*Horsetamer removes his hands slowly, spreads them wide. Staying
behind Midas, he begins to move in place like an eagle. His head
bobs, his spread forearms and wrists flick, and one foot stamps. His
chant is nearly a whisper.*

HORSETAMER (*cont.*) See her, Midas, beautifully! (*stamps*)
　　Over fields, flying beautifully! (*stamps*)
　　Over grain, beautifully! (*stamps*)

MIDAS Ah—?

HORSETAMER Over new green stalks (*stamps*)
　　Beautifully!
　　Over seeds shaking down (*stamps*)
　　Beautifully!
　　Over rivers clean (*stamps*)
　　Beautifully!
　　Water sparkling (*stamps*)
　　Beautifully!

MIDAS Hurts, you're—ah, ah.

HORSETAMER Over water oxen (*stamps*)
　　Beautifully!
　　Beautifully she comes now! (*stamps*)
　　Beautifully she comes now! (*stamps*)

MIDAS I can't see! Stop pressing, I can't see!

HORSETAMER Two lions sleep, beautifully! (*stamps*)
　　Deer grazing nearby, beautifully! (*stamps*)
　　Beautifully she comes gliding! (*stamps*)
　　Beautifully she comes gliding! (*stamps*)
　　Baby foxes in her talons,
　　Baby foxes bloody.
　　She comes beautifully! (*stamps*)
　　Beautifully! (*stamps*)
　　See Midas—

MIDAS Ahh!

HORSETAMER See Midas.

MIDAS Ahhh!

HORSETAMER See who is calling her.

MIDAS Ah, take your hands off my eyes!

HORSETAMER See rising out of earth now! (*stamps*)
　　Earth Mother calling her.
　　See Midas! (*stamps*) She is back,
　　See Midas! (*stamps*) Eagle stooping,
　　See Midas! (*stamps*) Foxes dropping,
　　See what the Goddess holds up,
　　Midas, beautifully! (*stamps*)
　　Beautifully! (*stamps*)
　　The egg, the new one, ready to be born.

MIDAS He's gonna blind me, stop him, stop!

CAPTAIN Soldier—

SOLDIER I can't budge his arms!

MIDAS Aaaah. Help me!

HORSETAMER In her arms the creature's egg! (*stamps*)
Egg begins to crack! (*stamps*)
Ai!

MIDAS Ai!

HORSETAMER Now the crack is widening. (*stamps*)

MIDAS (*gouging at his own eyes*) Ai!

HORSETAMER The half shells come apart.
Inside is what? What is it, Midas?
Inside is what is whole again,
Her powers being born again,
Her power have I shown you! (*stamps*)
Her power makes us well! (*stamps*)
It is the baby the new one! (*stamps*)
It is the baby the new one!(*stamps*)
The new one crying! (*stamps*)
The new one crying! (*stamps*)
Crying, Midas make us well again,
Midas make us well again,
We need Midas make us well again.
Midas! (*stamps*) Midas! (*stamps*)
Pick the foxes up! (*stamps*)
Lift the offerings, Midas! (*stamps*)
Lift them, Midas! (*stamps, then stops*)
Lift them.

Feed her.

Make us well again.

Midas holds his eyes up and faints.

HORSETAMER   Good come back. Toss evil men to hell.

CAPTAIN   Good God . . . Midas?

SOLDIER   Captain! Captain—!

GORDIAS   G–go, go for doctors, someone, quick, go!

Soldier goes.

HOLY MAN (*to Horsetamer*)   I knew your father. . . .

HORSETAMER   Just tell 'em at home. They were gonna have
my head anyhow.

CAPTAIN (*to Gordias*)   You cannot let this happen in front of
you and do nothing! Execute this savage. Immediately!

HOLY MAN (*to Gordias*)   Let no one touch this man, no one.

CAPTAIN   Immediately! (*raises sword*)

HOLY MAN   Nothing will be new here if you do! Look. Look.

*Mila, as if in a trance, slowly, awkwardly enters. She proceeds to
Midas, kneels, embraces him.*

GORDIAS   Leave the Horsetamer. I said, Leave him.

Enter DOCTOR.

GORDIAS (*cont.; to Doctor*)   Give him s–something. . . . He did
it to himself.

HORSETAMER   It would be no good if you touch him
now. . . .

Horsetamer takes Doctor's bag and ministers to Midas. Midas sleeps.

GORDIAS (*to Eteocles*)   As soon as it's p-p-possible, t-take him. Go.

Am-amba-ambassador: I am sending Persians this Holy Man and the knot he's made. It is our payment. He w-will explain its significance. Call it our guarantee of future friendliness. Holy Man, go with him. I heard you, yes. Be si-lent now.

The rest, watch what you re-report. If you are pressed by anyone with rumors, say an angry moneylender attacked Midas. We're investigating.

There is w-w-work to do, balance to be restored. Much to be made new again. S-s-stories veering wildly everywhere won't help. Get started now.

Holy Man, Ambassador, Soldier, and Guards go.

GORDIAS (*cont.*)   Captain, help my sister. Doctor, you too.

CAPTAIN   I don't want you taking chances with this man.

GORDIAS   I-I am a-a-aware. H-help my sister.

Man, Captain, Mila go.

GORDIAS (*cont.*)   G-greek, I want to hear what happened; you wait. (*to Horsetamer*)   A-and you, you, H-horsetamer: G-get to your feet. I va-va-vacate, I vacate your sentence. Go restore the shrine.

Gordias and Eteocles go. Horsetamer rolls a cigarette, sits by Midas, lights it, smokes. Enter Captain.

CAPTAIN   That old moron of a fraud out there, he's saying you're a Holy Man now. Well, that may be; I knew your pa. Or maybe not. But me you still owe twelve ponies.

HORSETAMER   I'll tell you where they are, maybe you try breaking them yourself.

CAPTAIN   You're the one with the hands. See to it.

HORSETAMER   Still just got one ass, Cap'n. Breaking ponies right takes time. Better figure waiting awhile.

Captain goes. Horsetamer smokes. Fade-out.

SCENE 15

The forest near the shrine. Sound of hammering, wood splintering. Enter Mila.

MILA   Hello?

Silence. Enter Horsetamer.

MILA (*cont.*)   I wanted to see it. What you were doing. I spent summers here. When I was small. I always wondered. Can I see?

HORSETAMER   I guess.

MILA   Do you mind?

HORSETAMER   Mind what?

MILA   Will you explain? The paintings. What they mean.

HORSETAMER   Just mean I'm not so good at painting, so far.

MILA   I want to know.

HORSETAMER   Come in.

They go. Enter Eteocles, leading Midas.

MIDAS   Where are we heading?

341

ETEOCLES   West. Stop here.

Eteocles sprinkles powder on grave.

MIDAS   Feel heat on my face. Like a hand.

ETEOCLES   Sunset.

MIDAS   Are we stopping for the night?

ETEOCLES   Not here.

Enter Horsetamer.

HORSETAMER   Heard your voice.

MIDAS   Who is it?

ETEOCLES   Local holy man.

MIDAS   Ask his blessing.

HORSETAMER   You have it.

MIDAS   I was Midas. I needed no one's blessing. Now no one
wants me. Not even my enemies. Thank you.

HORSETAMER   Greek, the work is going well. This painting
stuff. It's really something.

MIDAS   This smell of pines . . . so intense. . . .

HORSETAMER   I have to uncover the old walls first. They
were all wood—paneled over. That's okay. But painting is
clumsy for me. Hard.

ETEOCLES   Yes?

HORSETAMER   But the old sacred scenes I just know should be
on those walls—I am learning from what I find. They are
somehow coming along.

MIDAS   So strong, the pine smell. . . .

342

HORSETAMER   Dawn today, turned around from work: Been doing demolition—ripping the wood covering the walls off by night, painting by day—well, this female deer was watching me. You'd've thought the hammering—the wood ripping wood—anyhow, held the torch up to the old underwall of the shrine—there it was.

ETEOCLES   Yes?

HORSETAMER   My mother said she'd seen it in the old days: the big Heaven–Earth wedding mural, I guess. It was all faded. But you could make out what it was. It's still got some wood wall covering parts of it, but it'll be—I dunno—something. Really something. Deer just stood there, watching. What do you think?

ETEOCLES   Could be a good sign. Could be an unusually stupid deer.

HORSETAMER   Hey! I think it's a good sign.

ETEOCLES   Well, I was just leaving something. We can't stop, as you know.

HORSETAMER   No. Hey. Safe journey.

ETEOCLES   Come, Midas. We are moving on.

MIDAS   You know this scent, these pines . . . pine smoke . . . someone's burning needles, sweet-smelling, isn't it, Greek? Powerful, isn't it? It is, it is, Greek . . . so powerful . . . I can see green.

They go. Suddenly there is a sound of hammering, wood ripping. Horsetamer turns around, then goes. Fade.